Critical Perspectives on Women and Gender

Critical Perspectives on Women and Gender brings books on timely issues and controversies to an interdisciplinary audience. The series explores gender-related topics and illuminates the issues involved in current debates in feminist scholarship and across the disciplines.

Series Editorial Board

Titles in the series

Presence and Desire

Essays on Gender, Sexuality, Performance

Jill Dolan

Ann Arbor

THE UNIVERSITY OF MICHIGAN PRESS

Copyright © by the University of Michigan 1993
Published in the United States of America by
The University of Michigan Press
Manufactured in the United States of America

1996   1995   1994   1993   4   3   2   1

Library of Congress Cataloging-in-Publication Data

Dolan, Jill, 1957–
     Presence and desire : essays on gender, sexuality, performance /
Jill Dolan.
          p.   cm. — (Critical perspectives on women and gender)
     Includes bibliographical references and index.
     ISBN 0-472-09530-7 (alk. paper). — ISBN 0-472-06530-0 (pbk. :
alk. paper)
     1. Feminism and theater—United States. 2. Lesbianism.
3. Feminist theater—United States. 4. Sex role. 5. Feminist
criticism—United States.   I. Title.   II. Series.
PN2270.F45D65   1993
792'.082—dc20   93-32476
                                                                    CIP

A CIP catalogue record for this book is available from the British Library.

For Stacy . . .
partytime, excellent

Acknowledgments

These ten essays were written over a period of five years. During that time a number of people read and commented on them and provided feedback through their own critical work. I am grateful to all the students and scholars whose work has in many ways touched my own.

I also appreciate the institutional support I received for this work from the Graduate School at the University of Wisconsin–Madison, during the summers of 1989 and 1990. The Davis Humanities Institute at the University of California–Davis provided me a quiet place to finish the manuscript in Fall 1992; I thank Clarence Walker, the DHI acting director, and Kay Flavell, the associate director, for that much-needed place and time at the beginning of my Davis residency.

My colleagues at the University of Wisconsin–Madison, in Theatre and Drama and Women's Studies, have been encouraging and supportive of my critical writing and my University Theatre productions. I especially want to thank Bob Skloot, who, as theater department chair, sponsored my administrative work with the Women and Theatre Program and has been an astute editor of grant applications and an insightful procurer of essays that provoked my thinking; Phillip Zarrilli, who opened a space for me in the Asian/Experimental Theatre Program at Madison in which I could return to theater practice and who, as my tenure mentor, has taught me the ropes of institutional practice; Sally Banes, who, since her recent arrival in Madison, has provided a most important source of friendship and critical support; Betsy Draine, previous chair of women's studies, who offered me a place in the invigorating thickets of feminist pedagogy at Madison; Elaine Marks, whose institutional and critical savvy I gratefully acknowledge and always appreciate; and Mariamne Whatley and Dale Bauer, who, as the current chair and associate chair of women's studies, have been advocates of my writing, my directing, and my teaching. I thank all of them for their intellectual and institutional guidance and their valued friendships.

This work is inspired by all the students I've taught through my five years in Madison, whose responses to these essays, and to the field of feminist performance theory and practice, continue to shape my own thinking and commitments. I especially want to thank my students in "Theater and Society" (spring 1992), the graduate "Feminism and Brecht" and "Feminism and Postmodernism" seminars, and various semesters of "Introduction to Contemporary American Feminism and Theater" and "Feminism and Social Theory" for provoking me to rage and to laughter, for moving me and challenging me to sharpen and extend each of the ideas I've launched here. The actors and designers for *A Midsummer Night's Dream, Etta Jenks,* and *The Heidi Chronicles* were also instrumental in our translations of theory and practice during our production experiments.

These essays also echo with the voices of friends and colleagues who have pushed me to debate and to refine, to reaffirm and reassert, my commitments to feminism and performance. In particular, Peggy Phelan, Lynda Hart, Kate Davy, Gayle Austin, and Elin Diamond continue to provide smart hearings of my ideas and to motivate me with their own.

Vicki Patraka's commitment to her own work, and her critical acuity with mine, inspire me to keep writing and thinking and seeing performance. Her intensely felt and boldly performed political alliances, within the institution and in the feminist movement, have provided a model for my own. Many of the essays here are shaped by my dialogues with her.

Finally, for their continued support of my writing and productions I'd like to thank my parents, my sisters, my grandmother, and the rest of my family in Pittsburgh.

LeAnn Fields, editor at the University of Michigan Press, suggested my post-*Spectator* essays be published together; I'm grateful to her for seeing the project to fruition and for her continued commitment to publishing in feminist performance practice, theory, and criticism.

Permission to reprint the following articles, with editorial revisions, is gratefully acknowledged: "Personal, Political, Polemical: Feminist

Approaches to Politics and Theatre," from Graham Holderness, ed., *The Politics of Theatre and Drama* (New York and London: St. Martin's Press and Macmillan, 1992), 44–65, with permission of St. Martin's Press, Inc. "Staking Claims and Positions: The Women and Theatre Program, San Diego, and the Danger Zone," *Women & Performance Journal #8* 4, no. 2 (1989): 46–57, with permission of Julie Malnig, for the editorial board. "In Defense of the Discourse: Materialist Feminism, Postmodernism, Poststructuralism . . . and Theory," *TDR* 33, no. 3 (Fall 1989, T123): 58–71, and "Desire Cloaked in a Trenchcoat," *TDR* 33, no. 1 (Spring 1989, T121): 59–67, with permission of MIT Press. "Gender, Sexuality, and 'My Life' in the (University) Theatre," *Kenyon Review* 15, no. 2 (Spring 1993): 185–200, with permission of Martha Finan, managing editor. "Breaking the Code: Musings on Lesbian Sexuality and the Performer," *Modern Drama* 32, no. 1 (March 1989): 146–58, with permission of Patricia Howard, ed. "Peeling Away the Tropes of Visibility: Lesbian Sexuality and Materialist Performance Practice," *Theatre Topics* 2, no. 1 (March 1992): 41–50, and "'Lesbian' Subjectivity in Realism: Dragging at the Margins of Structure and Ideology," from Sue-Ellen Case, ed., *Performing Feminisms* (Baltimore: Johns Hopkins University Press, 1990), 40–53, with permission of The Johns Hopkins University Press. "Practicing Cultural Disruptions: Gay and Lesbian Representation and Sexuality," from Janelle Reinelt and Joseph Roach, eds., *Critical Theory and Performance* (Ann Arbor: University of Michigan Press, 1992), 263–75.

Contents

Introduction: Presence and Desire—Feminism and Theater Studies

I wanted to call this book *Presence and Desire* because these two terms have particular resonance for me, especially as they echo each other in performance. Within certain vocabularies of critical theory—psychoanalysis and deconstruction, most obviously—the terms generate more particular meanings and in more vexed ways than I want them to evoke here. Despite all I know theoretically about the ideological dangers and misuses of performative presence, and its implication in structures of power and authority, I continue to find women's presence onstage seductive.[1] I'm reminded that in practice such powerful, erotic, even authoritative presence is just now, and sporadically, seen and felt. Even as antimetaphysical theories such as deconstruction and poststructuralism move feminist critics away from their earlier valorizations of the female body onstage, I'm not ready to give up the intense pleasure I find in a powerful female performer. I still find radical her power to know, intellectually and psychophysically, how to wield the authority of stage presence, how to control the seductions inherent in the frame, and how to speak the language so that authority, seduction, and language mean something different about the status of women in culture.

The pleasure I take in such power ushers in desire, the second term of the title, which I want to use in a more theatrical than psychoanalytical way. Part of the pleasure of women's presence is the direct call it sounds to *my* desire, which doesn't require that I masquerade as a male spectator or that I translate the nouns, verbs, and other language markers to make something closer to my identity position appear in the representational frame.[2]

That these moments remain few is significant to me. I've felt presence and desire watching Peggy Shaw and Lois Weaver perform, in *Anniversary Waltz*, most recently, and with Deb Margolin earlier in *Little Women;* watching Sara Felder's Jewish vaudeville comic solo performance in *Beyond Brooklyn;* watching Geena Davis and Susan Sarandon bond to their deaths in *Thelma and Louise;* watching Christine Lahti and Meg Tilly run toward their own lives in *Leaving Normal;* and, most consistently, watching student actors perform in our University Theatre productions at Madison, informed by the feminist theories we discuss in class. These are large and important moments for me, ones I still can't take for granted.

Presence and desire remain key to my thinking and to my theater practice by keeping me attached to the potential of theater production and spectatorship. They fuel the search for different meanings in new and old productions and provide the power to model a reception strategy that will enable spectators to be competent to read these meanings. Presence and desire bend across gender, sexuality, and performance and across my own various and different locations as a writer and a teacher, a director and a scholar.

Mediations and Ruminations: Context and History

These ten essays chart my own growth and reassessments as my affiliations and commitments have changed and changed again over the last five years, in the context of a field of work and study that has become exponentially more sophisticated and visible. Thinking back over this work prompts reflection, not of a naive or nostalgic sort, but a self-reflexive, positioned retrospection.[3] I intend to write thoughtfully and self-consciously about one feminist writer's entanglements with the cultural preoccupations and moments in history whose web has grown to mediate and influence her work. The moving discourse of the field filters my rereading of all the texts I've assembled here; the various experiences I recount read as intertexts among those of my scholarship.

The essays collected in this book represent five years of thinking, writing, and theater practice produced in my first academic position, as an assistant professor of theater and drama and women's studies at the University of Wisconsin–Madison (UW). As Sue-Ellen Case notes in a recent article, "The material conditions of our own ideas

make them what they are and what they will become in their reception."[4] Although their production in an academic context marks their
style and contents, I also find the essays haunted by my first lasting
commitment, which was to feminist theater criticism in popular, as
well as university, settings.

From the earliest, perhaps most formative years in my theater
training, I considered myself a critic. As an undergraduate theater
student at Boston University (BU), writing about dramatic literature
and performance quickly replaced what had long been the pleasure
for me of acting and directing. As I've written in "Gender, Sexuality,
and 'My Life' in the (University) Theatre," my change in focus was
hastened by the training program in which I'd enrolled. The acting
program at BU in the mid-1970s prepared its students to perform
their dramatic roles but also fashioned them for cultural roles as
"normally" gendered young men and women. Rejecting this prepara-
tion for a social scheme I opted not to follow put me automatically in
a critic's position.

Assuming a critical role brought with it pariah status. I remember
mostly how quiet I was during my first year and a half at BU, frozen
by my inability to fit the gendered performance model taught as
desirable. The closed, awkward woman I became as an acting major
in college compared uncomfortably with the way acting, as a teenager, had always given me speech and mobility, through the media-
tions of text, character, and context. Since I could no longer embody
my own strength, through characters and exercises that now seemed
to drain it from me, writing about theater came to provide the outlet
I needed for presenting strong opinions and a highly constructed
sense of self. I took what I learned in dramatic literature classes
(where we sat safely behind desks) to the BU *Free Press* and surprised
myself by offering to write theater criticism with an emphasis on
women, a desire I'd never before consciously articulated.

Shortly after my move from the stage to the page, feminism
worked its way into my consciousness as an adept explanatory system for the kinds of awkwardnesses I'd experience as a young female
actor. The feminism I encountered at the BU Women's Center—fresh,
angry, excessive, and rollicking in 1977—was mixed with Marxism
and nuanced by lesbianism. As I gradually learned the feminist
analysis, I knew I'd found a method to explain what I felt and saw.

The acting experience had been so soured for me that returning to performance in some sort of feminist venue never crossed my mind. Feminist politics, already critical of dominant social values, seemed more clearly linked to my pursuit of a career as a cultural observer. But the Boston women's community in the late 1970s, although active and diverse, was much more committed to developing a political analysis than to engaging with my nascent feminist theater criticism. Women's culture was young and celebratory, but theater, as in other venues I've worked in since, was an anomolous stepchild, not at all as highly or closely regarded as film or television or, especially, the women's music scene into which feminism first poured its aesthetic energy and money.

During my two years living in Boston, post-BU, I wrote film and theater reviews for *Sojourner,* a feminist monthly produced out of Cambridge.[5] The editorial collective published my reviews, but no one seemed as convinced as I was of the importance of the performance critique I was trying to fashion. I was also growing cynical about the idealism and constraints of the feminist theater movement. Feminist theater workers, young and few in the late 1970s, insisted that feminist criticism function only as cheerleading. Reviewing a leftist/feminist production at Maxine Klein's Little Flags Theatre in Roxbury[6] with only halfhearted enthusiasm brought me her wrath, a reaction repeated by most of the political theater workers about whose productions I wrote. Unable to give up some sort of critical position to support any and all feminist endeavors, I found myself as a critic become anathema to the groups whose work I most wanted to engage.

Graduate school in the Performance Studies Department at New York University (NYU) became a place for me to work on a feminist theater criticism in a more systematic way. In the common room in the department I met women who shared my commitment to feminism and performance. We began to meet regularly as a support group and decided to publish what eventually became *Women & Performance: A Journal of Feminist Theory.*[7]

My determination to work on a methodology for feminist theater criticism that could accommodate feminist cultural debates and the various ways of looking at them was eventually bolstered by reading feminist theory. I was initially inspired by the French feminist model, which became more visible in the United States in the early 1980s. Like many other American feminists, I was captivated by the poetic descriptions of "writing with the body" that authors such as Hélène Cixous published and thought that *l'écriture féminine* might provide metaphors useful in the pursuit of feminist performance theory.[8] Four years of further reading, writing, and thinking produced *The Feminist Spectator as Critic*.[9] Suggesting that the ways we look at theater are marked by culturally generated identity positions that need accounting for was just beginning to be tried in theater studies in the mid- to late 1980s. Feminist film studies, of course, had created a useful model, one that was adapted and changed for feminist performance criticism.[10] *The Feminist Spectator as Critic* offers a kind of road map for other theater workers and feminist scholars who might find themselves, as I did, looking for new ways to think about their dissatisfactions (or their different pleasures) in the theater.

The metaphor of "stealing the seat" from the hegemonic figure of the white middle-class heterosexual male, and offering it instead to the feminist spectator who would look at representation with a productively critical eye, continues to offer possibilities to my thinking, even as I've come to critique the singularity of the replacement it promotes. The *Spectator* book also reflects my own immersion in performance styles I hadn't encountered in Boston. My location in New York gave me access to a wealth of theater and performance across genres and communities.

The feminist community in New York in the early 1980s was disparate and uncohesive (at least for a white Jewish lesbian living in the West Village), which gave it a refreshingly undogmatic face. Women Against Pornography toured Times Square, and other radical feminist groups asserted their values visibly, but there were also pockets of resistance and irreverence such as the WOW Cafe, which seemed to enact the complexities of the materialist feminist stance I'd come to adopt.

The *Spectator* book admires most the work that refused the principles of cultural feminism's emphasis on gender celebration and pacificism, which I saw at that time as a kind of feminist religion. The gender-bending experiments at WOW, and at the other Lower East Side clubs like Limbo Lounge and the Pyramid Club, seemed outlawed from the feminist core. These performances were sexy and politically inflected and used parody and satire to launch what I considered incisive social critiques. They also managed to be fun and entertaining, and I liked them for that.

Going to the lesbian performances at the WOW Cafe, and watching the performers experiment with sexuality and gender representation, not only challenged my theoretical and critical thinking but also profoundly stirred me as a typically disenfranchised spectator. Because for the first time I could see evidence of my own lesbian experience and my own materialist political perspective in the performances I wrote about, I went on to suggest that the performances at WOW offered the most potential for subverting the historically conservative performances of gender authorized by theater production. These lesbian producers offered what I called, borrowing from feminist theorist Teresa de Lauretis, a "view from elsewhere."[11] The *Spectator* book likewise suggests that lesbian spectators are most competent to read the subversion of gendered meanings in performance, because lesbians have perhaps the most at stake—or the most to lose—in buying into the coerced coincidence of biology and gender role.

Critical theory produced since *Spectator*, and my own shifting positionalities, has persuaded me to modify this reification of lesbian spectators. I think I was fortunate to be in New York at that time, to be able to witness, enjoy, and participate in the radical meanings generated by those performances. Since then I have lived for various periods of time in Pittsburgh, Pennsylvania, in Seattle, Washington, in Madison, Wisconsin, and in Davis, California, and I haven't seen anything quite like the WOW Cafe performances replicated in those places. What might be considered a gap in my theater experiences, though, has been filled in other ways, with other questions and other ideas about other communities of theater production and reception.

The current change in my thinking comes partly from my own reinvolvement in theater production, and partly from shifts in my own geography. Leaving New York, as the politics of location (geographically read) would predict, profoundly changed the focus of my writing.[12] Accepting a position at the University of Wisconsin and moving to Madison in early 1988, I suddenly found myself wrenched from what appeared to be the center of the action and panicked, for a while, over what performances I would write about.[13] Living in New York made me parochial, and, ironically, I had to relearn the first rule of thumb in performance studies: performance happens all around us, if you look at it that way.

The Professional Politics of History and the Local Context of Work: The Women and Theatre Program

When I enrolled in the graduate program at NYU in the fall of 1981, there was no track in feminism and performance and theory. Now *feminism* and *theater* are only two of many terms joined to describe the field's growing commitment to a diversity of critical and practical perspectives. Two of the articles collected here point out the growing complexities of negotiating an area of expertise whose cultural (and academic) capital grew exponentially in a very short time. This growth exacerbated the identity politics, academic politics, and aesthetic politics that clanged against one another as scholars and practitioners, critics and theorists, men and women, lesbians and heterosexuals, jockeyed for position. Many of these negotiations happened at the Women and Theatre Program (WTP) "preconferences," which take place before the Association for Theatre in Higher Education (ATHE) conference each year. As an event whose importance increased as feminism became more visible in theater studies, the preconference[14] became the crucible in which issues were ground together to create complex, rich, and sometimes painful reactions.

Since 1980, at least, these meetings have served as a lightning rod for feminist issues in theater studies. The first fight in the program was over feminism, as a politic and as a critique. Women playwrights and directors aspiring to a more humanist commitment to the profession responded angrily to critics (mostly academics) who insisted on a specifically feminist approach to work discussed. The feminists won that one, and WTP started producing performance artists instead of plays and presented work by WTP members, instead of inviting "outside" practitioners to speak on its preconference panels.

The next fight in the program was about theory, and subtextually, about lesbians. Theory became equated with "maleness," as it did elsewhere in feminist academic circles, which I thought then and think now was at least partly a code word for homophobia, since many of those promoting theory in the WTP were lesbians. (*Many,* of course, is a relative term, which in this context probably didn't exceed five.) The male-like lesbians traded in male-like theory, and both had to be resisted, mostly with language that reified the most passive stereotypes of femininity.[15] The so-called elitist language that liberated some women to consider expanded definitions of performance and representation alienated others, and the debates were heated and personal.

"Staking Claims and Positions" and "In Defense of the Discourse"—collected here under the first section, "Gender Polemics"—work with materials gathered from the WTP preconference in San Diego in August 1988, a historical moment at which the field's arrival threatened to simultaneously tear it apart. These articles discuss the vociferous debates about theory, the issue that dominated conference discussions that year, and both contextualize and take a position on these events. As the piece describes, the preconference meetings in 1988 got "bloody" because the year in some ways marked feminist performance theory's debut as a respectable academic venture.[16] The stakes were suddenly quite high and the claims quite visible.

Despite what Erika Munk referred to as the "blood on the floor,"[17] I still remember San Diego as a conference that set the terms for much of the work that followed in feminist performance theory, criticism, and practice. Marianne Goldberg presented the first of several theory pieces that she formulated for WTP participants; Kate Bornstein performed a narrative of her many gendered selves; and Anna Deavere Smith shared an "On the Road" installment compiled specifically for the program.[18]

"Staking Claims and Positions" is offered as "occasional" writing, in a style Nancy Miller, in her book *Getting Personal*, describes as narrative criticism. Such writing uses occasional events to contextualize theory that develops in feminist fields. Because the preconference was the one "place" at which many feminist theater critics, theorists, and practitioners met each year, it became a kind of local context for much of our critical and creative thinking. Miller argues that these "local contexts . . . need to remain a visible part of both the writing and our discussions of it." The article, then, analyzes an event at which "academics and critics perform[ed]," that "shape[d] critical practices trans-institutionally and publicly."[19] Because the preconference that year was vital to the growth of feminist performance theory, erasing the event from any writing I might do about the issues would have seemed false.

I wrote about the Women and Theatre meetings because they'd become my passion, the center of my intellectual and political commitments during my early years at UW. Since I was located in Madison, the ATHE conferences and the WTP annual meetings that preceded them became my lifeline to colleagues and ideas and performance styles and contents that now felt very far away. I think many of us felt that way, which is why San Diego in 1988 and New York in 1989 were so explosive and fraught. Feminist theater scholars and practitioners needed one another a lot, to abate the isolation we felt at our home institutions and in the rest of theater studies. There was a lot at stake in those two days prior to the ATHE conference: community to forge and rend; ideas to develop, extend, debate; performances to see and critique; arguments to have that we didn't feel safe enough to have at home.

But around us, or maybe because of us, theater studies was changing, eager to accommodate a feminist critique because it seemed the liveliest work in the profession. When jobs were offered on the basis of what had once been an outlawed perspective and book contracts were extended to distribute the work, our special area of expertise had to play by different rules. The community got bigger but seemed less intense. Everyone wasn't in it for the same reasons (if we ever were). Sue-Ellen Case wrote of these events:

> With success comes, for some, its spoils and that which it does spoil. For others, success brings a continuing and disappointing invisibility. The simple bonding, provided by the early outcast status of the movement is no longer to be taken for granted. Spoils bring power differences.[20]

In its move toward academic acceptance as a subspecialty feminist theater criticism lost its rebel status. I think that's partly what people mourned in some of those fights about theory and identity. This provided another part of the fight's complicated subtext.

There's an institutionally younger generation attending the WTP meetings now, feminist graduate students who have been trained academically at a time when feminism is a valued, vital part of curricular offerings. Energized in response to incursions into the political and social field by antiabortion activists and the New Right, these women are deeply political and very sophisticated, theoretically and practically.

This new generation has many more places to go to engage in

critical debates about theater and performance, gender and the "performative." Once theory really established itself in the academy, and once critical studies became its own interdisciplinary location, the WTP annual meetings no longer seemed as crucial an arena. Many interdisciplinary conferences were created and caucuses devised in others that siphoned off some of the intellectual and political energy of the WTP. One of the things the program hasn't yet accomplished—including under my own tenure as vice-president and president from 1988–92—is the legitimation of its own feminist performance theory as a discipline (interdisciplinary as it is) in its own right, as feminist film theory has so well established itself. The second-class status that haunts theater studies at large is particularly irksome around its feminist component, where so much important work has been done.

If feminist performance theory was reactive at its inception, borrowing from feminists in film, it has come to develop its own stamp, on its own terms. (Elin Diamond's article, "Brechtian Theory/Feminist Theory" comes to mind as exemplary.)[21] But that specific energy was too quickly redirected to forums where the stakes are larger, such as the Modern Language Association (MLA), and too quickly translated into cultural studies and gay and lesbian studies. Rather than forming affinity groups with these fields, feminist theater studies too often seems subsumed by or assimilated into them.

The WTP conferences continue to provide a key location in which the field pushes at its own limits and steadily redefines its concerns. There is usually, still, at least one disruption, for which I'm glad. The disruption in 1992 centered on racial tensions, an area in which the mostly white program has yet to do enough productive work. That year's debate was deeply and widely political and tore at the fabric of the program by challenging its own identity rather than its methods.

The disruption boiled over at *Eye to Eye: Telling Stories, Breaking Boundaries*, a performance by Jewish lesbian performance artist/writer Jyl Lynn Felman and African-American lesbian performance artist/writer Shirley Hayden Whitely, in which the two women listened to and seduced each other in performance with their modified autobiographical narratives. There was little movement in the piece, which resembled a poetry performance more than even performance art, but quite a lot of looking back and forth between Whitely and

Felman and much listening, reacting to, and sometimes speaking each other's tales. The dominating narrative in the piece, though, was Felman's, who reiterated her insistence on speaking of "*my* erotic, *my* desire." Her story (and her gravelly, East Coast–inflected voice) was laced with references to her Jewish ethnicity, the motivating ground of her desire.

The discussion afterward immediately focused on what was called Felman's silencing of Whitely's voice. Outraged spectators demanded to know how a Jewish woman could step so nonchalantly into the spotlight at the expense of her African-American sister. Many spectators' offense at the piece centered on an expectation of the equal representation of Felman's and Whitely's two different voices, which the performers insisted was not their intent. Whitely was nearly called an Uncle Tom, even though she spoke eloquently about her desire to hear Felman's story rather than speak her own. Felman was positioned as the dirty Jew, who'd once again usurped performative capital by presenting herself at the center. Her reasoned reply that Jewish women are sexually invisible and objectified at the same time, and are rarely represented as in charge of their erotic presence and desires, was disregarded.

A different hierarchy of race and ethnicity had been enforced by the discussion, one that did not acknowledge Jewish specificity but, instead, subsumed it under the category "white." Someone cried racism, and it suddenly became all right to be anti-Semitic, since some Jews have white-skin privilege. I was unsettled by my own response to the discussion, partly because the critique reminded me so much of the 1987 preconference, when Phyllis Jane Rose stood behind a group of women of color from At the Foot of the Mountain, who'd been invited to perform for the meetings, and appeared to speak for them. Author's intent didn't matter to me then, as I and other conference participants critiqued what we saw as Rose's authoritative and authorial control of the representational frame.[22] I was partly horrified that, in 1992, author's intent seemed to me a good enough explanation, that I thought the performers' choices were justified by a description of their process. Perhaps this time, from my position, I saw the visual power between the white Jewish lesbian and the African-American lesbian as much more equal, because I read the Jewish woman, too, as disenfranchised historically by representation. Watching Jyl Lynn Felman's performance was like leafing through photographs of seldom visited sites in my own identity; this Jewish lesbian who refused to be good seemed to be my own id, released.

This exchange placed me once again in a position in which my own identity markers flared in rage. Someone seems always to be excluded, the other in the binary on which the whole system depends. It's fashionable to talk now of multiple, intersecting identities, but very difficult to really think through and practice them all at once, without some consciously or unwittingly exclusionary gesture. As a Jew, I felt dirty and dismissed after that performance, placed within the outline of the historically derogatory cartoon that draws my race.

As my angry response to the conference discussion illustrates, I can't retreat from the reactions identity politics promote. In this postmodern moment some feminists are rejecting the strictures of identity politics and its insistence on visibility, and others want to temper postmodernism by reasserting the need to clearly mark categories such as "woman," which they argue have been fractured beyond efficacy by ever-splitting subjectivities. Many of my colleagues in theater and performance studies have theorized recently against visible identity as an origin of political action. Peggy Phelan, for example, on another 1992 preconference panel, insisted that our eyes can't secure identity and that the link between representation and the real must remain uncertain; otherwise, representation becomes servant to doxa.[23]

I'm persuaded and compelled by these debates. But I find myself unwilling and unable to give up identity, however constructed, positional, and unstable, as a place from which to begin my work—not as an ontologically meaningful home and a safe, idealized origin, but as a place of material circumstance that has deeply marked my own embodiments and movements through culture and discourse. If "lesbian" and "Jew" are the two labels through which I'm most easily disparaged and historically reviled, how can I stop reclaiming some even temporary, provisional version of them as part of my theoretical and theatrical project?[24] Although (or because) conference discussions seem to break down in moments of embodiment, theater practice is a likely place to risk experiment with how these intersections might productively be viewed.

Rethinking the Critical History: The Essays

The first section of *Presence and Desire* is called "Gender Polemics" and gathers essays that specifically address the implications of feminist theory for the representation of gender in theater and performance production. "Personal, Political, Polemical: Feminist Approaches to Politics and Theater" is meant as an introduction to the field. It offers paradigms and methods, historicizes the shifts in feminist thinking and activism, and charts the sea changes of feminist theater and performance and its attendant (or dissenting) criticism. From my experience using the piece in my own "Introduction to Contemporary American Feminism and Theater" course, it serves to illuminate the general vocabulary and methodologies in the field, for women's studies students without a theater background and for theater students who come to the course with little knowledge of even recent feminist history. My courses at Madison, especially on the introductory undergraduate level, have had to straddle these two audiences, which are sometimes unaware of each other's experiences and wary of what their very different political and practical positions will mean in class discussions. "Personal, Political, Polemical" works as an icebreaker by explicitly joining the two terms *feminism* and *theater* and by launching my own opinionated argument about how they're best employed together.

In the few years since I wrote the article I've grown to disagree with some of the basic premises on which the essay is built. For instance, I'm not sure we can say as safely, in 1992, that plays that receive prizes tend to be more conservative, as I once felt so surely about the Pulitzer-winning plays by women. I still think that *'night, Mother, Crimes of the Heart,* and *The Heidi Chronicles* don't represent the best plays written by women in the most dominant cultural contexts, but Jane Wagner's collaboration with Lily Tomlin, *Search for Signs of Intelligent Life in the Universe,* is a remarkable example of a play that won Broadway acclaim and success without compromising its political insights. The number of women playwrights I've since met or read through the Jane Chambers Playwrighting Award of the WTP persuades me that there are still playwrights determined to bring a political critique to regional and alternative theater forums whose work might someday be eligible (and deservedly so) for large prestigious prizes.[25] The lines between conservative and radical don't appear as clearly drawn to me as they once did.

"Personal, Political, Polemical" has been revised for publication here with material inserted about my experiments translating feminist theory and history into theater practice in a production of *The Heidi Chronicles*, which I directed in the summer of 1992 for the University Theatre at the University of Wisconsin–Madison. The essay articulates my antipathy for Wasserstein's play, but directing it in a summer theater season meant to be profitable for our department allowed me to tangle with all the contradictions of using feminist critical strategies and production practices to push at the limitations of an enormously popular text written by a woman playwright.

The current political situation in the United States also requires that the article be historicized. When I wrote the piece I hoped that a kind of radical political action might be resurrected in the 1990s through "attacks on women's reproductive rights and the reactionary backsliding of the Reagan and Bush administrations," one that might replicate the "ferment of the 1960s." But there's something qualitatively different about activism in the 1990s, changes wrought by communications technology and the media, which require activists to be sophisticated in manipulating representational power. Operation Rescue, which Peggy Phelan has written about so insightfully, is as successful (if not more so) in gaining media attention as Queer Nation and ACT-UP, which puts conservative and radical closer together in their choice of strategy, if not ideology. Conservatives in 1992 appear to be better at the old kinds of street activism than the radicals.

The acclaimed gender gap, prompted by the attack on Anita Hill during the Senate Judiciary Committee hearings in the fall of 1991, asserted itself in the 1992 national election, with senatorial and congressional seats being fought under the auspices of women's ire at their homeboys willful misogyny.[26] But grassroots feminism, and the theater that was born of it in the 1960s, can no longer communicate effectively in a postmodern era that deprecates the local while appealing to some superficial imperialist sense of the global through communication technologies. The country has become more complicated. The mediatization of the United States makes something quite different of "political theater" as a popular culture genre.[27] Too often political theater work either seems hopelessly nostalgic or naive, or it can't adequately address the multiple sites of oppression at which any radical politic now has to work. The paucity of strategies that take direct, embodied action in an era of simulation justify, in part, searching for new political methods that might be more efficacious.

If collective, grassroots feminist theater is a movement whose heyday has passed, the 1990s have so far seen more visibility for female solo performers, whose work has been described through a contemporary feminist critique that accounts for the complexity of media and representation. Porn star cum performance artist Annie Sprinkle shares the mantle with National Endowment for the Arts (NEA)–damned Karen Finley as the most voyeuristically desired female stage presences and the most sought-after objects of scholarly attention. Anna Deavere Smith has been in some ways more successful than Sprinkle or Finley, reaching the mass audience with *Fires in the Mirror*, a piece from her "On the Road" series, which chronicled the racial rage in Crown Heights, and *Twilight: Los Angeles, 1992*, which did the same for the aftermath of the Rodney King beating verdict. That these women have prompted discussion and debate, have been reviewed and grudgingly funded, have inspired writers and scholars looking for new models of feminist multicultural performance, indicates a shift in how and where we look for feminist theater activity. Work on feminist collectives is now a part of feminist historical scholarship.[28]

"Personal, Political, Polemical" somewhat foresees this shift by concentrating on work by Spiderwoman Theatre described as oppositional in form, content, and context to work by Wendy Wasserstein. Spiderwoman Theatre—which hasn't received the amount of attention garnered by performers whose work was generated at, for instance, the WOW Cafe[29]—could be seen as an eclectic collection of solo performers, bound together in a commitment to send their work into the hearts and minds of well-meaning liberal spectators. Describing Spiderwoman's *Winnetou's Snake-Oil Show from Wigwam City* as elaborating on and continuing the feminist history that Wasserstein's *Heidi Chronicles* elides points toward the importance of seeing ethnicity and race fully at the crossroads of gender and sexuality politics.

The article concentrates on the rage of exclusion that has galvanized various stages of American feminism. Feminists are still angry in 1992 and very much resistant to declarations of our movement(s)'s death(s).[30] But focusing on the very different angers that fuel the rage of white feminists and feminists of color is a productive step into the painful, imperative politics of difference. *The Heidi Chronicles'* erasure of any and all women's rage damns it still as a false, demeaning history.

"Personal, Political, Polemical," written in the late 1980s, cautions:

> Borrowing from so many of critical theory's most popular thinkers has lent feminism in the academy a peculiar respectability. This acceptance has prompted the curious incidence of "men in feminism," a phrase that ominously predicts the detachment of feminism from the experience—the personal, after all—from which it developed.

These "inside versus outside" debates have widened even further in feminist thinking. Tania Modleski's book, *Feminism without Women*, for example, worries not just about men dressed in feminist clothing but also about the abdication of actual women from feminism, prodded by the potential excesses of poststructuralism's anti-identitarian logic. "In the final analysis," Modleski writes, "it seems more important to struggle over what it *means* to be a woman than over whether or not to be one."[31] Well-intentioned feminist theorizing against binary thinking is sometimes mired in a series of peculiar inclusions and exclusions. Exploding and discarding the category "woman" allows men to be included as critical cross-dressers.[32] But, as Modleski argues, there are potential racial exclusions. She suggests, "Excluding women from a contested category on the grounds that there *is no category* may well be the latest ruse of white middle-class feminism."[33] There is much at stake, still, in the gender and racial identities of feminism, theory, and theater.

Part of the problem lies with the notion of feminism itself as an identity, rather than a practice. bell hooks argues eloquently for feminism as a politic one advocates, rather than an ontology one embodies.[34] Detaching feminist politics from ontology might open up more productive strategies for creating coalitions and affinity groups, rather than identity cliques that jealously guard their epistemological and ontological cores.

Yet there is something that can't be so quickly dismissed about the emotional charge of what identity politics has come to describe too fixedly. Ed Cohen, for example, adding his voice to the many currently theorizing identity politics as exclusionary and limited, cautions that critiques of gender and sexuality such as Judith Butler's, that insist these categories are only repeated surface enactments, fail to account for how "local 'strategies of subversive repetition' crystallize into new constellations of relationship and position, i.e., how they cohere as 'movements.'"[35] Cohen argues for a modified notion of somatic depth, in which "(e)motion" allows people to be moved into political action. "You see," Cohen writes, "I *feel* there *is* something 'different' about the body: I *believe* feeling is the difference that bodies make, a difference that *moves* people to action."[36] This argument for the importance of feeling to political movement, however destabilized and perhaps performed, is enormously useful to theatrical representations that would have some political and (e)motion(al) effect on spectators.[37]

"In Defense of the Discourse: Materialist Feminism, Postmodernism, Poststructuralism . . . and Theory" takes up questions of identity and efficacy through poststructuralist and postmodernist logic. Written in a polemical but introductory style, "In Defense of the Discourse" was meant to frame issues about identity, language, and representation in feminist performance theory that were becoming more and more obviously entrenched and dichotomous. I looked at a number of reviews of recently published books of feminist theater criticism for clues about how the field was being received and perceived and ways in which to speculate about the underlying (and overriding) ideological factions forming the critical camps.

My implicit use of military metaphors here must be evidence of the "return of the repressed," since, as "In Defense of the Discourse" explains, so much of the criticism of feminist performance theory was couched in complaints about its so-called militaristic maleness. These fights about the genderedness (and whiteness) of theory unfortunately continue, especially in women's studies. But getting past the gender block is the first step toward seeing methodologies as differently capable tools that depend quite a lot on the context in which they're articulated for how useful and/or radical they become.

As "In Defense" describes, the antitheory drum was beat to rally women against the direction certain writers had decided to take. The published response to books such as Case's *Feminism and Theatre* and Hart's edited volume, *Making a Spectacle,* and to my own *Feminist Spectator as Critic* seemed illuminating about the horizon of expectations established by the field. The dichotomy between critic and artist, academic and professional, woman and feminist, was clearly marked in most of the reviews I surveyed for the article and profoundly ignored the challenges to binary thinking postmodernist and poststructuralist feminism provided.

"In Defense of the Discourse" takes the first two articles collected here under "Gender Polemics" and builds on them, referring once again to recent feminist history, to the WTP preconferences as an important site of theoretical and practical engagement,[38] and to the complications of identity politics as an originary system for feminist activism or feminist representations. The essay stands as another "occasional" piece, but one in which my own passion for theory's complicated explanations grounds my descriptions and my arguments.

As I look back over the article, it's striking that the publications I survey are mostly literary critical and/or performance-oriented studies, rather than historiography or discussions of practice. The critical and theoretical writings in feminist performance studies introduced the field, but by the early 1990s feminist historians such as Tracy Davis and Ellen Donkin have contributed new methods and questions to fill in the shortfalls of a solely critical approach.[39] The new historiography, with its mixture of sociohistorical and cultural/critical inquiry, has rounded out the edges of the field since "In Defense" was written.

Upstaging Big Daddy, Ellen Donkin and Susan Clement's coedited anthology of articles on feminist directing strategies, will add a much needed theoretical spin to studies of performance practice. *Acting Out,* Lynda Hart and Peggy Phelan's coedited sequel to *Making a Spectacle,* will engage critically, theoretically, and historically with many of the women solo and performance artists that the *Spectacle* book chose to overlook in its emphasis on women playwrights.[40]

In all, "In Defense" would be a much different essay if written today, because of the wealth of published feminist theater studies writing to which it would now have to respond. But even at this remove I'd agree with its main premises. I worry about the potential excesses of postmodernist and poststructuralist approaches that might lead to an enervating relativity for political movements, but I still fear the imposition of universalist truths trumpeted by an unproblematized humanism. I still think that "truth is changeable, permeable," as I write in the article, but I no longer think it's "irrelevant." "Provisional" is a more apt description for how truth might best stake its claim in the cultural landscape.

In theater, however, my recent experiences with production have confirmed the need to approach truth-claims with a healthy suspicion. As the last essay in this section, "Gender, Sexuality, and 'My Life' in the (University) Theatre," describes, mounting a resistant, postmodern/poststructuralist production of Marlane Meyer's *Etta Jenks* proved with almost frightening clarity how forcefully spectators demand truth-claims to be advanced in the theater. Our insistence, with *Etta Jenks*, to bring spectators into the epicenter of a debate about pornography and female sexuality, rather than clearly offering them one side or the other with which to align themselves, provoked a disgruntled, disturbed response from many of our University Theatre's spectators. What is theater if not a place for affirmation of values and beliefs and ways of inculcating them? they seemed to ask. What kind of "unethical" mind could create a production concept in which a polemic could be advanced but not answered?

The article describes a process of theorizing in practice some of the questions raised by "In Defense of the Discourse" and other writing about identification, subjectivity, and reception. Trying to thwart, from a director's perspective, the exigencies of the male gaze, in a play about pornography that could otherwise allow a director to cultivate the prurience of looking, challenged ideas expressed in my own writing. But my experience with the production reasserted the pedagogical function of feminist praxis, for me and for the actors, dramaturgs, and designers. We never sought a single truth from our work but looked for all the provisional ones that might open up the options through which Etta and her cohorts—and the actors and theirs—might express a fuller subjectivity.

That production, and the article that came of it, allowed me to test hypotheses I'd been making in my writing and profoundly deepened my respect for theater practitioners working resistantly under the weight of its apparatus. I found presence and desire rekindled for me, in performances and in rehearsals, and, in writing about the play, a renewed faith in my own commitments to performance as a laboratory for culture.[41]

Visibility as Epistemology, Sexuality as Ontology

The next essays gathered in *Presence and Desire* are grouped in a section called "Sexuality and Visibility," the conjunction of which is now highly debated by gay and lesbian activists and theorists. Butler, for example, challenges profoundly a lesbian and gay politic built on asserting the visibility of marginalized identities:

> There is no question that gays and lesbians are threatened by the violence of public erasure, but the decision to counter that violence must be careful not to reinstall another in its place. Which version of lesbian or gay ought to be rendered visible, and which internal exclusions will that rendering visible institute? Can the visibility of identity *suffice* as a political strategy, or can it only be the starting point for a strategic intervention which calls for a transformation of policy? Is it not a sign of despair over public politics when identity becomes its own policy, bringing with it those who would "police" it from various sides?[42]

Butler's reading forecasts a theoretical climate in which the exclusions of identity politics have been thoroughly routed, along with their stabilizing claims to a totalized, fixed assumption of lesbian subjectivity.

The articles in this section must be read through this recent theoretical castigation of identity politics. Historicized this way, however, the essays also can be placed in counterpoint to Butler's argument, asserting the remnants of efficacy for the visual while arguing that the subjectivities and sexual practices brought into view don't necessarily have to dictate public, fixed, totalizing identity policies.

The earliest of this set of articles, "Desire Cloaked in a Trenchcoat," was written in 1987 and presented in a draft version at the ATHE conference in Chicago that August. Five years later the article already seems historical, since the issues it worries have since become part of the regular discourse of theater studies. But it continues to stir my imagination and to point toward research and thinking that remains to be done.

I wonder, now, if "the image of the woman sitting in a darkened theater wearing a trenchcoat is incongruous at best." Lesbian pornography has become much more visible since I wrote this article, and many more theorists have suggested ways for women in general to take pleasure in representations of their own and others' sexuality.[43] With Susie "Sexpert" Bright a published and widely distributed author,[44] and with more and more lesbian magazines with a markedly sexual slant vying for consumption, the woman in the trenchcoat might not even find herself alone in the theater. Scholars, critics, consumers, producers, and performers might surround her, congenially laughing and whistling at the not-so-grainy, wry, and witty representations screened for their pleasurable contemplation. They might not find themselves congregating at a local porn house, parking in a seedy lot and entering the dingy theater furtively, but might experience their spectatorial community as a celebration, at a gay and lesbian studies conference, at a lesbian film festival, or around the VCR in their homes and community spaces. The openness and sexiness of pornography as a topic, in the academy and in gay and lesbian culture, inflects "Desire Cloaked in a Trenchcoat" differently in this revised context.[45] It couldn't be written in quite the same way today.

Nonetheless, the basic paradigm still holds. I'm fascinated by how often the influence of sexuality on representation is borne out, in plot or form, in genres as diverse as mainstream theater and film, television, popular culture, and performance art, and in contexts as different as subscription-based regional theaters, coffeehouses, and art clubs. Some of this fascination is teased out in other articles collected here: "'Lesbian' Subjectivity in Realism" looks at the paradigmatic love story for instances of realism's control over the structure of sexual relations and their cultural expression, and "Practicing Cultural Disruptions" suggests that the love story's erotic tone—whether the doomed or lucky lovers are heterosexual or not—might productively be exploded by the baser, more physical, excessive, bodily based representations of pornography.

"Breaking the Code: Musings on Lesbian Sexuality and the Performer" refashions questions about the link between sexuality and representation by looking at the performer, rather than theorizing the spectator. The essay is very much informed by Teresa de Lauretis's key article, "Sexual Indifference and Lesbian Representation," which cautioned not to reify a lesbian subjectivity based only on sexual identity.[46] As she did in her important introduction to *Feminist Studies/Critical Studies*, de Lauretis argued the necessity of looking at differences within and between women, rather than taking one un-problematized instance of identity (such as lesbian) as determining.[47]

de Lauretis's article influenced my thinking about lesbian representation quite a lot, but in "Breaking the Code" I skirted the dangers of the very essentialism against which she cautioned. The terms on which I suggest a lesbian theater community of performers and spectators might be built appear restrictive to me now, as the article argues for a correspondence between performer, identity, and role. Such a strict correlation makes a biologism of lesbian identity, rather than seeing it as a less constricting, more fluid, less congruous instance of cultural performance crossed by multiple identity positions.[48]

Some of my examples, though, come from wondering about the choices confronting performers and producers in actual production settings. In my explication of Cherríe Moraga's *Giving Up the Ghost* I say that the play "demands the presence of a Chicana lesbian body to carry its meanings. Who, then, can perform this text, and under what production circumstances? And who can comprise the social audience it requires to change the conditions of what can be seen?" Reading work by women of color such as Moraga seemed at the time of my writing to demand a distance from white feminists, a respect for the difference of the community it speaks from and to. The most radical suggestion seemed to be to let white lesbians into the theater but to keep them respectfully and appropriately watching from the door. Perhaps now, after new phases of feminist multiculturalist theorizing that point out the impossibility of uncrossed identities, it becomes important to rethink my own work at the intersections of multiple communities and to find new metaphors to describe how people might congregate at the theater.

In reading writing by feminists theorizing in various disciplines, I'm trying to rethink the notion of what "radical" can mean in the context of feminist theater practice and reception. This word seems contingent upon the context in which it's posed, and very much connected to the ways we build audiences for our productions and for our theoretical and critical writing. Rather than the closed communities based on singular identity positions from which I charted my argument in "Breaking the Code," I'm lately persuaded by writers such as sociologist Iris Marion Young on the imminent fascism of certain communities, that breed inside/outside boundaries from which only totalizing, exclusionary definitions of identity can be posed.[49] As Diana Fuss, in her introduction to *Inside/Out*, argues cogently:

> The problem, of course, with the inside/outside rhetoric, if it remains undeconstructed, is that such polemics disguise the fact that most of us are both inside and outside at the same time. Any misplaced nostalgia for or romanticization of the outside as the privileged site of radicality immediately gives us away, for in order to idealize the outside we must already be, to some degree, comfortably entrenched on the inside. We really only have the leisure to idealize the subversive potential of the power of the marginal when our place of enunciation is quite central.[50]

For example, in the context of lesbian "community" theater, then, where do radical politics lie, in production by some comfortably "inside" group reifying its "outsidership" or in the reception of these meanings by those, by virtue of identity or ability to read the signs, outside of them? Is *radical* a term that, in some ways, is only protected by its inside/out community of origin? Aren't the ways theaters "do" radical contained by the practices of the communities that foster them?

At the end of *The Feminist Spectator as Critic* I questioned whether lesbian work in subcultural performance spaces such as the WOW Cafe could retain its radical meanings when it moved into larger venues, away from primarily lesbian spectators, or whether it might be neutralized as a commodity consumable in a more mainstream economy.[51] I'm no longer sure this is the right question to ask of lesbian performance. I think my definition of *radicality* is simple and even naive, given that, in more recent theory, the category "lesbian," for only one example, has been productively multiplied by other categories, which makes the ideal of a radical, transgressive space, based on a single identity, a rather utopian and exclusive assumption.

While "Breaking the Code" points again and again to a coherent, "true" lesbian identity, there are questions posed in the article that I still find productive. Must sexuality be seen to be known? What can be seen in representation, and who is seeing? "Because the signs of sexuality are inherently performative," as I asserted in the article, does "the assumption of heterosexuality prevail unless homosexual or lesbian practice is made textual"?

Much of the recent scholarship in gay and lesbian studies addresses these questions by studying sexuality and gender as cultural performances. Butler, for instance, argues that heterosexual identities, "those ontologically consolidated phantasms of 'man' and 'woman,' are theatrically produced effects that posture as grounds, origins, the normative measure of the real."[52] But, she goes on to insist, "Sexuality always exceeds any given performance, presentation, or narrative which is why it is not possible to derive or read off a sexuality from any given gender presentation. . . . Sexuality is never fully 'expressed' in a performance or practice. . . . Part of what constitutes sexuality is precisely that which does not appear and that which, to some degree, can never appear."[53]

If sexuality is an always incomplete performance, fashioned continually through the exigencies of context and authority, discourse and the subconscious, it excites desire as much by what it leaves invisible as that which it openly performs. Fuss writes, "Sexual identity might be less a function of knowledge than performance, or, in Foucauldian terms, less a matter of final discovery than perpetual reinvention."[54] The articles in this section of *Presence and Desire* think about how sexualities, if incomplete and only partially visible, perpetually reinvent themselves in various situations of performance and reception and how the parts of sexual practice that do enter the visible can be politically effective in disrupting the heterosexual norm.

At the end of "Breaking the Code" I argue that, "for lesbian spectators, a heterosexual woman would not be believable as a lesbian. As much as she might empathize or do visualization exercises to project herself into a lesbian role, a heterosexual woman will never know, in her body, what it feels like to be queer in a homophobic culture." This bodily knowledge remains evocative for me.[55] Through discourse, the body becomes a palimpsest of experience and resistance. The lesbian performer can demonstrate her various bodily and discursive texts, in a Brechtian fashion. But, if sexuality is performance (and if, as I quote in "Breaking the Code," "performance is sex"), why can't a woman first taught heterosexuality learn to perform some variant of lesbian sexual practice onstage? Sexuality is part of material existence, semiotized on the body. I now think it's productive for a heterosexual woman to imaginatively write on her body the experiences of a lesbian, performed in a kind of Brechtian laboratory of "not" and "but." Otherwise, sexuality is only expressive, transparently spoken from and toward a biologized origin of lesbian identity.

"Peeling Away the Tropes of Visibility: Lesbian Sexuality and Materialist Performance Practice" was written in honor of the feminist/postmodernist/revisionist production of *A Midsummer Night's Dream* I codirected with Phillip Zarrilli at the University of Wisconsin–Madison in 1991. The article works as a useful companion piece to "Breaking the Code," because my experience in production allowed me to reverse some of the claims about correlating performers' and characters' identities I had made earlier. In the rehearsal process we created together we let chance and imagination replace a neat coincidence of identity, and, as a result, authorized performances of sexuality that were much more open and diverse, pleasurable and complicated, theatrical and performative, than they might have been had we auditioned only lesbians and gay men for roles we'd rewritten as lesbian and gay. *Midsummer* was all about playing with gender and sexuality as constructions. As codirector and only one of the many resident lesbian performance theorists working on the production, I encouraged everyone in the cast to play with the possibilities of working against their assigned (or chosen) sexuality and gender. As the essay reports, the experience was pleasurable and productive, an ironic coda to work that tried to circle the wagons around an idealized lesbian community.

Form, Content, Context: Sex in Sight

The last three essays in the "Sexuality and Visibility" section of *Presence and Desire* regard more closely the question of what might enter the visible and in which contexts and the political effects of representing disruptive sexual practices. "'Lesbian' Subjectivity in Realism: Dragging at the Margins of Structure and Ideology" performs a close reading of exemplary dramatic literature through which white lesbian identities have been described and constituted in modern American drama. The essay raises questions, in the process, about the historical and social contexts in which plays by or about lesbians have been allowed into the visible, that is, read and produced in U.S. culture.

The article engages with feminist critical debates about the efficacy of realism as a style and genre, a conversation that has perhaps been feminist performance theory's most valuable contribution to critical studies of representation.

There are feminist scholars still determined to advocate realism's usefulness to a feminist social critique and certainly feminist and female playwrights whose positions require that their formal strategies be what Jeanie Forte calls "readable" and accessible to wide audiences.[56] But the resounding rejection of the form through feminist critical thinking in the 1980s, in which my article participates, was an important gesture toward focusing a feminist critique not only on content—images of women in theater and performance—but also on form. Materialist feminism's borrowing of Marxist critical methods facilitated this focus and sent a generation of feminist theater and performance scholars to write about avant-garde and experimental performance. As I suggest in "'Lesbian' Subjectivity," this prompted a focus on performance art and subcultural performance, a healthy search at the margins of theater practice for work that might belie the domestic conformity of realism's style and contents.

Dramatic literature by and/or about lesbians, as a result, hasn't won the same enthused critical attention as less text-based work. I was led to return to anthologized and published plays partly because of my location in Madison, away from a proliferation of experimental lesbian performance activity. In the article I disagree with Forte's reading of realism's potential for social change, but I think now that it's important to continue looking at theater productions offered under realism's auspices. The limitations of mimesis have been usefully theorized, but the seductions of the search for reflection and validation, especially for marginalized communities, must still be reckoned with by feminist critics. Doesn't it mean something important, for example, that some women of color working in supportive critical, artistic, and ethnic communities who desire to reach a kind of "social audience" often employ realism?[57] Why has realism come to occupy the naive position on the critical hierarchy if it continues, like it or not, to fulfill an important function for spectators disenfranchised at dominant cultural production sites?

Shelia Stowell, in "Rehabilitating Realism," launches a vitriolic attack on much of the feminist performance theory that used Catherine Belsey's work to argue that the form is ideologically conservative in its contemporary usage. Stowell calls the feminist critique "ahistorical thinking" and uses mostly turn-of-the-century English and American realist playwrights to argue that realism doesn't, for example, mystify the process of its own production. I find her use of mostly male writers from the early twentieth century makes her critique ahistorical in itself, since the feminist work explicitly focuses on mostly American playwrights after 1945.

But Stowell does make several important points that suggest rejecting realism out of hand is presumptuous. She argues against the notion of Althusserian interpellation, on which much of the feminist performance critique is based: "The audience is not some sort of monolithic tabula rasa unwittingly acquiescing to its inscription by an author."[58] She's right in suggesting that the notion of interpellation, in which subjects are "hailed" through ideology, leaves little room for resistance or for spectators' different reactions to realism's address. Current methods in cultural studies are offering ways to rethink the spectatorial paradigm on which the critique of realism relies.[59]

But Stowell belies her own criticisms of the feminist work when she acknowledges the site specificity of the critique of realism: "As practiced, much realist drama warrants challenge from feminists";[60] practice and production were exactly the point. But the realism debates were never about "silencing women writers who don't 'write right,'"[61] as Stowell suggests, but, rather, depended on a commitment to thinking about the importance of form in launching effective cultural change. Because of critiques such as Stowell's, and ever new methods for thinking about form, returning to realism frequently to check its status and its meanings seems inevitable, even though the basic critical outline of its conservative ideological implications has been thoroughly established.

Writing "'Lesbian' Subjectivity in Realism," I was intrigued by how neatly the plays I studied formalized a structural pattern with moral and ideological implications, in plays that crossed historical moments in American culture. Although I'm not a formalist critic, this pattern of form and meaning became very persuasive. I don't believe that structure is transhistorical or universal and agree with Stowell's assessment that "dramatic forms are not in themselves narrowly partisan."[62] But the important question for feminist critics to ask is why these forms, consistently employed to tell these particular stories, and similarly structured by exposition, crisis, denouement, are so useful to the maintenance of specific patterns of cultural organization.

The questions I raise in "'Lesbian' Subjectivity" about readability, spectatorial competence, and the complications of form rehearse those asked in "Breaking the Code," but already point to a wider range of answers and are broached through a critique of the essentialism that the earlier article espouses. But "'Lesbian' Subjectivity in Realism," too, remains invested in an antiassimilationist discourse that damns realism for its comforting bourgeois familiarity and too easily reifies lesbian reception communities as unquestionably radical. Critiquing Holly Hughes's performance piece, *World without End*, in a footnote, for example, I remarked that, since the piece seems coded to read for a wider audience, and since it describes bisexual content, "Hughes has been domesticated by her own bisexual, bourgeois narrative." I now find this assessment harsh. I do think Hughes's piece is more fascinating as a piece of literature than it is as a performance text, but the notion that playing it to mixed audiences domesticates Hughes's work now seems much too simple.[63] Lurking in the notes and margins of this article is the beginning of a more complex reading of how inside-versus-outside status in marginalized communities appears to "authenticate" lesbian texts and their readings, a reading that rejects the essentialism of such claims and looks for other ways to formulate the issues.

The essay collected in *Presence and Desire* written most recently is "The Body as Flesh: Or, the Danger of the Visual," which reiterates questions about visibility. I argue in this essay that feminist and lesbian criticism and productions must, in fact, militate for images that are the most difficult to see, the ones that profoundly upset our sense of ethical cultural organization. If many of the articles collected in this second section debate the politics of visibility through lesbian subjectivity's performance and reception, "The Body as Flesh" asks what state authority allows to be seen and why and looks at systems of discursive and material power for how they organize the visible and map it across "othered" bodies. This essay briefly considers state power through the NEA censorship controversies and through the antipornography and antisadomasochism debates in 1980s American feminism. The "danger of visual" is defined morally—picking up on Peggy Phelan's provocative suggestion that feminists and the Left might reclaim the power of moral imagining—but also politically, looking at what is considered by normative culture as too dangerous to see, too powerfully perverse to circulate through dominant visual channels.

There is much grist left to mill here. This brief, unpublished essay was presented as a paper in two different versions, one at the 1990 ATHE conference in Chicago, another the same year at the first Performance Studies International Conference in New York. I was captivated by debates around lesbian sadomasochism at that time and eager to think through Pat Califia's seering essays and stories from a Foucauldian perspective. The conjunction of several critical and political moments contributed to my beginning this work: reading lesbian porn, critical theory about power and the body, and accounts of the NEA debates; talking with my friend and colleague Vicki Patraka about the body in pain and how it's figured differently in Holocaust literature and lesbian s/m pornography; and thinking about the fixed meaning of images and whether or not lesbian discourse can really make something different of forms and contents inscribed with long and meaningful and mostly conservative histories.

But once begun I found that the discursive struggles I wanted to chart felt much too material, and the complications of my many identifications with many different positions vis-à-vis the work made me dizzy. My Jewishness tangled with my lesbianism, one chiding the other for various readings of the swastika and other Nazi-like images of dominance and submission; my postmodernism goaded my ethics, one refusing to fix meaning, the other yearning for an image that mattered enough for people to rally their politics behind it. I was very much stirred by the things I read. Califia's introduction to *Macho Sluts*, for example, was beautifully evocative to me, and surprisingly spiritual, in its invocation of the truth of the flesh. Here, at the site of lesbian s/m practice, seemed to be a place to stop the spin of postmodern indifference to the material, to contemplate for a moment, with passion and conviction, the damage that history, exclusion, and conservative morality inflicts on the body. But "The Body as Flesh" was all I could produce. I think the essay is marked by my own questions, ambivalences, doubts, and fears at the entangled identifications I confronted in this material and, for that, remains a turbulent, unfinished piece of thinking.[64]

The last essay I've collected here asks similar questions as "The Body as Flesh," but in the context of representational structures that differently mark choices made under their auspices. "Practicing Cultural Disruptions: Gay and Lesbian Representation and Sexuality" reflects a return to theater, away from social performances back to those rehearsed, performed, and watched with a different intention. I looked at local performances as one of my case studies, finding in Madison, Wisconsin, a variety of lesbian work that helped make my argument. I also looked at a gay male text produced by a straight theater, opening up the sites at which a wider variety of texts might be studied. I remain preoccupied here with the possibilities of pornography as a kind of explicit excess, rather than erotics as a safe, romantic, idealized image. The article writes something of an enduring commitment to challenging the body politic by insisting on making visible practices from which normative culture hides its eyes. I don't propose it's the only politically effective route to follow, but I don't think it's exhausted its potential to unsettle and enrage.

Melding Feminist Practices and Theories

It occurs to me, reading over these articles together, that much of my thinking over the last five years has maintained a critical, political, and theoretical dichotomy between cultural and materialist feminists. The taxonomies of feminism developed in the mid- to late 1980s were enormously useful in historicizing the social and intellectual movements of feminist thought and activism and, in theater studies, described more specifically the various kinds of feminist criticism and productions. But now that the important sifting and distinguishing work has been accomplished and productively employed, feminist theater criticism and theory can move beyond the binaries of materialist and radical thought and practice, to look vigorously at how they can be combined and thought in tandem to create an even more vital critical method and creative practice. Writing theoretically about historical cultural feminist productions has still to be done in feminist theater and performance studies and, in conjunction with methods in cultural studies, can be explored to productive result. The women's music and comedy productions, for example, that first spurred me toward mixing feminism and performance, have not yet been theorized, critiqued, or historicized as important sites of cultural feminist production. Feminist performance theories that take the "risk of essentialism"[65] might find rich objects of analysis in much of this work.

I ended "Peeling Away the Tropes of Visibility" with another call toward the theater as a laboratory for theory: "For many years I've been starting with the theory. I think for awhile I'm going to start with the theater." When the article was published in *Theater Topics*, some people read it to mean that I'd disavowed theory. I have to say they were wrong.

But, in the continuing balancing act between theory and practice that theater studies conducts, the productions on which I've worked recently have allowed me to simply reorder my thinking, rather than rejecting one side of the binary for the other. One of the commitments of feminist theater and performance criticism has been to finding ways to meld theory and practice into praxis, to challenge the hierarchical function of the two terms.

My involvement in *A Midsummer Night's Dream* as codirector and *Etta Jenks*, *The Heidi Chronicles*, and, most recently, *Machinal* as director has allowed me to engage with praxis in a way that I once refused or was refused to me. Early in my five years at Madison I was invited to come to a rehearsal of a feminist play that another faculty member was directing. At the rehearsal's end I was told to feed my comments to the director, later, because as a "theorist," I didn't know how to talk to actors.

It occurs to me that we keep skewering one another over language. If you know some of the intricacies of theory, how can you possibly translate them into a clear, workable acting suggestion? Likewise, if you trade in the language of superobjectives, how can you possibly see past The Method to theorize resistant feminist practice?

Given my own chance to work against these binaries, I find it's possible to keep switching languages, to mix them in a fashion as erotic and forbidden as Gloria Anzaldúa or Cherríe Moraga, when they mold their English with Spanish and other dialects.[66] The point is not to assimilate everything into one accessible, universal patois but, rather, to keep the stew simmering, to encourage actors and dramaturgs and critics to be multilingual in theater studies as well as in the cultural scene. This is what "the Madison experiments," as my colleague Phillip Zarrilli describes much of our production work, have enabled me to do.

One of my fondest memories of the *Midsummer* rehearsal process was the night I first played Gloria Gaynor's 1970s disco song "I Will Survive" for the cast. We intended to use the song to mark the play's move into the forest, which we'd reconfigured as a subcultural gay disco. Gaynor's anthem had anchored my early experiences of liberated dancing in lesbian and gay bars. When we played it for the cast, I introduced it enthusiastically and told them they would eventually come to love it as much as I did. The song, in fact, became a high point of the production and a favorite request at the two cast parties we had afterward. I enjoyed sharing this bit of subcultural lore.

It's this kind of talking on two levels that's become more exciting to me in my recent work. Just as working at theory through practice allows a kind of bilingual code switching that's astute and articulate, working cross-culturally, speaking the codes of gay and lesbian sub-cultures into dominant cultural sites, offers multivocal meanings. Rather than suggesting that only other lesbians can break the codes of subcultural sexual identity, I'm eager to teach the codes I know so that others can trade in them, performatively and playfully. I'm eager to learn the codes I don't know, about sexuality and race and ethnicity, so that I can better educate myself to difference. The point is not to form exclusive clubs with secret codes in which essential identities are transparently expressed but, instead, to make these various de-stabilized, multivocal positions of sexuality visible and available. Theater studies and production have a lot to offer to cultural reimaginings.

NOTES

I'd like to thank Stacy Wolf and Vicki Patraka for their careful readings of drafts of this introduction.

1. Sue-Ellen Case and Janelle Reinelt, in their introduction to their edited volume, *The Performance of Power: Theatrical Discourse and Politics* (Iowa City: University of Iowa Press, 1991), discuss the gender markings and authoritative structures of presence in a number of performative examples. See particularly their discussion of "strategies of surveillance" in performative discourse (xvii). Michael Peterson, whose dissertation "Performance Art

Monologues and White Heterosexual Male Identity" was completed at the University of Wisconsin–Madison (1993), theorizes at length the political pitfalls of an unselfconscious use of presence and "charisma" by white heterosexual male solo performers such as Spalding Gray and Eric Bogosian.

2. Mary Ann Doane, in particular, has theorized the cross-gender effects of spectatorship for women, in *The Desire to Desire: The Woman's Film of the 1940s* (Bloomington: Indiana University Press, 1987), although more recent feminist film theory has found other, more resistant positions for female spectators. See also Doane's recent *Femme Fatales: Feminism, Film Theory, Psychoanalysis* (New York and London: Routledge, 1991).

3. The movement toward (or some would say the return to) more self-reflexive, self-revealing writing in feminist theory and criticism has been performed and remarked upon recently by many feminist scholars. See, for example, Nancy Miller's *Getting Personal: Feminist Occasions and Other Autobiographical Acts* (New York and London: Routledge, 1991), for a white feminist theorist's description of the ramifications of writing her own autobiographical, positioned reflections on her work and her field; and Patricia Williams, *The Alchemy of Race and Rights: Diary of a Law Professor* (Cambridge: Harvard University Press, 1991) for an African-American feminist's combination of theorized life narratives with insightful cultural critique. See also Susan David Bernstein, "Confessing Feminist Theory: What's 'I' Got to Do with It?" *Hypatia* 7, no. 2 (Spring 1992): 120–47, for a thoughtful critique of Miller's, Williams's, and Jane Gallop's first-person, "personal" writing, in which Bernstein usefully points out the limits and liabilities of the "confessional" mode (121).

4. Sue-Ellen Case, "Theory/History/Revolution," in Janelle Reinelt and Joseph Roach, eds., *Critical Theory and Performance* (Ann Arbor: University of Michigan Press, 1992), 427.

5. *Sojourner* is still publishing and is now distributed nationally.

6. Klein had been on the faculty at Boston University when I began there; in fact, she was my freshman acting teacher, before she left her position to create her own theater company. Her *Theatre for the 98%* (Boston: South End Press, 1978) was the first book on political theater I'd ever encountered.

7. *Women & Performance Journal*, too, is still publishing. The journal usually appears now on an annual basis, with issues organized around a central topic. See, for example, the most recent issue, "Feminist Ethnography and Performance," Susan Slyomovic and Judy Burns, guest eds., *Women & Performance Journal #9* 5, no. 1 (1990).

8. See early literature on and translations of *l'écriture féminine* in Elaine Marks and Isabelle de Courtivron, eds., *New French Feminisms* (New York: Schocken Books, 1981). The question of useful metaphors persists for feminist performance theory, and for theater in general, which is becoming more and more a metaphor itself in contemporary critical theory.

9. Jill Dolan, *The Feminist Spectator as Critic* (1988; reprint, Ann Arbor: University of Michigan Press, 1991).

10. See, for example, Doane, *The Desire to Desire*; Teresa de Lauretis, *Alice*

Doesn't: Feminism, Semiotics, Cinema (Bloomington: Indiana University Press, 1984); Kaja Silverman, *The Subject of Semiotics* (New York: Oxford University Press, 1983); and E. Ann Kaplan, *Women & Film: Both Sides of the Camera* (New York and London: Methuen, 1983).

11. Teresa de Lauretis, "The Technology of Gender," *Technologies of Gender: Essays on Theory, Film, and Fiction* (Bloomington: Indiana University Press), 25, as quoted in Dolan, *The Feminist Spectator as Critic* (cf. chap. 6).

12. Adrienne Rich's essay, "Notes toward a Politics of Location," in Muriam Díaz-Diocaretz and Iris M. Zavala, eds., *Women, Feminist Identity, and Society in the 1980s: Selected Papers* (Philadelphia: John Benjamins, 1985), 7–22, has been instrumental in defining the ramifications of spatial and psychic geography. Linda Alcoff's article, "Cultural Feminism vs. Post-Structuralism: The Identity Crisis in Feminist Theory," *SIGNS* 13, no. 3 (Spring 1988) (reprinted in Micheline Malson, Jean O'Barr, Sarah Westphal-Wihl, and Mary Wyer, eds., *Feminist Theory in Practice and Process* [Chicago: University of Chicago Press, 1989], 295–326), is a cogent description of the efficacy of "positionality" as a political strategy as well as a provisional location marker.

13. This description isn't meant to position New York City as the center of lesbian performance action. Reinelt and Case, in their introduction to *The Performance of Power*, point out very usefully the problems with such "scopic centrality" (xii). Since I've left New York, I've taken up the more useful challenge of theorizing theater productions that happen locally and regionally and have found that, indeed, lesbian performance activity of different kinds is not just a New York–based phenomenon. See also Stacy Wolf's dissertation-in-progress at the University of Wisconsin–Madison, which theorizes theater audiences locally through cultural studies methods.

14. The Women and Theatre Program annual meetings came to be called the "preconference" because they are scheduled before the ATHE conference (the WTP's "parent" organization) each year. Because some women now only come for the WTP meetings, and because the prefix *pre-* seems to defer to the parent organization's authority and larger importance, some women have militated to drop the prefix. Juli Burk, current WTP president, for example, feels strongly about such a semantic change.

15. The "mythic mannish lesbian" whose specter was best described and put to rest by Esther Newton comes to mind here as an explanatory description of one of the dynamics motivating the WTP theory debates. See Newton's "The Mythic Mannish Lesbian: Radclyffe Hall and the New Woman," *SIGNS* 9, no. 4 (1984): 557–75.

16. This increase in visibility and respectability was due in large part to the efforts of Vicki Patraka, who, as WTP president from 1988 to 1990, worked tirelessly to bring theory and practice together at the preconference meetings and actively advocated and administered the sophistication and vigor of the WTP panels at the ATHE meetings.

17. Erika Munk, "Representation and Its Discontents," *Village Voice*, September 6, 1988, 86.

18. Bornstein, a male-to-female transsexual, has gone on to perform her piece, *Hidden Agender*, which represents and narrates her various genders, in San Francisco and New York, and Smith has received the acclaim she deserves with *Fires in the Mirror*, an "On the Road" installment that chronicles the violent ethnic entanglements between Jews and African-Americans in Brooklyn's Crown Heights. Her piece, *Twilight: Los Angeles, 1992* renders the insurrection in L.A. prompted by the original Rodney King beating verdict. For a partial version of the text of *Chlorophyll Post-Modernism and the Mother Goddess: A Conversation*, the piece Smith presented for the WTP in San Diego, see "Celebrating the Women and Theatre Program," *Women & Performance Journal #8* 4, no. 2 (1989): 26–46. See also Sue-Ellen Case's introduction to Smith's performance in the same issue (20–25).

19. Miller, *Getting Personal*, xi.

20. Case, intro. to Smith, "Celebrating," 24.

21. Elin Diamond, "Brechtian Theory/Feminist Theory," *TDR* 32, no. 1 (Spring 1988): 82–95.

22. See *The Feminist Spectator as Critic*, especially chapter 5 (92–95), for "occasional" writing about this conference event.

23. Peggy Phelan made these remarks on a panel at the August 1992 WTP preconference in Atlanta. They reiterate ideas presented fully in her book, *Unmarked* (London and New York: Routledge, 1993).

24. Janelle Reinelt, in a 1992 ASTR paper, "Bodies in Space: Doing the Work of Identity," suggests that spectators need to be "hailed" through provisional positions of identity for certain theatrical subversions of dominant discourse to work. I find persuasive Reinelt's proposal that the "goal of performance should [not] be the denial of identity but rendering visible its contingency and historicity" (MS., 13).

25. For example, Sherry Kramer's evocative play, *David's Red-Haired Death*, which won the Jane Chambers Award in 1992, is a formally unusual, politically insightful piece that would certainly deserve additional prizes. As of October 1992, the play is available from Theatre Communication Group's *Plays in Process* series. Naomi Wallace's play *In the Fields of Aceldama*, which won the Jane Chamber's Student Playwrighting Award in 1992, would also be worthy of national honors.

26. For lively critical and theoretical readings of the Hill/Thomas hearings, see Toni Morrison, ed., *Race-ing Justice, En-gendering Power* (New York: Pantheon, 1992).

27. See Philip Auslander, "Live Performance in a Mediatized Culture," *Essays in Theatre/Etudes Théâtrales* 11, no. 1 (November 1992): 33–40, for a persuasive reading of the effects of mediatization on theater production and reception.

28. See, for example, Charlotte Canning's 1991 dissertation at the University of Washington, "Working from Experience: A History of Feminist Theater in the United States, 1969–Present," *Dissertation Abstracts International* 52, no. 5, sec. A, 1574.

29. An exception is Rebecca Schneider, "See the Big Show: Spiderwoman Theatre Doubling Back," in Lynda Hart and Peggy Phelan, eds., *Acting Out: Feminist Performances* (Ann Arbor: University of Michigan Press, 1993), 227–56.

30. For a useful critique of feminism's betrayal by popular and media culture, see Susan Faludi, *Backlash: The Undeclared War against American Women* (New York: Crown, 1991).

31. Tania Modleski, *Feminism without Women: Culture and Criticism in a "Post-Feminist" Age* (New York: Routledge, 1991), 20.

32. See Elaine Showalter, "Critical Cross-Dressing: Male Feminists and the Woman of the Year," in Alice Jardine and Paul Smith, eds., *Men in Feminism* (New York: Methuen, 1987), 116–32.

33. Modleski, 21.

34. See bell hooks, *From Margin to Center* (Boston: Beacon Press, 1984), 29.

35. Ed Cohen, "Who Are 'We'? Gay 'Identity' as Political (E)motion (A Theoretical Rumination)," in Diana Fuss, ed., *Inside/Out: Lesbian Theories, Gay Theories* (New York and London: Routledge, 1991), 83.

36. Ibid., 84.

37. Vicki Patraka, in her interview "Robbie McCauley: Obsessing in Public," *TDR* 37, no. 2 (Summer 1993): 25–55, says, "I'm always curious about the kind of audience who prides itself on certain knowledgeability and resistance to being moved . . . they understand the 'trick' of it . . . almost past the point where it can be effective" (MS., 20). Something of Cohen's proposal that emotion be employed to move politics resonates here.

38. In its original version, when published in *TDR*, this article also included an analysis of events at the 1988 San Diego WTP preconference. That analysis has been incorporated into "Staking Claims and Positions," in this volume, to avoid redundancies between essays.

39. See, for only a few examples, Tracy Davis, *Actresses as Working Women. Their Social Identity in Victorian Culture* (New York and London: Routledge, 1991), and her article "Questions for a Feminist Methodology in Theatre History," in Postlewait and McConachie, eds., *Interpreting the Theatrical Past*, 59–81; Ellen Donkin, "Mrs. Siddons Looks Back in Anger: Feminist Historiography for Eighteenth-Century British Theater," in Reinelt and Roach, eds., *Critical Theory and Performance*, 276–90. Other recent work on theater studies and new historicism can be found in Reinelt and Roach, *Critical Theory and Performance* (291–350); Postlewait and McConachie, *Interpreting the Theatrical Past*, which includes an excellent bibliography (273–305); and Case and Reinelt, *The Performance of Power*, especially Bruce McConachie's "New Historicism and American Theatre History: Toward an Interdisciplinary Paradigm for Scholarship" (265–71), and Marvin Carlson, "The Theory of History" (272–79).

40. See Ellen Donkin and Susan Clements, eds., *Upstaging Big Daddy: Directing Theater as if Gender and Race Matter* (Ann Arbor: University of Michigan Press, 1993) and Lynda Hart and Peggy Phelan, eds., *Acting Out: Feminist Performances* (Ann Arbor: University of Michigan Press, 1993).

41. See my early article "Gender Impersonation Onstage," *Women & Performance Journal* 4 (1985) (reprinted with addendum in Laurence Senelick, ed., *Gender in Performance: The Presentation of Difference in the Performing Arts* [Hanover: University Press of New England], 3–13), for an explication of the notion of theater as laboratory in feminist performance.

42. Judith Butler, "Imitation and Gender Insubordination," in Fuss, ed., *Inside/Out*, 19.

43. For a feminist theoretical analysis of pornography in representation, see Linda Williams, *Hardcore: Power, Pleasure, and the "Frenzy of the Visible"* (Berkeley: University of California Press, 1989). Williams doesn't discuss lesbian pornography. For an excellent, revisionist reading of lesbian pornography's potential to rebuild a nonstatic, "becoming" community, see Terralee Bensinger, "Lesbian Pornography: The Re/Making of (a) Community," *Discourse* 15, no. 1 (Fall 1992): 69–93. Vicki Patraka has also pointed out, in "Split Britches in *Little Women the Tragedy*: Staging Censorship, Nostalgia, and Desire," *Kenyon Review* 15, no. 2 (Spring 1993): 6–13, that Split Britches' work is now imagining not just lesbian sexual pleasure but heterosexual and autoerotic possibilities as well, which seems to point toward a wider consideration of representations of pleasure for women across sexuality practices.

44. Susie Bright, *Susie Sexpert's Lesbian Sex World* (Pittsburgh and San Francisco: Cleis Press, 1990), and *Susie Bright's Sexual Reality: A Virtual Sex World Reader* (Pittsburgh and San Francisco: Cleis Press, 1992).

45. For writing about pornography's fashionability in academic discourse, in particular, see Deborah Cameron, "Discourses of Desire: Liberals, Feminists, and the Politics of Pornography," *American Literary History* 2, no. 4 (Winter 1990): 784–98, and "Pornography: What Is the Problem," *Critical Quarterly* 34, no. 2 (Summer 1992): 3–11, in which she argues that feminists do have to take a moral stand on the issue of pornography.

46. Teresa de Lauretis, "Sexual Indifference and Lesbian Identity," *Theatre Journal* 40 (1988): 155–77 (reprinted in Sue-Ellen Case, ed., *Performing Feminisms: Feminist Critical Theory and Theatre* [Baltimore: Johns Hopkins University Press, 1990], 17–39).

47. Teresa de Lauretis, "Issues, Terms, and Context," *Feminist Studies/Critical Studies* (Bloomington: Indiana University Press, 1987), 1–19.

48. There is, of course, much debate in recent feminist theory about which "troubled" gender position might be most politically effective. Modleski, for example, critiques many of Butler's assumptions in *Gender Trouble* by suggesting "the kind of 'gender trouble' advocated by Judith Butler and others in which gender, anatomy, and performance are at odds with one another does not necessarily result in the subversive effects often claimed for it. . . . [O]n the contrary, in certain cases, such as those involving the woman of color who has often been considered . . . 'not quite' a woman, this kind of 'play' may have extremely conservative implications" (132). Modleski's chastising stance is both compelling and disturbing, partly because, although she might be right about race, she ignores the importance of incongruous perfor-

mances of gender and identity in sexuality subcultures such as the gay and lesbian community (which complicate racial "play" even further for gay people of color).

49. See Iris Marion Young, "The Ideal of Community and the Politics of Difference," in Linda Nicholson, ed., *Feminism/Postmodernism* (New York and London: Routledge, 1990), 300–323.

50. Diana Fuss, "Inside/Out," *Inside/Out*, 5.

51. Dolan, *The Feminist Spectator as Critic*, 119–20.

52. Butler, "Imitation and Gender Insubordination," 21.

53. Ibid., 25.

54. Fuss, "Inside/Out," 7.

55. As Case notes in "Theory/History/Revolution," "At this point in the history of scholarship . . . old bodiless pursuits are giving way to a full-blooded cultural materialism" (427).

56. See Jeanie Forte, "Realism, Narrative, and the Feminist Playwright—A Problem of Reception," *Modern Drama* 32, no. 1 (1989); and Sheila Stowell, "Rehabilitating Realism," *Journal of Dramatic Theory and Criticism* 6, no. 2 (Spring 1992): 81–88.

57. For other engagements with the question of women of color and realism, see Patricia Schroeder's work on African-American women and realism, including her 1991 ATHE paper, "Recovering the Disremembered: Realism, Feminism, and the Harlem Renaissance," which is part of a longer piece in William Demastes's forthcoming anthology on American drama and realism. Schroeder's 1992 ATHE paper, "Re-reading Alice Childress" also explicates Childress's play *Wine in the Wilderness* through an affirmation of the political potentials of realism. On the other hand, African-American performance artist Robbie McCauley, in the *TDR* interview with Patraka, suggests that, if black theaters are about business, they have to be more conservative formally.

58. Stowell, "Rehabilitating Realism," 82.

59. John Fiske's *Television Culture* (New York and London: Routledge, 1987) is perhaps most useful in laying out the cultural studies strategies.

60. Stowell, "Rehabilitating Realism," 87.

61. Ibid.

62. Ibid.

63. For other readings of Hughes's work, see Kate Davy, "From *Lady Dick* to Ladylike: The Work of Holly Hughes," in Hart and Phelan, eds., *Acting Out*, 54–84. See also the exchange of letters between Sue-Ellen Case and Holly Hughes around the question of assimilation and reception context in *TDR* 33, no. 1 (Spring 1989) and 33, no. 4 (Winter 1989).

64. Lynda Hart is now at work on *Between the Body and the Flesh: Performing Lesbian S/M*, which systematically theorizes lesbian s/m practice, for the gay and lesbian studies series at Columbia University Press.

65. Teresa de Lauretis, "The Essence of the Triangle, or, Taking the Risk of Essentialism Seriously: Feminist Theory in Italy, the U.S. and Britain," *differences* 1, no. 2 (Summer 1989): 3–37.

66. See Gloria Anzaldúa, "Haciendo caras, una entrada: An Introduction," in her edited collection, *Making Face/Making Soul: Creative and Critical Perspectives by Women of Color* (San Francisco: Aunt Lute, 1990), particularly xxii, for an elaboration of such code switching.

PART 1
Gender Polemics

Chapter 1

Personal, Political, Polemical: Feminist Approaches to Politics and Theater

As for women in other areas of social and political life, a great deal has been accomplished by women in theater in the United States over the last two decades, and a great deal remains to be gained. The 1970s are remembered, from a 1990s' vantage point, as an era when theater for women—and more precisely "feminist" theater—was born and proliferated. In tandem with the political movement from which it sprang, activist women's theaters with radical techniques and manifestos were organized in major urban centers around the country. The groups were innumerable and local, since the theater they produced spoke directly to its constituents.

The 1980s might be remembered as a decade when, on one hand, the radical, collective theater work of the 1970s sputtered and failed and, on the other, women who aspired to careers in professional, mainstream theater began to gain ground. The visibility of women playwrights, in particular, led to three Pulitzer Prize in Drama awards for women in the 1980s: Beth Henley, for *Crimes of the Heart* (1981), Marsha Norman, for *'night, Mother* (1983), and Wendy Wasserstein, for *The Heidi Chronicles* (1989). After many years of ignoring women playwrights, the Pulitzer committee—along with the Tony Awards, which honored Wasserstein's play as the first written by a woman ever to win the Best Play award in 1989—seemed finally to take notice of the "new" talent.[1]

But the apparent success of women playwrights in mainstream theater obscures several political issues that continue to frame the field of feminism and theater. The plays most honored by the prize committees, and subsequently most published and produced, tend to be the most conservative in content and form. Henley's *Crimes of the Heart*, for example, is a Southern domestic comedy in which three sisters overcome their individual quirks to bond together as family. Few references are made to a larger political setting or to women outside their comfortable white, middle-class, heterosexual situation. Norman's *'night, Mother* generated much controversy in the feminist press over its protagonist's a priori choice to commit suicide and the hopeless, isolated quality of her life. The most recent winner, Wasserstein's *The Heidi Chronicles*, is a critique of the feminist movement launched by a character whose individual liberal humanism is comfortably promoted by the realist dramatic frame she inhabits. The play's rendition of feminism in the 1970s implies that the movement is over and its achievements bittersweet.

While Wasserstein's popular play tolls the death knell of feminism from its safe position in a costly Broadway theater, something very different is happening on the streets outside. Although alternative feminist theater remains dormant except for several long-lived companies, the liberal and radical feminist movements in the United States are regaining an activist stance, prompted primarily by attacks on women's reproductive rights and the reactionary backsliding of the Reagan and Bush administrations. At the onset of the 1990s the political climate in the United States and especially abroad, in Eastern Europe, seems potentially reminiscent of the ferment of the 1960s. With abortion and now AIDS activists taking once again to the streets in the United States and jarring the complacency of their upwardly mobile generation, one wonders if feminist theater, too, will once again become a site for political activism.[2]

Historicizing Feminism and Theater

The potential for renewed theatrical radicalism in the 1990s is best viewed through the historical context of the late 1960s and early 1970s, when the second wave of U.S. feminism followed on the heels of the civil rights movement and the formation of a vocal, active New Left. From within the political upheaval of the late 1960s activists tried to revise interpersonal relationships and cultural value systems according to more egalitarian ideology.[3]

But within the Left's rhetoric of racial and economic liberation, and a rethinking of cultural values, gender politics remained conservative. The contemporary women's movement in the United States rekindled itself partly out of profound disaffection with the misogyny of the male Left. Through a network of ad hoc consciousness-raising groups, white middle-class women with some background in radical politics spoke to one another for what seemed like the first time, without mediation. These consciousness-raising groups allowed women to exchange previously unheard details of their personal lives. The apparent commonality of their shared experience provoked a political analysis based on the private sphere their lives inhabited, and the slogan The Personal Is the Political gained currency.[4]

What began in the late 1960s as a grassroots political movement became, through the 1970s, a political and ideological movement with organized impact and increasingly divergent strains. Networks such as the National Organization for Women, for example, developed strategies for influencing existing social and political systems around women's issues. The liberal feminist movement generated by women within these organizations works to reform U.S. systems toward women's equality.[5]

Radical feminism, in contrast to the reformism of liberal feminism, theorized women's oppression as systemic and began to analyze how patriarchal domination relegated women to the private sphere and alienated them from the power men wielded in public life. Radical feminism in the late 1960s and early 1970s proposed that gender roles were socially constructed and could be changed only after a revolutionary restructuring of cultural power.[6]

Early women's and feminist theater began as a voice of radical feminism and the first manifestations of what eventually came to be celebrated as women's culture.[7] The It's Alright to Be a Woman Theatre in New York, for example, one of the earliest groups, transposed the political movement's consciousness-raising format to performance and used the new public forum to help validate women's personal lives. The troupe used agitprop techniques with a long tradition in political theater as well as street theater and guerilla tactics that they borrowed from the Left-oriented experimental theaters that had multiplied in the United States in the late 1960s and early 1970s.[8]

The Living Theatre, the Open Theatre, and the Performance Group, for example, broke with the psychological realism that dominated professional U.S. stages. These experimental theater groups formed collectives that disrupted the politically constricting hierarchy of the playwright/actor/director triumvirate and the separation of spectators and performers formalized by the proscenium arch.[9] The importation of Grotowski's poor theater, Brecht's alienation-effect, and Artaud's Theater of Cruelty from the Continent also radicalized experimental theater aesthetics in the United States. The text was no longer sacred; happenings and rituals became the primary base of theater work; and social issues and politics explicitly informed every performance choice.

Although the experimental theater work of the period addressed in vital ways civil rights issues and the protests against the Vietnam War, it did no more for women than the Left in general. Women such as Megan Terry and Roberta Sklar, who'd both worked in the shadow of Joseph Chaikin's fame at the Open Theatre, left to form specifically women's theater groups. At the Omaha Magic Theatre and the Women's Experimental Theatre, respectively, they brought along many of the experimental theaters' innovations with theater form—including ritual-based theory and borrowings from Grotowski, Brecht, and Artaud—but set them in a political arena in which the spectators and performers moved along a revised gender axis.[10]

While such examples of separatist-inclined women's culture thrived through the 1970s, in the 1980s liberal feminism continued to gain viability. The movement's achievements saw Geraldine Ferraro placed on the Democratic presidential ticket in 1984. Although dogged attempts to pass the Equal Rights Amendment failed, marches on Washington and consistent lobbying around women's issues instituted a focus on the "gender gap" in U.S. politics. The situation of urban black women and other racial and ethnic groups received little attention on the liberal feminist agenda, but the movement's focus on political and economic equity for white middle-class women became a force with which the dominant culture had to contend.

Mainstream theater in the 1980s—no doubt as a result of liberal feminism—began to dole out its major awards to women such as Henley, Norman, and Wasserstein, and Lily Tomlin and Jane Wagner's *Search for Signs of Intelligent Life in the Universe* (1985) proved a major Broadway success.[11] Women's caucuses in professional theater organizations and the vitality of Julia Miles's Women's Project at the

American Place Theatre helped women playwrights, directors, producers, designers, and actors seem suddenly to appear where they'd
never been before in the ranks of Broadway and regional U.S. theaters.[12]

Because of increasing economic burdens and the fractionalization
within radical feminism, however, the tradition of alternative feminist theaters that had flourished in the 1970s failed to sustain itself
into the 1980s. Of the numerous radical feminist theater groups that
began in the 1970s, only Spiderwoman Theatre, a collective of American Indian women operating in New York, and At the Foot of the
Mountain Theatre in Minneapolis continued to produce and tour by
the end of the 1980s.[13] The founding of Split Britches, a popular
feminist and lesbian troupe that began in the 1980s in the East Village
lesbian community in New York City, was an anomaly in an otherwise stagnant scene.[14] But, while alternative feminist theater practice
declined in the 1980s, the decade witnessed the beginning of committed feminist criticism and theory that has become a vital site for
activist and intellectual work in the theater profession and in the
academy.

Materialist Feminism and the New Critical Theory

Feminist theater criticism in the 1980s began commenting on feminist
and women's theater in an effort to distinguish ideological viewpoints within work by women. Borrowing from such distinctions in
other fields, theater critics and theorists began to sort out the differences in form, content, and context among liberal, radical, and materialist feminists. In feminist criticism and theory, materialist feminists
influenced by the Marxist equation of form and content and by materialism's emphasis on ideology have been at the forefront of the
movement to examine not simply images of women in theater but
also the whole meaning-producing apparatus under which theater
operates.

Materialist feminist theory is concerned with more than just the
artifact of representation—the play, film, painting, or dance. It considers the entire apparatus that frames and creates these images and
their connection not just to social roles but also to the structure of
culture and its divisions of power. The theater apparatus, then, includes the stage, lights, sets, casting, blocking, gestures, the location

of the auditorium and the cost of the tickets, the advertising, the length of the run—all the material and ideological forces that shape what a theater event means. Such theories of representation also consider the spectator an active producer of theater's meanings.[15]

According to materialist feminist performance theory, placing a woman in representation—the site for the production of meaning in theater—is always a political act. Female bodies inscribed in the representational frame offered by the proscenium arch, and the frame created simply by the act of gazing through gender and ideology, bear meanings with political implications. Rather than promoting positive or negative images of women—as sociological, liberal feminist criticism first proposed—the materialist feminist approach suggests a new poetics of performance embracing radical revisions of content and form, which might more fully express women's various subjectivities across race, class, ethnicity, and sexual preference.[16]

This "new poetics" insists on the inseparability of content and form. This stance has provoked a critique of mimesis in feminist theater work that suggests long-held assumptions that theater mirrors reality—or, following Aristotle, is an imitation of life—mask the dominant ideology that shapes the image in its mirror. Mimesis is not so much reflective, the theory suggests, as didactic.[17] Materialist feminism's critique of realism proposes that, similarly, the form's attempt to recreate reality through psychological identification processes that objectify women renders it unable to frame subject positions that differ from representation's white, middle-class, heterosexual, male ideal spectator.[18]

These suggestions, needless to say, are unpopular with liberal feminists in the profession still determined to write popular realist plays for mainstream theater and who believe politics can be separated from aesthetics and "art."[19] Materialist feminist theater and performance theory and criticism developed in the academy, rather than in the profession, at a time when universities in the United States were reeling with the influences of Continental theories that stressed the importance of politics and ideology in shaping a culture's representations.[20] The performance theory described by materialist feminists draws on various French feminist positions espoused by psychoanalytic critics Luce Irigaray, Hélène Cixous, and Julia Kristeva; the deconstructive strategies of Jacques Derrida; Michel Foucault's analysis of power and sexuality; revisions of the structuralist psychoanalysis of Jacques Lacan; and poststructuralism's claims for an incoherent, shifting subjectivity that has correlaries in American postmodernism's pop and pastiche style.

Borrowing from so many of critical theory's most popular thinkers has lent feminism in the academy a peculiar respectability. This acceptance has prompted the curious incidence of "men in feminism," a phrase that ominously predicts the detachment of feminism from the experience—the personal, after all—from which it developed. Similarly, liberal feminism seems to have been so widely accepted—or perhaps, more accurately, co-opted—in U.S. culture and its political systems that the dangerous term "postfeminism" has also gained ascendancy. The uneasy alliances radical, or "essentialist" or "cultural," feminism has made with the New Right in the antipornography debate and with the New Age movement's retreat into spirituality and psychic recovery has made it vulnerable to critique by other branches of feminism and also to satire in popular culture, both of which neutralize its efficacy.[21]

The trend of recuperating these various ideological strains of feminism into more conservative institutions or cultural contexts can be seen in the use of feminism as content in mainstream realist plays. But the potential for resistance to dominant cultural hegemony remains in the alternative forms of feminist theater and theory, in which an activist sense of rage at exclusion from power and culture remains potent.

Two exceedingly different theater texts will serve as examples of U.S. feminism's place in this historical moment. Wendy Wasserstein's *The Heidi Chronicles* is a "postfeminist" mainstream play that distorts the political history of U.S. feminism from the mid-1960s to the late 1980s. The play trivializes radical feminist gains, suppresses feminist rage, and acquiesces to the dominant culture's reading of the end of feminism. The play's traditional realist form helps to promote its essentially conservative ideology.

Winnetou's Snake-Oil Show from Wigwam City, a piece written and performed collectively by Spiderwoman Theatre, uses Brechtian and ritual technique to break from the ideological and formal constraints of realism. *Winnetou* eloquently expresses racial rage over the appropriation of American Indian culture and, through its use of alternative form, expresses the potential for feminist subjectivities. *The Heidi Chronicles* authorizes the dominant culture's view of the end of feminism, while *Winnetou* offers evidence that those marginalized by the dominant culture are still filled with a rage that might productively be channeled into reinvigorated activism in the 1990s.

The Heidi Chronicles: Choking on the Rage of Postfeminism

Wendy Wasserstein's *Heidi Chronicles* narrates the uncomplimentary view of the feminist movement promoted by the dominant culture. The recent play serves as an ironic bookend to Wasserstein's *Uncommon Women and Others* (1979), which, for all its problems as an upper-middle-class white women's play, still manages to launch some pungent observations about a group of college women's dawning awareness of the necessity of their own liberation through a gender analysis. *Heidi Chronicles* is *Uncommon Women*'s older sister, bitter and chagrined by the unfulfilled promises of the social movement. Heidi is a cipher, who never gives voice to an incisive or adequate political or artistic analysis. While Wasserstein's story is told against the backdrop of feminism, Heidi distances herself from the movement by calling herself a humanist; she reiterates that all people deserve to fulfill their potential. The feminist movement appears to end with the narrative closure of Wasserstein's realist text.

The *Heidi Chronicles* is told in flashbacks, as art historian Heidi Holland uses the occasion of lectures for a course at Columbia University to reflect on the shape of her life. Heidi's lectures, which open each act, represent a facile liberal feminist art criticism that focuses on images and analogies. For example, Heidi describes Lily Martin Spencer's painting of a solitary young woman, "We Both Must Fade" (1869), in her opening lecture. She reminds her students (i.e., the audience, to whom she obliquely speaks) of high school dances, at which "you sort of don't know what you want" and "you're waiting to see what might happen."[22] The analogy reduces art to the reflection of a universally assumed experience and describes Heidi's reactive, passive position within the history Wasserstein narrates.

The play's series of scenes bound through twenty years of U.S. history, covering many of the era's most vital, turbulent moments. But history recedes into the background of the relationships on which the play focuses. The first scene returns Heidi to a high school dance in a Chicago suburb in 1965, at which Heidi's friend Susan inculcates her into heterosexual mores. The scene's music is period appropriate and inspires a jolt of recognition that conjures up a sentimental nostalgia, rather than a more thoughtful consideration of the history the music recalls.

Wasserstein's ahistorical approach continues into the next scene, a rally for McCarthy's presidential bid in 1967, at which Heidi meets Scoop, the arrogant editor of *Liberated Earth News*. Wasserstein positions Scoop as the social prophet who knows more about Heidi and her future than she knows herself. When Heidi tentatively explains her nascent feminist politics, Scoop remarks sardonically, "You'll be one of those true believers who didn't understand it was just a phase" (17).

Scoop's prophecy, of course, is borne out by the remainder of the play, in which Heidi witnesses the progress of the feminist movement, according to Wasserstein, from a radical separatism to an upwardly mobile, liberal reintegration into the country's economic and political systems. Wasserstein's position on the shift in American— and feminist—values over the last twenty years is provided by Scoop and Susan, while Heidi, bemused and never changing, watches passively.

In an early scene Susan brings Heidi to a consciousness-raising meeting at the University of Michigan in 1970. The women present are white and middle-class, some are housewives, some are students, and all appear superficial and foolish as they encounter one anothers' lives. They speak the rhetoric of 1970s pop psychology more than the language of early consciousness-raising, self-righteously explaining that they're "trying to work through" things, and ending the session with a pep rally cry backed by Aretha Franklin's song "Respect" (30). Missing in this trivializing scene are the painful exchanges of the stories women had never before told. In their place are glib jokes at the characters' expense and a facile emotionalism. The characters hug continually and repeat that they love one another, as if consciousness-raising were simply about unconditional love between women.

Wasserstein shies away from exploring female sexuality, one of the more important topics consciousness-raising essayed. The presumption of heterosexuality is maintained, as Fran, the scene's only lesbian character, is treated with blatant homophobia. Fran's army fatigues and "macho" behavior mark her as lesbian, since Wasserstein trades in dominant cultural stereotypes to create an easy mark for the scene's humor. When Fran confronts Heidi over her choice to sleep with women, Heidi scrapes her chair back an extra foot from the visitor's position outside the circle of women she already inhabits. Heidi's uncomfortable response to Fran indicates Wasserstein's need to distance herself from any display of radicalism, sexual or political. When asked by the other women if her work in art history is feminist, Heidi qualifies, "Humanist" (26), once again opting for the middle ground.

Even liberal feminist struggles for women's equality appear radical and extremist in the play. For example, a demonstration Heidi joins at the Chicago Art Institute in 1974 is ridiculed in Wasserstein's treatment. Heidi's friend Peter is present on the picket line, but his well-meaning support throws the scene's focus to men's responses to feminist activism and belittles the feminist analysis of women's exclusion from art history the scene might have launched. The feminist organizer of the demonstration is costumed in black and played as an arch man hater, which encourages Heidi to opt again for humanism: she remains outside the museum with Peter when he is barred from the women-only demonstration inside.

Peter comes out as gay in the Art Institute scene, announcing his sexual preference by way of insisting his struggle for equality is as valid as women's. In an invidious manner Wasserstein pits two marginalized positions against each other in competition for audience sympathies. Ultimately, the struggle of male homosexuals is valued more than feminism's struggle for gender equality. Near the end of the play, for instance, as Wasserstein sweeps into the 1980s with a nod to AIDS, Peter dismisses Heidi's individual angst as a luxury, compared to the emotional demands of his difficult, dedicated life among people with AIDS.

The male characters in the play continually predict the women's futures. Susan, for example, represents the separatism of early radical feminism, choosing to live and work on an all-female dude ranch in the western United States. But at his wedding the ever-prescient Scoop insists Susan will soon be working on Wall Street. Dancing one last song with Heidi before he honeymoons with someone else, Scoop brings down the act 1 curtain predicting: "You quality-time girls are going to be one generation of disappointed women. Interesting, exemplary, even sexy, but basically unhappy" (52). And, of course, he proves correct.

Act 2's dip into the upwardly mobile consumerism of the 1980s is not a critique of the materialism of "baby boomer" values so much as a pointed discounting of political idealism in the concerted rush toward "having it all." The text safely ensconces feminism in the academy, where the next generation of women reads all about the women who fought for their opportunities. Women's studies replaces the experience of women's lives, and bourgeois feminism dissipates into an aggressive movement toward success, acquisition, and money.

Susan, the once "radical shepherdess," becomes a vice-president for a television production company that wants a feminist with a business background, a combination that in the previous decade would have been an oxymoron. But in the 1980s Susan happily becomes a power broker, parlaying friendships into business contacts. Scoop, too, although less surprisingly, disposes of his once radical politics, leaving *Liberated Earth News* to start *Boomer*, a power magazine for the 1980s. When he sells the magazine for a large sum of money at the end of the play, Scoop intends to run for Congress, neatly completing the reintegration into political and economic systems that characterizes the U.S. baby-boom generation. He also expects Heidi's and Peter's votes, assuming that women and gay men will be complicit once again in the white heterosexual male's bid for power.

Heidi, however, remains alone at the play's end. She wonders what the social movements of the 1960s and 1970s were all for and wonders still what she and other women want. Her long monologue in the second act employs self-pity as a political strategy, as she complains that feminism left her isolated. Just as Scoop predicted, Heidi believed, when the others knew feminism—and maybe even humanism—was just a fad. Even Susan, in one of the harshest reversals the text constructs, says: "I'm not political anymore. I mean, equal rights is one thing; equal pay is one thing; but blaming everything on being a woman is just passé" (79). Heidi, though, feels stranded and sad, because she "thought the point was we were all in this together" (84). The woman who pushed her chair back from community finally notices that she is alone.

In the best 1980s fashion Heidi buys herself the family she has been unable to acquire otherwise. She adopts a Panamanian baby and predicts that things will be better for her daughter. The text eternally defers feminist achievements to more and more distant generations. Heidi sits rocking her baby in a huge, empty loft somewhere in New York, for which—in the "real life" Wasserstein emulates—the maintenance fees would be enormous. Wasserstein's play and its Broadway context glorifies consumption just as promiscuously as Scoop's magazine.

According to Wasserstein, this is the sadness of liberal feminism—that it isn't possible to have it all and that to have any of it, for women, requires great personal compromise. Heidi rocks alone with her adopted daughter, but there is no man in her life. Under the system of values the play constructs life without man is a supreme sacrifice. By the end of the play Heidi feels silenced and sad, without the agency promised by the movement to which she supposedly subscribed.

Missing from Wasserstein's play and from the feminist history her realist narrative distorts is the motivating fuel of women's rage at their marginalization and oppression by dominant discourse. Rather than acknowledging the political power of rage and mourning its repression in the "new age," Wasserstein's political project explicitly trivializes women's anger. In the art history lecture that opens the second act, Heidi intends to be showing slides of paintings by Lila Cabot Perry but accidentally inserts an image of Artemisia Gentileschi's "Judith Beheading Holifernes," which is an important site of early feminist discourse in art history.[23] Heidi jokes snidely that Perry went through a little known period of hostility; the painting depicts a woman and her maid viciously cutting off a man's head.

The text scores a laugh with this image; the joke is that the upper-class pretentions of Perry's work have nothing in common with Gentileschi's violence. But the joke underscores the repression of Heidi's hostility and rage, which is never described in the text as part of her feminist development. That the Gentileschi slide is shown accidentally and removed from the scene is typical of Wasserstein's treatment of the history of feminism. Key moments are trivialized, and the legitimacy of women's rage is neatly elided. Women aren't supposed to be angry anymore.

The Heidi Chronicles is an example of misdirected rage, in which white feminist anger is suppressed by the realist text and erupts inappropriately to trash the history of the movement. *The Heidi Chronicles* uses feminism as content: the movement becomes a historical backdrop against which the same domestic stories traditionally recounted by American realism play out. The play also suppresses race and class difference in its white-washed, consumer-oriented portrait of late-1980s America. Wasserstein fails to see that the roots of gender oppression are systemic, not a result of feminism's failure to help white women succeed in "having it all."

A Postproduction Tangent

Despite my strong reaction to Wasserstein's play, I agreed to direct it for the University Theatre's 1992 summer season at the University of Wisconsin–Madison. The play had been suggested to the selection committee because of its popularity and what the committee considered its salability as a summer title. Worried that it might be presented "as is," I took on the challenge of seeing where and how Wasserstein's text might be subverted, while retaining enough of its appeal to guarantee the department some necessary summer income.

My attempt centered around challenging Wasserstein's view of recent feminist history by taking a more affectionate than malicious attitude toward the 1960s and 1970s and by satirizing the excesses of the 1980s more than the play does as written. By ending the play with Scoop's choice to run for election, Wasserstein seems to condone the power structure bolstered by the "yuppie-ism" of the 1980s. We tried to even out the hierarchy by satirizing the 1980s as much as the 1960s and 1970s.

The production concept hinged on exploding Wasserstein's "light comedy" into a full-blown parody of cultural mores. Most of the parody was either visual or performative. The designers aimed to produce recognizable historical markers and overextend them, and the actors' goal was to create characters with whom the spectators could laugh, rather than stereotypes whom they could laugh at. We worked carefully to mark these fine distinctions, imagining a Madison audience that was mostly white, mostly college educated, and mostly baby boomers themselves. To speak to younger spectators, whose memories of the 1960s and 1970s are filtered through "golden oldies" stations and syndicated television, we historicized the play by inserting music and visual fragments borrowed mostly from popular culture and the mass media.

Designers Dawn Lanphier and Laura Carlson worked with dramaturgs Susan McCully and Patty Gallagher and assistant director Stacy Wolf and me to flesh out the presentation of feminist and progressive history on which the play cheats. A lengthy slide show, presented before the play began and at intermission, represented wry and strong images of women in art history and social history and was played to accompanying evocative sound bites. The montage set the mood for a production located in discussion with the vicissitudes of historical movement, rather than against a superficial background of facile historical memory. The images juxtaposed objectified or romanticized women in art and social history with women in communities, fighting to change their status. We selected many images of women working, to evoke women's active participation in historical change.

Slides became a visual and thematic linking device between scenes in the episodic play. Since Wasserstein labels the year and location of each scene, we moved the play by producing a collage of photos, texts, and sound bites in each transition that echoed the complexity of the historical event or cultural icon against which each scene plays. For instance, before Scoop and Lisa's wedding at the end of act 1, the slide montage inundated spectators with pictures of brides and grooms, from the wedding of Prince Charles and Lady Diana to clippings from *Bride Magazine,* from Miss Piggy and Kermit the Frog to a lesbian couple kissing each other in bridal gowns over a caption that read, "Look Mom, no groom!" The sheer number and variety of images displayed was meant to persuade spectators to read the play's wedding scene as one union among the many possible, rather than as the ultimate heterosexual goal from which Heidi is exiled by her own wrongheadedness. If nothing else, the set of slides presented marriage ironically, rather than naturally.

In addition to the slide images, the minimal props and set pieces we used were designed to be iconographic and excessive, each representative of a Brechtian social gest. The punch bowl in the high school dance scene was mammoth and pink, decorated with tiny punch glasses from which Peter and Heidi drank. The presents in the "power" shower that opens the second act were enormous, towering over the women who opened them and containing tiny, tiny baby gifts. The obviousness of these parodies was meant to signal to spectators the irreverent approach we encouraged them to take to material Wasserstein holds more sacrosanct.

The prop key to our subtle deconstruction was the baby that ends the play. Determined not to romanticize Heidi's choice to adopt a Panamanian baby to alleviate her self-induced feminist gloom, we decided to continue the parody to the end and use a baby doll to represent Judy Holland. We tried a Raggedy Ann doll in the first dress rehearsal, but it didn't work; it was too clearly a toy and made Heidi look like she'd lost her mind. We returned instead to using the weighted baby doll prop we'd used in rehearsal (and affectionately called the "dead baby"), since it really did look like a baby but obviously wasn't real.

When she introduces the baby to Scoop—who sits in the oversized, Edith Ann rocker we'd created as the center of the scene—Heidi's manner was nonchalant and casual. Scoop treated the baby much more reverently and, in fact, left with it accidentally at the end of the scene, returning chagrined to hand Judy back to Heidi. When Scoop exited and Heidi's romantic final moment as mother-with-child began, accompanied by the song, "You Send Me," Heidi was blocked to dance around the stage with the doll in her arms, gradually increasing her speed and fervor until she swung the doll by the arms, then the hands, then only one hand, flinging the baby around her head. We offered a biting critique of Wasserstein's idealized final moment.

Darcey Engen, who played Heidi as one of her MFA thesis roles, read against the grain of the character as written by performing her as a strong, active woman. Joan Allen's work in the Broadway production I saw in 1989 was passive and indistinct, and she was directed to hang back from the center of the action. We put Heidi squarely in the middle, rooting her at the apex of the triangle of chairs in the consciousness-raising scene and, wherever possible, blocking her to initiate an action rather than reacting to someone else's. Engen's work in psychophysical acting techniques served her well, as she was conscious of the different effects each set of muscles she used would have on her movement and her reading of a line. Her physical strength, and the clarity of her choices, showed through the dialogue to give Heidi nuance and power she doesn't have on the page.

We combined Engen's strength with readings of the two male

leads that disallowed the overriding sympathy they achieve in the text. Peter was played (by Chris Tallman) as much more selfish and self-centered than altruistic, as a handful for Heidi to manage rather than as the martyr who betters Heidi by devoting himself to a higher cause. Their relationship became more complicated, as Engen worked to show Heidi's compromises for Peter as choices, rather than as the natural outcome of their friendship. Scoop was also played (by Josh Stamberg) as less sympathetic, more slickly arrogant than charismatic. We couldn't change the prophetic role Wasserstein writes for him, but we made him oily enough that some spectators reacted out loud, in what sounded like disbelief, to his sexist predictions.

I did find that Wasserstein's writing is so slick that it's impossible to completely subvert the facile (usually conservative) humor of many of the one-liners that structure the play. Her ear for laughs is impeccable; once we had an audience it was clear that even the resistant blocking we created ourselves seemed modulated to allow time for the laughs she'd anticipated. In many cases, despite our efforts, the play won. For instance, the consciousness-raising scene in the first act was difficult to turn into an example of "laughing with" instead of "laughing at." I regret that we didn't keep trying to come up with alternate ways of pointing out how easily Wasserstein dismisses an important ritual of white middle-class feminist history. We parodied the scene as we did others, costuming the women in bell-bottoms, knitted caps, platform shoes, and army jackets to evoke the sartorial protests of the early 1970s. The actors were directed to overemphasize all those assertions of sisterly love Wasserstein assigns them, but to really mean them, too, to show how deep and real was these women's regard for one another. That strategy worked partially, but the scene was still funny for the wrong reasons.

For a University Theatre community, part of which is predisposed to seeing feminist theater production as humorless and dour, our version of *The Heidi Chronicles* worked to make them think while they laughed. We capitalized on a well-paced, funny play to score a few points about the continuing vitality of the feminist movement in the United States. We also tried to recuperate a sense of appropriate feminist rage. Heidi got angry more than she sank into self-righteous bitterness (although the "I thought we were all in this together" speech at the gym was a challenge to resist), and none of the female

characters were allowed to whine without parodying the choice vocally and physically. When Heidi accidentally shows "Judith Beheading Holifernes" in her lecture at the beginning of the second act, we
let the slide haunt the lecture instead of obediently removing it from
view. Every time Heidi turned around the image would reappear on
the screen, surrounding her with the enormity of the emotion it depicts. In our production feminist anger accompanied Heidi into the
second act of the play.

Alternative Theater and the Potential
for Renewed Radicalism

The rage that *The Heidi Chronicles* represses finds a more productive
expression in Spiderwoman Theatre's *Winnetou's Snake-Oil Show from
Wigwam City*. The piece's nonlinear, nonrealist style accommodates
the troupe's guiding ideology of gender and racial marginalization
and allows the performers to directly address their political statements to their spectators. Spiderwoman is one of the oldest producing feminist theater groups in the country. The backbone of the
troupe are three Cuna/Rappahannock American Indian sisters, Lisa
Mayo, and Gloria and Muriel Miguel, who borrow the troupe's name
from a Hopi goddess:

> We take our name from Spiderwoman, goddess of creation, the
> first to create designs and teach her people to weave. She always
> wove a flaw into her designs to allow her spirit to find its way
> out and be free. We call on her inspiration in the development
> of our working technique, "storyweaving," creating designs and
> weaving stories with words and movement.[24]

Spiderwoman's story-weaving technique results in pieces that
are loosely compiled around various themes, all of which relate to
the women's gender and ethnicity. They have also injected their
own subjectivities into various parts of the dramatic canon, mounting, for example, versions of *Lysistrata* (*The Lysistrata Numbah* [1977])
and *The Three Sisters* (*Three Sisters From Here to There* [1982]), in
which the sisters' unrealized dream is to move to Manhattan from
Brooklyn. The male characters in this piece were represented by
life-sized dolls, and the sisters' home movies were interjected into

the narrative. The mix of media and an interweaving of various narrative threads characterizes Spiderwoman's productions, which are often incoherent and diffuse. The nonlinear, improvisatory style, however, is intentional and allows the members of Spider-woman to explore and celebrate their gender and ethnic heritage in an alternative theatrical form.

In *Winnetou's Snake-Oil Show from Wigwam City* Spiderwoman satirizes the nineteenth-century conventions of popular culture's medicine shows and "wild west" shows and the more recent phenomenon of New Age spirituality to formulate a sharp critique of the dominant culture's appropriation of American Indian symbols and shamanism.[25] The piece's structure is loose and unconfining: a cheat sheet of sorts with the production's essential structural elements is pinned to the back curtain and frequently referred to by the cast. The eclectic setting is strictly "poor theater": a patched quilt of multicultural images confronts the spectators as scenery, and a large plastic garbage pail and several cardboard crates provide set pieces to be transformed as necessary.

The piece opens on a film clip of an American Indian pow-wow, accompanied by theme music from the quintessentially "American" Marlboro cigarette commercials. This juxtaposition of cultural elements is both humorous and pointed, as it refers to the infiltration of American Indian culture by the imperialist mythology of the United States' western expansion. Film clips recur through the production, projected on a white sheet hanging from the theater's three-sided balcony. The clips are often cued visually or vocally by the actors, breaking the realist convention of masking production elements. Such Brechtian pointing to the means of production continues throughout the piece.

In the first episode a German-accented trapper appears, accompanied by a scout who intends to tell him "how we hunt in the west." Their exchange employs cultural stereotypes of cowboys and Indians, but the roles are cast across gender and deliberately overacted to hold such images up for critique. The trapper's German accent waxes and wanes, mutating frequently into the performer's native Brooklynese. But the character comes and goes equally fluidly, as scenes move through various sites in Indian and western lore. The two "men" appear to be captured or confronted by a local tribe: Chief Winnetou enters wrapped in an American Indian blanket and a headband adorned with symbols of snakes. Under his outfit the colorful lamé jumpsuit that each of the four women performers wear as their basic costume can be seen shimmering.[26]

Spiderwoman appropriates freely and promiscuously from both high and low culture, often at the same time, to lend texture to its cultural juxtapositions. The characters begin a ritual ceremony that mixes slapstick physical comedy with allusions to the witches' scene in *Macbeth*. The garbage pail becomes a cauldron for witches' brew, parodying the notion of American Indian rituals as superstitious. The mops that jut from the pail are soon transformed into horses that the characters ride—accompanied by fabricated clopping sounds—to the site of Spiderwoman's next parody.

The subsequent construction of a wild west extravaganza recalls those that helped to promote the mythology of the American west as an untamed wilderness in which brave white men conquered fearsome, savage Indian tribes. The cultural imperialism of this history is explicitly satirized in this section of *Winnetou's Snake-Oil Show*, since the entertainments are provided by American Indian women with names like Minnie Ho-Runner, Mother Moonface, Princess Pussywillow from the Mish Mash Tribe of Brooklyn, and Ethel Christian Christianson.

The women perform a variety of tricks, all of which are intentionally demystified for the spectators. Whip tricks are performed in which hats are knocked off the heads of assistants by the assistants themselves. Horse tricks are accomplished by using the mops as capable steeds. A sharpshooter aims at balloons held over an assistant's head, after the assistant is not-so-surreptitiously instructed to burst them with a sharp ring he or she is given to wear. A trick roper performs tricks "so fine they can't be discerned by the naked eye," for which, of course, the rope is mimed. The demystification of these tricks points explicitly to the mystifications of the American west mythology.

The Spiderwoman troupe ad libs enthusiastically and is not at all concerned about presenting a slick illusion of professionalism or reality. Throughout this free-form, circus-style segment, for example, the performers clearly improvise much of the dialogue and often mistake one another's stage names. They laugh at their own mistakes and, like stand-up comics before a live audience, invite spectators to share their jokes.

These moments of energetic, erratic slapstick parody are inter-
spersed with more expressionistic or ritualistic moments of American
Indian storytelling in *Winnetou*. Often one of the women will narrate
a story, while the others act it out behind her or provide atmospheric
sound effects. The first of these stories refers to the "bones of our
ancestors," evoking a mystical history of connection to earth that has
been trampled by white people's invasion.

The final section of *Winnetou* is a sharp critique of the appropriation of American Indian spirituality by the dominant culture's New
Age movement—and, one might interpolate, by the spiritualists of
radical, or "metaphysical," feminism. The performers turn a medicine show parody into a "plastic pow-wow workshop," at which, for
three thousand dollars per weekend, people can be transformed into
American Indians. A spectator is chosen to participate and is run
through the process. After performing an improvisatory ceremonial
dance, he is ushered into a sweat lodge, where he is first given a
choice of tribes then a choice of Indian names.[27]

The names Spiderwoman concocts emphasize the stereotypes
American culture has generated for American Indians; the tribes are
Rappahamburg, Mish Mash, and Wishee Washee, and the Indian
names are Two Dogs Fucking, Old Dead-Eyed Dick, Two Sheets in
the Wind, and Punctured Eardrum, among others. The participant's
choices are presented to him on cardboard placards, which are held
up Vanna White–style for all the spectators to see. When the spectator has made all his choices and completed the ceremony, he is given
a photocopied picture of a "traditional" Indian, with long hair and
headband, which he must wear in front of his face for the rest of his
life. The two-dimensionality of the image he receives refers to the
equally flat stereotype promoted of Indian culture, even by liberal
New Age types eager to participate in—and, implicitly, to appropriate—its spirituality.

The comic tone set by the proceedings is carefully reversed at the
end of the piece, when another story is related of a "face without
borders" that refers to the disintegration of American Indian culture
and identity. The storyteller directs her remarks to the audience,
saying with bitter irony, "Thank you for discovering me," and "Don't
take your spirituality out on me." The audience becomes the target
of *Winnetou*'s pointed humor and is forced to ponder its complicity
in the imperialism the piece describes.

The piece's last moment is also tinged with irony. "The death of Winnetou" is announced epic theater style and enacted in a presentational way. All the seams show, and the scene's performance conventions are pointed to emphatically. A kind of eulogy is chanted for Winnetou. "He sat down and he died" is repeated three times, and the purported moral of the story is delivered sardonically: "Winnetou, lose a two." But the comic death scene transforms gradually in the final opportunity for Spiderwoman to deliver its more serious political statement.

"There lies Winnetou," the performers intone. "There lies the Indian, a sick and dying race." The digging metaphor used through many of the stories is used to suggest that the American Indian must return home to the land underneath white culture. The performers remove even the tenuous, haphazardly constructed mask of character they have worn throughout the piece, to insist that the spectators look at them. "See me," they chant in syncopated rhythm. "I'm talking, loving, hating, drinking too much, performing *my* songs, stories, dances, and now I tell *you*, discover your own spirituality." Rather than being objectified and appropriated by the spectator's gaze, Spiderwoman insists that their ethnic identities be respected as differently constructed.

The charge to white spectators is unavoidable, a moment in which Spiderwoman's rage at their culture's marginalization and commodification is directly expressed. The comedy used to satirize dominant cultural conventions turns sharply poignant, as Spiderwoman issues a challenge to white spectators to think about their responsibility for the history the piece presents.

The women in Spiderwoman always use their bodies—which are large and brown and middle-aged—and their lives to fashion political theater statements. *Winnetou's Snake-Oil Show* retains the best of Spiderwoman's eclectic nonlinearity while offering its thematic content with such a clear political and emotional investment that its various meanings become difficult to miss or dismiss. The risk Spiderwoman takes in crafting what could possibly be an unpopular message among the liberal audiences to whom the troupe plays gives *Winnetou* a vitality that alternative feminist theater desperately needs to resuscitate and to sustain itself through the 1990s.

In its advance press material Spiderwoman writes:

Challenging the "one-size-fits-all view of feminism," this seven woman company uses their diverse experiences as women, as American Indian women, as lesbians, as scorpios, woman [sic] over fifty and women under twenty-five, as sisters and mothers and grandmothers to defy such old generalizations as: "All blondes have more fun," and "All women's theatre is the same."[28]

Spiderwoman refuses to be subsumed under a heading that might align it with Wendy Wasserstein, whose "women's theater," if it fits that rubric at all, speaks from a very different position within dominant cultural privilege than Spiderwoman will ever have the leisure to inhabit. *Winnetou,* in the best Brechtian style, forces political contemplation from its spectators. *The Heidi Chronicles'* realism panders to its spectators' assumed, self-congratulatory apoliticism and, despite its foray into feminism, authorizes the dominant culture's conservative ideology.

By exploding the constraints of the realist form, as well as those of a hegemonic notion of feminism or "postfeminism," groups like Spiderwoman have the potential to transform feminist theater once again into a site of radical political action for the 1990s, by working at the intersections of race, ethnicity, and gender.

NOTES

1. See, for example, Mel Gussow, "Women Playwrights: New Voices in the Theatre," *New York Times Sunday Magazine,* May 1, 1983, in which he highlights Marsha Norman as foremost in a wave of new women playwrights changing the American theater scene. Gussow's article was sharply criticized for completely overlooking the long history of women working in American theater, both mainstream and alternative. This kind of ahistoricism, however, continues to mark popular media accounts of women's accomplishments in theater.

2. The theatricalism of social activism that so characterized American antiwar and other demonstrations in the late 1960s seems to be returning to the streets of the United States. Operation Rescue, a rightist antiabortion activist group, has co-opted leftist guerilla and street theater tactics to launch its attack on abortion clinics. Perhaps more in the spirit of leftist political theatricality is ACT-UP, an AIDS activist group that lobbies for a legislative and financial commitment to people with AIDS. See, for example, Alisa Solo-

mon, "AIDS Crusaders Act Up a Storm," *American Theater* 6, no. 7 (October 1989): 38–41, 120–21.

3. Although there are many political and social histories written on this period of American history, see, for example, Todd Gitlin, *The Sixties* (New York: Bantam, 1987).

4. See Hester Eisenstein, *Contemporary Feminist Thought* (Boston: G. K. Hall, 1983), for an insightful and informative description of feminist thought and political strategies in the early 1970s. Her chapter on consciousness-raising (35–41) is particularly useful here.

5. For an insightful analysis of liberal feminism in the United States, see Zillah Eisenstein, *The Radical Future of Liberal Feminism* (New York: Longman, 1981). Feminist theorists across disciplines, especially in the 1980s, have taken to drawing distinctions between various strands of feminist ideology. Liberal feminism is generally characterized as a reformist branch of the movement, since its efforts are concentrated on gaining equality for women without radically changing existing social or political systems. The movement is sometimes called "bourgeois feminism" and continues to be one of the more visible strains of American feminism.

6. See Eisenstein, *Contemporary Feminist Thought* (3–41), on this period in the history of radical feminism.

7. Radical feminism's initial focus on gender difference emphasized the constructedness of polarized social roles and sought to change them. Many feminist historians and theorists since have charted radical feminism's subsequent move into a celebration of entrenched gender differences (see ibid., 45–136). See Alice Echols, *Daring to Be Bad: Radical Feminism in America, 1967–1975* (Minneapolis: University of Minnesota, 1989), for a comprehensive history of the ideological changes in the movement. In an earlier article Echols termed the new version of radical feminism "cultural feminism," since it explicitly fosters the creation of a separate women's culture (see "The New Feminism of Yin and Yang," in Ann Snitow, Christine Stansell, and Sharon Thompson, eds., *Powers of Desire* [New York: Monthly Review Press, 1983], 439–59). Other theorists call the subsequent ideological position "essentialist feminism," since it considers women's nurturing roles to be innate and desirable (see, for such a discussion, Diana Fuss, "Reading like a Feminist," *differences* 1, no. 2 (Spring 1989): 77–92. Still others characterize variants of this position as "metaphysical feminism," since it theorizes women's spirituality—as opposed to social activism—as the site of their liberation (see Eisenstein, *Contemporary Feminist Thought*, 125–45).

8. See Dinah Leavitt, *Feminist Theatre Groups* (Jefferson, N.C.: MacFarland, 1980), 18–19, for a brief description of It's Alright to Be a Woman Theatre. For information on other early feminist theater groups in the United States, see Helen Krich Chinoy and Linda Walsh Jenkins, eds., *Women in American Theatre*, rev. ed. (New York: Theatre Communications Group, 1987).

9. See Richard Schechner, "Six Axioms for Environmental Theatre," reprinted in Brooks McNamara and Jill Dolan, eds., *The Drama Review: Thirty*

Years of Commentary on the Avant-Garde (Ann Arbor: UMI Research Press, 1986). Schechner's tract, written in 1968, proposed among other things breaking the proscenium arch by mingling the performers with spectators. The totally rearranged spatial relationship offered the potential for interaction that disallowed the separations of mimesis that realism demanded.

10. See Megan Terry's interviews in Kathleen Betsko and Rachel Koenig, eds., *Interviews with Contemporary Women Playwrights* (New York: Beechtree Books, 1987); and David Savran, *In Their Own Words: Contemporary American Playwrights* (New York: Theatre Communications Group, 1988). Writings on the Women's Experimental Theatre and Roberta Sklar's involvement can be found in Chinoy and Jenkins, as well as in Karen Malpede, *Women in Theatre: Compassion and Hope* (New York: Drama Book Publishers, 1983). See also Jill Dolan, "Feminists, Lesbians, and Other Women in Theatre: Thoughts on the Politics of Performance," in James Redmond, ed., *Women in Theatre: Themes in Drama*, vol. 11 (London: Cambridge University Press, 1989), 199–207, for an analysis of the Women's Experimental Theatre's work in relation to radical feminism.

11. See Jane Wagner, *The Search for Signs of Intelligent Life in the Universe* (New York: Harper and Row, 1986). *Search for Signs*, although quite a mainstream success, is much more radical in form and content than plays by Henley, Norman, or Wasserstein. Its one-woman show format allows Tomlin to use the transformation technique pioneered in feminist theater by women like Megan Terry and to break with the expectations of dramatic realism. As a result, the play's content is a much more sympathetic, politically invested discussion of American feminism from the early 1970s to the middle 1980s than Wasserstein's play, discussed below. *Search for Signs'* popularity, however, remains an anomaly on a Broadway scene that generally disallows the presentation of overtly political work.

12. The Women's Project has since left the American Place Theatre and incorporated on its own. The Women and Theatre Program of the Association for Theatre in Higher Education (formerly the American Theatre Association) is a good example of a professional organization that straddles mainstream and alternative theater and advocates for professional and academic women in theater. In the last several years, thanks to Vicki Patraka's leadership as president, the WTP's orientation has become more theoretical and scholarly. But, as a result, its annual conferences have produced some of the most interesting, alternative performance work by women in the United States. See the special issue of *Women & Performance Journal*, "Celebrating the Women and Theatre Program," 4, no. 2 (1989), for critical and historical information on the organization and its recent work.

13. While the Women's Experimental Theatre produced a series of performances in the early 1980s, it stopped actively creating new performance work by 1986. For information on At the Foot of the Mountain, see Chinoy and Jenkins, *Women in American Theatre*, 44–50 and 321–25; and Leavitt, *Feminist Theatre Groups*, 66–78. For a theoretical analysis of their recent work, see Jill

Dolan, *The Feminist Spectator as Critic* (1988; reprint, Ann Arbor: University of Michigan Press, 1991), 92–95.

14. Split Britches—a collective composed of Lois Weaver, Peggy Shaw, and Deborah Margolin—presented its signature production, *Split Britches*, in 1981 and has consistently produced works in repertory since. *Beauty and the Beast* (1982), *Upwardly Mobile Home* (1984), and *Little Women* (1988) are original, intricately constructed pastiches that rewrite popular and high culture from the perspectives of those marginalized by gender, ethnicity, and sexuality. Although Margolin tends to write their scripts and Weaver to direct them, the three women generate their material collectively by improvising around the often eccentric characters they create. Their nonlinear scripts work by a kind of accumulation of detail, so that atmospheres and quirky, incoherent personalities are created instead of unifying themes or action-based plots. Their pieces are episodic and repetitious and often simply end, rather than arriving at the point of full disclosure and apparent understanding that realism usually promotes.

Split Britches, and its affiliated producing space, the WOW Cafe, relies on community rather than government funding to produce its work, and frequently tours London, Amsterdam, and other European cities to make its livelihood. The attention materialist feminists in the academy (discussed below) have focused on the group has also provided them with sustaining residencies at various college campuses throughout the United States. Peggy Shaw and Lois Weaver met while working with Spiderwoman, a group discussed extensively below. For more information on this feminist theater troupe, see also Dolan, *The Feminist Spectator as Critic,* chap. 4; Sue-Ellen Case, "From Split Subject to Split Britches," in Enoch Brater, ed., *Feminine Focus* (New York and Oxford: Oxford University Press, 1989); and Vivian M. Patraka, "Split Britches in *Split Britches:* Performing History, Vaudeville, and the Everyday," *Women & Performance Journal* 4, no. 2 (1989): 58–67.

15. For a description and application of materialist feminist performance theory, see Dolan, *The Feminist Spectator as Critic;* and Sue-Ellen Case, *Feminism and Theatre* (New York and London: Methuen, 1988).

16. See Case's chapter, "Towards a New Poetics," *Feminism and Theatre,* 112–32.

17. See also Jill Dolan, "Gender Impersonation Onstage: Destroying or Maintaining the Mirror of Gender Roles," *Women & Performance Journal* 2, no. 2 (1985): 5–11, for a discussion of the gender implications of mimesis. Much work has been generated around the topic of realism and mimesis since this early article. For a theoretical extension of the question of mimesis, see Elin Diamond, "Mimesis, Mimicry, and the 'True-Real,'" *Modern Drama* 32, no. 1 (March 1989): 58–72. This issue of *Modern Drama* is a special issue on "Women in Theatre" and contains several articles useful to illuminate this discussion. See also the work in Sue-Ellen Case, ed., *Performing Feminisms: Feminist Critical Theory and Theatre* (Baltimore: Johns Hopkins University Press, 1990).

18. See Dolan, *The Feminist Spectator as Critic,* for an explication of the ideal spectator of representation.

19. See Jill Dolan, "In Defense of the Discourse: Materialist Feminism, Post-modernism, Post-structuralism . . . and Theory," *TDR* 33, no. 3 (Fall 1989): 58–71, for a discussion of the parameters of this debate within the field of feminism and theater.

20. For an explication of the ramifications of feminist theory in the academy and its influence on theater research, see Case's introduction to *Performing Feminisms.*

21. For example, *The Kathy and Mo Show,* a popular comedy revue with a long, off-Broadway run through 1989 and into 1990, which was subsequently taped for broadcast on the HBO cable channel, satirizes radical feminism in a scene in which two elderly women enrolled in a women's studies course attend a performance at a feminist coffeehouse. The construction of the scene indicates its authors' familiarity with radical feminist tenets, but its subsequent ridicule of women's culture (though somewhat affectionately conceived) also indicates they believe radical feminism is archaic in the context of 1980s values.

22. Wendy Wasserstein, *The Heidi Chronicles* (New York: Dramatists Play Service), 2. All subsequent page references will appear in the text. See also Phyllis Jane Rose, "Dear Heidi," *American Theater* 6, no. 7 (October 1989): 26–29, 114–16, for additional feminist commentary. My observations are drawn from my reading of the unpublished text as well as the Broadway performance with Joan Allen in the title role, which I attended on July 29, 1989.

23. See Rozsika Parker and Griselda Pollock, *Old Mistresses: Women, Art, and Ideology* (New York and London: Routledge, 1981), 20–26, for a materialist feminist critical discussion of the Gentileschi painting. I am indebted to Vicki Patraka for helping me make these connections.

24. From Spiderwoman's promotional material. See also Chinoy and Jenkins, *Women in American Theatre,* 303–5, for more historical information on the troupe.

25. The *Winnetou* manuscript is unpublished. My observations are based on the performance I attended, which was presented at At the Foot of the Mountain in Minneapolis on October 8, 1989.

26. Lisa Mayo and Gloria and Muriel Miguel were joined in this performance by Hortenisa Colorado.

27. At the performance I attended the participating spectator was a man. I have since heard that other volunteers have been women, so the participant's gender here can be switched.

28. From Spiderwoman's advance press material.

Chapter 2

Staking Claims and Positions: The Women and Theatre Program, San Diego, and the Danger Zone

This moment in feminism seems to me an awkward one. The movement is fractious and afraid, subject to external influences that make our issues loaded and divisive. The 1980s have moved us from a conception of women and feminism as monolithic and universal, to an investigation of differences prompted by an insistence on identity politics, toward an inquiry into the ways in which the differences among us and within us are crafted by discourse and reside in the very language we use to describe ourselves.

The factions and contentions currently dividing feminist critics, theorists, and practitioners in theater and performance seem to reflect the social movement's historical progress and the tensions caused by changing perspectives so rapidly. The Women and Theatre Program (WTP) of the Association for Theatre in Higher Education (ATHE) has not been exempt from the internecine struggles within the feminist movement and, in recent years, has become a crucible for the often fractious debates between liberal, radical, and materialist feminists and their various critical and practical strategies. After many years as an organization devoted primarily to networking between academic and professional theater women, WTP's focus began to shift into considering the intersections of feminist, critical, theoretical, and practical concerns around its 1986 preconference, which then-president Rhonda Blair organized at New York University. The New York preconference began the contentious debates between feminist theorists determined to stake a claim in the only active national organization for women and theater and those women for whom feminism—let alone theory—was still an irritating irrelevancy in their professional lives.

The 1987 Chicago preconference organized by then-vice-president Vicki Patraka insisted on addressing feminism and theory from the outset. Patraka sent out packets of reading material to conference participants and invited panelists to address the burgeoning role of theory in feminist performance and critical thought. The preconference textualized what had long been subtextual in the organization—the tacit hostility between people with different approaches to women, feminism, and theater.

The debates at the Chicago preconference began at a work-in-progress presentation, presented by At the Foot of the Mountain (AFOM) theater, of a reworked version of *Story of a Mother II* and a revived adaptation of Brecht's *The Exception and the Rule* called *Raped*.[1] The participants divided into two groups over the response to the performance. The division among the preconference spectators neatly paralleled that between feminists who practice poststructuralist, postmodernist, or materialist readings of representation and those who concentrate on theater's mirroring of stable identities.

Feminist theater people who continue to hold the text sacred and the playwright primary and to view character action as the cornerstone of the dramatic event found themselves provoked by those who want to use the expanded boundaries offered by theory to rethink the nature of representation and the role of gender, sexuality, race, and class within it. These women found their faith challenged; theorists found their hard-won tools attacked.

Spectators who supported AFOM perceived the critical discussion of their performance as a virulent, "male-like" attack by theorists. They claimed the performers were being purposefully misunderstood by women who refused to accept the work on its own terms and who would not position themselves in the manner demanded by the ritualized performance text and its performers. The critics/theorists were positioned as unfeeling and soulless by spectators who appreciated the woman-identified, healing nature of AFOM's work.

Racial politics were unarticulated but embedded in the skirmish, a state of affairs that was to be replicated a year later at the San Diego preconference. The multiculturalism of the AFOM ensemble provided a focus for the attack on theory. In a perversion of critical intent the theorists were called racist for supposedly silencing the performers of color. The theorists were trying to describe the racial politics of the work by analyzing the ideology behind the group's manipulation of the representational apparatus.

The 1988 WTP preconference was held at the Horton Grand Hotel in San Diego. Reporting on the conference presents a personal challenge for me, since I both organized the event and was embroiled in much of the controversy it raised. All I can hope to do here is to provide an accounting of my own experience of the events, filtered through my own various, often conflicting, positions as a white-materialist- feminist- lesbian- Jewish- poststructuralist- postmodernist critic and theorist. As preconference coordinator, I was determined to push theory and practice further, in panels on which we could look closely at the differences among us and our disparate work. Called "Staging Feminisms: Theories and Practices," the preconference began Sunday evening, July 31, with a keynote address by Erika Munk, senior editor and columnist at the *Village Voice.*

Munk proved an interesting choice. Her periodic "Cross Left" column always offers trenchant examinations of the relationship between art and politics through her own brand of socialist feminism. Munk has been peripheral, however, to the WTP. Asking her to address theory, practice, theater, and feminism meant inviting an outsider's opinion on the state of our arts and our issues.

Munk met the challenge by delivering an incendiary address. Her remarks were aimed at her own preconceived notions of feminist academic theoreticians, whom she intended to chastise into an awareness of the material world outside their so-called safe ivory towers. Munk thought she was talking to women who talk to themselves and whose discourse doesn't affect the public sphere in which she and other journalists participate. She harshly criticized theorists for failing to use their privilege to advance the agenda of social change; she called theory "careerist, masculinist jargon that insults the reader and the artist" and said that theory "speaks dangerous ideas harmlessly" and that "abstraction strips ideas of their excitement."

Munk's talk immediately set up a polemic in which theory was positioned as irrelevant to the "reality" of movements for social change. Although her position as a Marxist feminist may have been alien to many of the women present, her antitheory sentiments seemed popular and provided grist for the debates that were to follow.

Sue-Ellen Case, then editor of *Theatre Journal* and associate professor in the School of Drama at the University of Washington, was the respondent to Munk's remarks, a choice carefully structured to showcase the polemical points and counterpoints I wanted the preconference to offer. Case had delivered the keynote at the 1987 Chicago preconference. Her provocative piece called "Towards a Butch-Femme Aesthetic" textualized lesbian issues for the WTP and implicitly charged the group with a kind of tacit homophobia.[2] Her lecture was applauded but largely ignored in Chicago. I hoped to reraise some of the issues left open by Case's 1987 address and to maintain a sense of historical continuity by asking her to respond to the 1988 keynote.

Case situated Munk as a feminist eager to return to the socialist realist position of inscribing the hero into the text. She accused Munk of being melancholy over the loss of the author, whom Case said "we don't believe in anymore." "What is reality?" she asked, pointing out that the "public, journalistic discourse" Munk defined in opposition to abstract "academic discourse" remains constructed. Case insisted that we are in a revolutionary moment, in which our newly found ability to theorize is throwing us from the windows of the ivory tower, leaving us dangling by our fingertips from the ledges. Where Munk saw theory as a safe escape from direct political action, Case countered that theory is a radical position that threatens the hegemonic institutions in which it's based by bringing the social movement onto their doorsteps.

The exchange between Case and Munk set the tone for the proceedings that followed and raised all the hard questions. Who is the readership for the kinds of theoretical writing many of us do? To whom are all of us talking? Are we even talking to one another? As Case asked, who is the "public" to whom Munk insisted we are responsible? Case's response pointed out the myths of origin implicit in much of Munk's reasoning. Case suggested that we can't point to institutions like the academy and lay blame within them. She proposed that discourse is more elusive and more insidious and that language, too, is an institution that carries power. Theory is centered within language and discourse and aims to reorient their circulation.

"Elucidating Terms and Issues," the opening panel discussion Monday morning, August 1, was designed to address the question of language directly and to give participants a common vocabulary with which to work through the preconference. Moderator Janelle Reinelt, professor of theater at California State University–Sacramento, was articulate about the need to put ourselves into the flux of the historical moment, to admit that all of our positions vis-à-vis the dominant culture are unstable. Through a materialist feminist perspective she addressed the nature of hegemony and admitted that she has been thinking of representation as a monolith, rather than as a structure that is itself unstable. "How is social change possible?" Reinelt asked, and she proposed that, rather than coming to a single conclusion, we continually challenge ourselves and discard solutions that seem too pat.

Gayle Austin, who was then directing the Southeast Playwrights' Conference and had recently completed a dissertation at the City University of New York on feminist theory and playwriting, sketched out her own history within feminism and theater to delineate what she sees as a conflict between grassroots feminism and theory. Resisting the labels and categories often drawn around feminist women, Austin described herself as a woman "in the cracks," whose liminality makes it impossible for her to rest within any one area of theory or practice. Austin works to bridge the distance between the two. She described her introduction to theory as analogous to listening to a kind of alien music that becomes clearer as you grow accustomed to it.

Noreen Barnes described her decision to leave academia and the increasingly difficult position of being a woman in theater companies supposedly dedicated to collective operations that remain girded in misogynistic structures. Judy Stephens, an associate professor in theater at the Schuylkill Campus of Pennsylvania State University, eloquently described her position as a feminist on a rural campus, where her attempt to present images counter to dominant discourse is met with mixed responses. Stephens also reraised the question of authorship. As a critic who has written on the female characters in Eugene O'Neill's plays and subsequently wondered about the compatibility of feminism and realism, she asked if the playwright is a valid position for feminists to assume. Stephens pointed out the lack of black feminist women in the WTP and posed the question of sexuality differences among us, suggesting that we need to be able to ask and answer questions around these issues honestly.

The panel broke into small groups to explore various topics: articulating differences in subject positions prompted by sexual preference; how liminality allows you to straddle positions; the relationship between theoretical pursuits and developing a body of new plays to produce, discuss, and write about; how to attack the hegemony of representation with counterimages; how feminism relates to mainstream theater; and the new boundaries drawn in the juxtaposition of playwriting with performance art.

The afternoon panel, "Generating Texts," was moderated by Juli Thompson Burk, then assistant professor of theater at the University of Hawaii. The panel was constructed to address the production of meaning in performance/text situations that vary according to differences in race, class, and sexuality among authors, performers, and spectators. To illustrate how meaning varies across these differences the preconference packet of background reading materials included excerpts from Cherríe Moraga's Chicana lesbian play *Giving Up the Ghost;* Holly Hughes's white lesbian satire *The Well of Horniness;* Karen Finley's performance art piece *The Constant State of Desire;* and Aishah Rahman's play, *Unfinished Women Cry in No Man's Land while a Bird Dies in a Gilded Cage,* which is published in Margaret Wilkerson's *Nine Plays by Black Women.*

Participants' responses to these texts varied and produced some surprising, sometimes disturbing remarks. For example, one woman felt excluded by the Spanish sections of Moraga's play and called it "elitist" because the typical modes of entry into the text were closed to her by the language. In contrast, although the WTP group is overwhelmingly heterosexual, most of the women at the preconference found Hughes's lesbian text accessible. *The Well's* parody and humor gave the participants a level on which to relate to the text, and they subsequently refused to acknowledge their differences as heterosexual women from *The Well's* lesbian references and subcultural meanings.

To complement such textual issues three panelists presented their thoughts on narrative and meaning. E. Beth Sullivan, an assistant professor in theater at Ohio State University, writes on the narrative strategies of contemporary women playwrights. On the "Generating Texts" panel Sullivan discussed the nature of "enplotment," of how events come together to form stories. She said her task as a feminist theorist is to be aware of the ideological interests at work in the construction and reception of narrative. Sullivan suggested that people are trained to see themselves in narrative but proposed that its movement toward resolution has ramifications that diverge according to a reader's gender (and—as the discussion of Moraga's and Hughes's texts proved—class, race, ethnicity, and sexuality).

Panel participant Katherine Griffith, who heads the women's division of New Dramatists in New York, described herself as someone who, like Austin, straddles several different theatrical and feminist realms. She recalled her unease as a performer-in-training at Julliard with traditional texts that erased her own experience. As a performer in East Village work, she refocused her concerns on how to sabotage texts instead of supporting them as commodities.

Kay Carney, a performer and theater educator, suggested that we consider the spirituality and aesthetics of theater rather than its politics. Carney proposed that employing women's intuition and authenticity in theater can reveal a deep level of experience. She proposed that self-revelation can be political power and that spirituality enables people to see the whole of their identities. Clearly, the panel presented divergent, provocative viewpoints on the construction and representation of identity as meaning in performance.

The cumulative issues raised by the two opening panels were addressed in practice at the "Performing Bodies" panel the next morning, Tuesday, August 2. Organized and moderated by Rhonda Blair, the panel presented work by Marianne Goldberg and Kate Bornstein, Joan Schirle and Elinor Fuchs, that explored the mutual impact of theory on performance practice.

Schirle, a member of the Dell'Arte Players in Blue Lake, California, showed clips from her work and discussed the importance of physical performance training for women. Schirle said women have generally been left out of circus training, which explains their absence from the New Vaudeville performance genre currently in vogue. Dell'Arte offers *commedia* workshops, at which Schirle said finding masks for women becomes a challenging practical and ideological concern. Schirle proposed that *commedia*'s physical, presentational style can help women analyze their material in ideological terms.

Elinor Fuchs, who writes for the *Village Voice* and teaches at

Emory University, wondered how the feminist critic can extend a hand to the artist, whether or not a woman's work has feminist content. She described puppet and mask work by sculptor/performance artist Julie Taymor, Maria Irene Fornes's play *Fefu and Her Friends*, and pieces by performance artist Rachel Rosenthal. Fuchs analyzed the three women's work through their use of female bodies and the female performer's position in relationship to the spectator.

Kate Bornstein and Marianne Goldberg presented pieces that offered some of the conference's most provocative moments. Bornstein is a male-to-female postoperative transsexual who first attended a WTP preconference in Chicago in 1987. Her participation there brought issues from the social movement into focus for the WTP, as participants grappled with the physical and ideological implications of her presence. Bornstein revealed herself as a transsexual halfway through the Chicago preconference, approaching various women individually for their response.

Her revelation prompted a great deal of gossip and much soul-searching about the nature of gender and its construction. Could someone who had lived most of her adult life as a man relate to her newly adopted sex and gender in the same way as women who have been socialized as female? Bornstein's lesbianism complicated many women's responses, as they grappled with the implications of such a variety of past and present sex, gender, and sexuality positions combined in one body.

Since Bornstein stated her continued commitment to the WTP in Chicago, Blair and I decided to invite her to address her transsexualism openly on the "Performing Bodies" panel in San Diego. Her performance of her experiences of gender identity was brave and explicit. She delivered a male character's monologue as she once played him as a male actor, aware of her imprisonment in her theatrical role. She then performed a female character as she once did as a male actor, protected by the theatrical convention of gender impersonation while her body enacted this impersonation in everyday life. Her monologues traded among shifting, constructed identities, layered on a body that has experienced all of these constructions.

Standing before us, unprotected by the formal trappings of the representational frame, Bornstein threw the question of gender and sexuality construction right into our laps. Where do you locate gender on an altered body that bears the echo of its past? Bornstein recast herself biologically to play an alternate sex and gender role. She hired a surgical knife to allow her to play the gender role she desired in a body that would look the part. Confined by gender construction, Bornstein opted to reconstruct her body to fit herself into gendered discourse. Or did she subvert gendered discourse by her choice to tamper with biology?

Watching her perform, I was unsettled by my awareness that Bornstein has no neutral body, that even her biology is not immutable but, rather, constructed. Spectators pointed out that a certain Brechtian distance is implicit in Bornstein's position, that her body editorializes on itself the moment her choice is made textual. Bornstein performed a noncoincidence of body and language, a postmodern dissociation of presence and discourse.

Marianne Goldberg, a performer/theorist and editorial board member of *Women & Performance Journal*, presented pieces of work that has been through many permutations both in performance and in print.[3] Goldberg refuses the traditional dichotomy of theory and practice. Casually standing behind a lectern, Goldberg delivered a lecture/demonstration on the body as language and on the location of gender in the body as meaning. Her performance was a literarization of the body à la Brecht, not an incidence of *l'écriture féminine;* in fact, Goldberg insists, "We can claim our bodies only if we stop claiming that they give us truth." Her body became a text written in space, and she played self-reflexively with the meanings it created.

Her wry observations editorialized the typical expectations of the performer positioned as "naive art object," to be viewed and consumed through the spectator's desire. By calling attention to the ideological markings and potential disruptions of her own presence, Goldberg shifted the discussion into the performer's possibilities for resisting the domination of the gaze. Her body, she says, is "in motion and at risk,"[4] present in a discourse in which she is engaged and competent. She speaks to spectators and points out that she is exchanging the gaze with them. She is an author who refuses authority, a subject intent on shifting her identity even as she speaks.

The final preconference panel Tuesday afternoon, "Feminist Criticism and Theater," grappled with the language of theory and the ideological differences between various strands of contemporary American feminism. Pat Rice, an associate professor of theater at California State University–Sacramento, suggested that feminists in theater should practice looking through the ideologies that divide us and that the liberal, cultural/radical, and materialist categories of American feminism might bleed together usefully.

Linda Walsh Jenkins, then a professor of theater at Northwestern University, positioned herself as a materialist feminist activist/theorist, although she does not call herself a critic. She remarked on the different ways in which women speak according to class and race and suggested that feminist criticism must address its own racism. Jenkins said she attempts to use texts outside of Western culture and that entering their narratives makes her look critically at herself.

Jeanie Forte, then an assistant professor in the English Department at the University of Tennessee, discussed feminist uses of the body in performance art, suggesting that the form allows the female body's relation to representation to frustrate its gender-biased conventions. Forte said feminism brings a critical component to creative work by offering a process of self-examination. She wondered whether feminists can refuse the conventional, masterful, authoritative critical stance to be accountable to the performers' work, to bridge the distance between the language of the text and theoretical language used to describe it.

Elin Diamond, associate professor at Rutgers University, who moderated the panel, suggested that we offer what we know of theater to invigorate the field of critical theory. She emphasized theater's materiality and the way in which it poses the question of who is speaking, who is listening, and the sharing of the look and suggested that these theoretical issues are far from depleted. As critics, Diamond said, we become arbiters and interpreters of ideology, yet we must historicize our own positions so that we don't impose new hegemonic rules.

Diamond proposed that we revel in the instability of positionality, rather than fighting turf wars or protecting ourselves with ideological boxes. Words are a site of struggle, she said, in the continuing conflict between humanist notions of the self and poststructuralist notions of shifting subject positions that are constructed historically. Diamond pointed out that the critic is never heard the way she wants to be heard, but she cautioned that only a "fascist mentality wants to arrest the circulation of words."

The summary session Tuesday evening analyzed a disruption that had occurred during a discussion of Anna Deavere Smith's performance Monday night. Smith's "On the Road" series uses oral history techniques to perform topical issues and familiar personalities in community settings. She was commissioned by the WTP to produce a performance piece for the preconference based on the organization's nine-year history. The piece was called *Chlorophyll Postmodernism and the Mother-Goddess: A Conversation*, a tapestry of nearly one hundred interviews conducted with women involved with the WTP who vary across age, race, class, sexuality and the context in which they work on women or feminism and theater.[5]

Smith's montage of these interviews provided several juxtapositions hospitable to a feminist postmodernist reading of the representation of identity. She performed on a formal proscenium stage, with rudimentary lighting and sound, and emblematic props that recalled the conventions of one-woman shows. She created the semblance of an environment as much as the semblance of character in a traditional, realist way. But her presence as a black woman performer—the only black woman of the one hundred women attending the conference—was continually foregrounded through the piece, since the personas she assumed were often noncoincident with her race. Instead of building characters through psychological, empathetic identification techniques, Smith glossed the recognizable, personal attributes of the women she performed, which allowed spectators simply to identify them, not necessarily to identify *with* them. She moved from "character" to character very quickly; her changes of gesture and voice were broad and presentational.

Smith used the words of black women and white women she had interviewed to create versions of their identities and the WTP. The spectators could identify the subjects of Smith's performance—many of whom were in the audience—but were encouraged to see her performing them, to hear her choose their words, and to grapple with the foregrounding of race and ideas.

In a sense her performance maintained a mimetic function anathema to postmodernism. But, if she provided a mirror, it was insistently, usefully cracked by her presence as a black woman, which conveyed an editorial comment on the personalities and issues she interwove. Some spectators expected a more traditional mimesis and railed against their absence from Smith's opaque mirror. Because they didn't see the radical implications of Smith's performance, and because they didn't hear her critique, they proceeded to attack the history of the program instead. Lost in the ensuing struggle among white women was a confrontation with the ideas about race and representation in the performance text Smith constructed. By searching for an "authentic" representation of their own experience, and focusing on their dissatisfaction with its absence, the spectators erased the residue of Smith's commentary on her experience.[6]

Yet the performance struck some sort of nerve related, perhaps, to the assumptions of mimesis. Since the piece was ostensibly about the history of the program, there were people in the audience who chose the postperformance discussion as the moment to critique the WTP's composition. Those who didn't see themselves reflected in the mirror of the piece, in however editorialized a fashion, read it as a piece about power and felt silenced, since their own voices went unheard within its frame. The fact that the piece was presented by a black woman, herself critical of the group's ideological base, particularly about race issues, eluded the audience, who argued more literally about their own lack of representation in the piece and the organization.

Many of the women who complained after the performance took the occasion to attack the WTP's theorists, although no one was named explicitly. The spectators climbed on the antitheory bandwagon Munk rode in on Sunday night and proceeded to decry the WTP's move toward theory.[7] Although the issue remained unarticulated publicly, the fear of theory some women evinced seemed linked to sexuality differences. The group's more visible and vocal theorists have been perceived as lesbians. (Whether they are or not is almost—not quite—beside the point.) When the assumption of their sexuality is compounded with these theorists' insistence on the decenteredness of the subject, some heterosexual women seem to feel their privilege threatened. If sexuality is suddenly thrown into a shifting, poststructuralist space in which it is seen as constructed through discourse, the presence of a lesbian position—and a vociferous one, at that—seems to be discomforting.

Some observers suggested that the postperformance discussion was shaped in response to a heated exchange at the "Elucidating Terms and Issues" panel that morning. When the question of textual intervention arose at that panel, Elinor Fuchs wanted to discuss a production of *Don Juan* that Richard Schechner had directed at Florida State University. Two women at the preconference had worked with

Schechner on the production. As Fuchs stood up to describe the work, I found myself resenting the amount of time we were taking to valorize a male director. Although Fuchs ironized her characterization of Schechner's work as feminist, several of the women present agreed with me that an extended discussion of his production would be inappropriate in the preconference context. The debate about whether to discuss the work quickly became loaded and intense. Some preconference participants felt that the theorists present had joined as a block to "silence" Fuchs and the women whose work contributed to Schechner's production. The discussion after Smith's performance Monday night seemed to vent resentment left over from the morning's skirmish.

The postperformance discussion was troubling for many reasons, and my description of it here is inevitably shaped by my own position within that moment as one of the theorists under reproach. Since the preconference I have heard a variety of stories about what happened and can only hope to share my own clearly biased version. In my interpretation of the discussion the language of victimization was employed to launch an attack against the group's theorists. Radical feminist ideology that valorizes healing was suddenly pressed into service to harm. Words like *savagery* were used to describe an exchange that was perhaps intense but certainly not violent. Old dichotomies were revived; theorists were implicitly charged with maleness, and those they critiqued were positioned as passive victims.

The discussion caused a rupture in the preconference, not because the issues it raised weren't valid but, rather, because the discussion was veiled and ugly, and the vocabulary on which it relied linked materialist feminist poststructuralist/postmodernist theorists with the worst radical feminist nightmare of male-like behavior. Rather than confronting our differences productively and trying to respect and learn from one another, the theorists were silenced and attacked, and much personal hurt was inflicted all around. Most of the preconference participants spent a long night in the Horton Grand's lobby and rooms, rehashing what had happened and what might be done. The evening was exhausting and, in hindsight, too dramatic and emotional. But, clearly, the issue of theory and practice, and the ideological variations among feminisms, were suddenly clarified, and members of the WTP were forced to decide where they stood.

I maintain that naming and claiming responsibility for your position regarding feminism and theater, theory and practice, is a positive act. But speaking as the newly elected vice-president of the WTP—an election was held during the summer of 1988, before the San Diego preconference—I hope that it's not necessary for our organization to falter and split over the issue of differences, which continues to plague feminism at large. The WTP is still small but growing large enough that the recognition of difference within and outside of our ranks should be our prime concern in the coming years. I am determined to bring issues from feminist performance theory that have revitalized feminism and theater together in our meetings. Yet I hope that President Vicki Patraka and I are sensitive to the needs of our diverse membership and to the fact that, for some of us, identity politics are absolutely vital to our sense of oppression and victimization as women. Patraka and I are committed to finding mutually beneficial ways to bring these conflicting perspectives together.

Some women would prefer our meetings to be safe and uncritically supportive, a time of comfort and healing. Feminism has never been such a safe place for me; it has always challenged and pushed me, never held my hand and comforted me. Feminism has strengthened me, perhaps even empowered me, but it's also made me realize how dangerous I am and that my position, however it shifts historically, will never be safe. Feminism has made me confront racism and classism, and locating myself in front of them makes me completely unsafe. Feminism has given me an analysis of homophobia; I don't feel safe knowing there are people who hate me for my sexuality. Feminism has given me theory, and that is where I live. I believe that opting to work in feminist practice and theory leads you right into the ubiquitous danger zone.

What I deplore, and what haunts me from the San Diego preconference, is an attack on theory that comes from ignorance and an unwillingness to confront the changing tides of feminist history. The feminist movement has moved into an era in which theory has been instrumental in recognizing the differences among and within women. Theory is not a so-called male game of divide and conquer but, rather, a deeply political, committed effort to divide and name, to liberate one another from the yoke not only of cultural oppression but also of a monolithic feminism that would coerce us into sameness. The theory that it's become so fashionable to denigrate tries to discern difference and its construction. Poststructuralism and materialist feminism chart the movement of power through the culture, in ways that will allow women, people of color, and the working class to stake their claims to it. Theory is not about amassing power but about its more equitable distribution.

I know there is a common assumption that theory is in vogue, that doing theory gives you the power of publishing and the ability to move in rarefied academic circles. Much of what Munk, in her summary of the event, called the preconference bloodletting,[8] was prompted by the perception that feminist theorists are the ones with the jobs, the books, the tenure, and the acclaim, while other feminist women remain the unsung workhorses of theater departments across the country. These women are training actors, designers, technicians, and future theater educators and don't have time to train themselves in the pursuit of theory.

I understand and respect their positions. I am also aware that the liaison between feminism and theory within the conservative halls of the academy might eventually pose dangerous threats to the radical potential of both pursuits. My aim is not to make feminists in theater and performance worship at the altar of contemporary critical theory. I simply believe that we all choose where we work best and that there's no need to place theory and practice in a judgmental, jealous, hierarchical relationship.

Theory is another place to work on the question of how our culture shapes us and how we can intervene in its representations in the effort toward social change. Theory and practice must inform each other and combine to make feminist theater and performance and criticism a formidable cultural force. The WTP preconferences can be used as precious time to learn from one another, to challenge one another's commitments and perspectives on common issues.

NOTES

1. See my book *The Feminist Spectator as Critic* (1988; reprint, Ann Arbor: University of Michigan Press, 1991), chapter 5, "Cultural Feminism and the Feminine Aesthetic," 92–95, for a thorough, if biased, description of that event.

2. See Sue-Ellen Case, "Towards a Butch-Femme Aesthetic," in Lynda Hart, ed., *Making a Spectacle: Feminist Essays on Contemporary Women Playwrights* (Ann Arbor: University of Michigan Press, 1988), 282–99.

3. For one permutation of the piece she presented, see "Ballerinas and Ball Passing," *Women & Performance Journal #6* 3, no. 1 (1987–88): 7–31.

4. See Elin Diamond, "Brechtian Theory/Feminist Theory," *TDR* 32, no. 1 (1988): 82–94.

5. See the script of this performance, and Sue-Ellen Case's introductory notes to it, in *Women & Performance Journal's* special issue on the Women and Theatre Program, 4, no. 2 (1989): 20–45.

6. After publishing this analysis of her performance and the response to it, I learned that Smith took exception to my understanding of how race functioned in the piece. She told me later that she hadn't intended race to matter or to filter the testimonies she shared through her perspective as an African-American woman. Smith and Sydné Mahone, dramaturg at Crossroads Theatre in New Brunswick, New Jersey, both told me they felt my analysis was racist in its insistence on reading Smith's perspective as "black."

7. Erika Munk's position, after her keynote address, shifted significantly during the preconference. Case and Munk sat together to watch Smith's performance, an ironic image, given the debacle that followed. Spectators couldn't perceive that two women who had argued so vehemently the evening before were able to respect each other's differences and realize that the work they do, ultimately, is mutually rewarding. Munk was very surprised by the personal investment, vulnerability, and commitment she found in women she had tried to describe as removed from the passionate struggle for social change. In her "Cross Left" summary of the event Munk wrote, "All in all, considerable blood on the floor. And, all in all, a good thing, proving that there's new life in the theatrical academy, where theatre thinking came late to the kind of questions literary, film, and mass-media criticism have been examining for a decade.... [E]xperimenting ... with the large hypotheses Women in Theatre [*sic*] posed could change American theatre" ("Representation and Its Discontents," *Village Voice*, September 6, 1988, 86).

8. Ibid.

Chapter 3

In Defense of the Discourse: Materialist Feminism, Postmodernism, Poststructuralism... and Theory

Ten years ago feminist theater and performance criticism was something of an oxymoron. Like most avowedly political criticism, feminist work in the late 1970s and early 1980s seemed caught in conflicting demands of aesthetics and ideology. Feminist critics of feminist work teetered uneasily among a desire to support women's production efforts, to investigate the ramifications of an unprecedented switch in gender perspective, and to compare women's theater and performance with an aesthetic standard that had not yet been formulated. Critics writing for feminist presses usually chose to validate what they saw; those writing in academic venues generally took a sociological approach to theater's reflection of women's social roles. The bulk of the critical effort was toward redressing the historical invisibility of women in the field.

When French theory began to find its way across the Atlantic, it changed the contours of feminist criticism in the academy. Elaine Marks and Isabelle de Courtivron published their landmark anthology *New French Feminisms* in 1981 and suddenly gave American feminist criticism a whole new vocabulary and new territories to cover. Hélène Cixous, Luce Irigaray, and Julia Kristeva, among others, seemed powerful and poetic in their descriptions of female sexuality as a subversive, antipatriarchal textuality. If women could write with their bodies, as *l'écriture féminine*'s florid manifestos proposed, could the body also be a site of a new theater practice and textual analysis?

Could the French feminist pantheon's borrowings from Derrida and Lacan give feminist theater and performance critics new tools for describing the field?

American feminist criticism in the 1980s has also been shaped by the field of cultural studies. The influx of British materialism, with its focus on ideology formation in representation, has allowed critics to dig deeper, farther, and wider in the investigation of representation as an ideological apparatus with an active role in preserving social arrangements. The materialist approach has moved academic feminist criticism away from sociological analysis based in assumptions that theater serves a mimetic function for the culture into an analysis of representation as a site for the production of cultural meanings that perpetuate conservative gender roles.

Deconstruction, poststructuralism, psychoanalysis, and materialism often appear to be unlikely traveling companions along the critical terrain, but, if nothing else, they have prompted an increased focus on theory over sociology. Feminist theater and performance criticism, as a result, has arrived at the end of the decade with its contours shaped roughly by three different analytical methods based in divergent ideologies: (1) a liberal feminist insistence on traditional criticism that supports the play as the basis of the dramatic experience; (2) a radical feminist reification of theater as a mimesis that validates women's identities; and (3) a materialist feminist approach to theater and performance as ideologically marked representation, which borrows variously from psychoanalysis, poststructuralism, and Marxist criticism.

These three approaches to feminist theater and performance criticism have recently been at odds. At the Women and Theatre Program's (WTP) annual preconferences, liberal and radical feminist critics and practitioners have butted against materialist theorists' methods and ideologies. Poststructuralism, especially, seems to challenge many long-held theatrical assumptions that many liberal and radical feminists aren't eager to release. The heralded "death of the author"[1] displaces the playwright's primacy and locates the responsibility for producing meaning in the hermeneutic sphere. The traditional triumvirate of playwright-director-actor has been disrupted by the spectator's insertion into the paradigm as an active participant in the production of meaning.

Author's intent has become suspect or irrelevant, the director's

authority challenged, and the actor's position as manipula
traded for one of resistance. Poststructuralism's sacrileg
to those who deplore its theory, is its unwillingness tc
text and its insistence on the shifting, historical nature of tne ᵢₙ꜀ₐₓₓ
ings representation produces.

Poststructuralist theory threatens what some see as feminist criticism's role in validating women's identities in theater and performance. The issue of identity is particularly vital in theater, which has
historically solicited its responses based on empathetic identification
techniques. The larger struggle in feminism over how to reconcile its
conflicting theories of identity and the self, then, is particularly ur-
gent in theater and performance.

Poststructuralism versus Identity Politics

Over the last several years the popularity of poststructuralism and
the prevalence of identity politics in feminism have prompted the
development of opposing feminist theories of the self. Identity politics claims to define women's subjectivity by their positions within
race, class, or sexuality that the dominant culture—and often the
dominating voices in feminism—have effectively squelched.
Poststructuralist practice suggests that any such coherent concep-
tions of identity are specious, since even race, class, and sexuality,
as well as gender, are constructed within discursive fields and
changeable within the flux of history. According to poststructuralism,
subjectivity is never monolithic or fixed, but decentered, and constantly thrown into process by the very competing discourses
through which identity might be claimed.

These opposing feminist camps base their arguments in definitions of experience, as the old slogan The Personal Is the Political
comes back to haunt in unexpected ways. Feminism at this historical
moment seems caught between reifying experience as truth and pro-
claiming that, although experience does dictate a certain material
reality, it's totally constructed and is not the basis of objective truth.

The two camps split on the issue of identity. Radical feminists
propose that female identity is coherent and whole and defined in
opposition to male identity. The politics that stem from this position
carve out places in gender, race, and class that are solipsistically
unified and that elide the differences within and between women.

Radical feminist performance texts, as Elin Diamond has written, tend to romanticize female identity by assuming that a transcendent female self can be mirrored in "woman-identified" theater.[2]

Asserting a ground of experience from which to theorize feminism is not romanticized or totalized under materialist feminist analysis, which borrows some of its tenets from poststructuralism. Teresa de Lauretis, for instance, cautions that the assertion of identity is not the goal, as it is in feminist identity politics, but a point of departure for a multivalent, shifting ground of subjectivity, a "self-contradictory identity, . . . made up of heterogeneous and heteronomous representations of gender, race, and class."[3] Identity becomes a site of struggle, at which the subject organizes and reorganizes competing discourses as they fight for supremacy.

Materialist feminist performance criticism uses poststructuralism to deconstruct both traditional, male-identified realism and alternative, woman-identified ritual drama and performance art for their belief in coherent, unified identities. If feminist poststructuralism is the tool of this critique, postmodernism is the style that offers potential performance applications. Logically, a postmodernist performance style that breaks with realist narrative strategies, heralds the death of unified characters, decenters the subject, and foregrounds conventions of perception is conducive to materialist feminist analyses of representation.

The intent of the growing, diversifying field of feminist postmodern performance theory is to develop theater and performance strategies that will create new meanings at the site of representation, which has historically outlawed or silenced women within its frame. Feminist postmodernist performance theories intervene in representation to encourage spectators to think differently about their positions within culture, differently than the comfortable conventions of realism ever persuade them to think. Feminist performance theories give critics a language that unmasks the seeming transparency of performance texts and that articulates the insidious ideology of any representation that presents experience as truth.

Continually watchdogging themselves and their bedfellows, feminist performance theorists have also chastised the commodified brands of postmodernist performance that devolve into an endless plurality of meaning; a chic, politically apathetic ennui; or a retrograde nostalgia for master narratives.[4] The project of feminist theory is unflaggingly political, as it studies not simply the superficial structure of performance but also its effect on the culture and the search for modes of effective social change.

A wealth of invigorating thinking and criticism has come from pondering the alliance of feminist criticism and postmodern style. But, concurrently, feminist criticism's struggle between poststructuralism and identity politics has provoked a metadebate over theory in feminism. Theorists who subscribe to poststructuralist analysis are accused of oppressing radical feminist identity politicians with the privileges of an elite language. Accusations of silencing are hurled about, since this argument takes place in discourse and is very much about the power of language.

Struggles in Discourse

Tensions between these opposing camps have been exacerbated by the increasing visibility of critical and theoretical work in feminist theater and performance. Feminist panels sponsored by the WTP at the annual Association for Theatre in Higher Education conferences, as well as at the Modern Language Association conventions, have been very well attended over the last several years, and publishers are beginning to seek out feminist books in the field. Helen Krich Chinoy's and Linda Walsh Jenkins's anthology *Women in American Theatre*, originally published by Crown in 1981, was revised and reissued by Theatre Communications Group in 1987. Karen Malpede's collection *Women in Theatre: Compassion and Hope* was published in 1983, Helene Keyssar's *Feminist Theatre* in 1985, and Kathleen Betsko and Rachel Koenig's anthology *Interviews with Contemporary Women Playwrights* appeared in 1987.[5]

These four editions essentially reflect the sociological approach to feminist criticism and theater history. The Chinoy/Jenkins anthology is a valuable sourcebook of information on women playwrights, producers, directors, and actors that provides a solid introduction to the wealth of women's work overlooked in distant and present theater history. The collection is marked, however, by its early 1980s perspective on feminist theater criticism as an ill-defined plurality of approaches. The reissued volume surveys more recent critical methodologies in the field, such as semiotics, materialism, and poststructuralism, but shies away from a rigorous investigation of the ideological meanings of different feminist analytical styles.

The Betsko/Koenig collection of interviews is grounded in the liberal feminist assertion of the text's primacy. The book succeeds in providing women playwrights an important, public forum in which to speak for themselves about their politics, their creative processes, and their projects but, like the Chinoy/Jenkins anthology, fails to provide an overarching, specific framework for feminism, aesthetics, or ideology. The editors intentionally avoid such distinctions.

Three books published in 1988 take on the task of sorting through feminist ideologies and their various critical perspectives: *The Feminist Spectator as Critic,* my own book; Sue-Ellen Case's *Feminism and Theatre;* and *Making a Spectacle: Feminist Essays on Contemporary Women's Theatre,* edited by Lynda Hart.[6] My book applies critical theory to investigate the feminist spectator's position vis-à-vis the representational frame and favors a materialist feminist approach. Through case studies of work by Marsha Norman, Richard Foreman, At the Foot of the Mountain, the Women's Experimental Theatre, Spiderwoman, and other performance groups, I attempt to specify the ideological underpinnings of various performance theories and practices.

Case's *Feminism and Theatre* is a handbook that introduces feminist critical theory in theater and performance. Case rejects the assumption of theater as mimesis and argues that theater history and dramatic literature cannot be read for information about actual women's lives. The book begins with an attack on the Aristotelian, Greek, and Elizabethan theater traditions as forums for patriarchal ideology that repressed actual historical women. Case suggests that the feminist reader studying *The Poetics* and other canonical texts that gird the Western theater tradition can "discover the methodology and assumptions of patriarchal production" in which they are based.[7]

Hart's anthology mixes liberal, radical, and materialist perspectives under sections that address women playwrights' metaphors, their use of aesthetics and history, and their disruptions of the patriarchal ideology Case describes. Hart characterizes the articles in her collection as documenting the "shift in feminist perspective from discovering and creating positive images of women in the content of drama to analyzing and disrupting the ideological codes embedded in the inherited structures of dramatic representation."[8] The book serves as a focal point for applications of diverging feminist critical thought on contemporary theater.

The published response to these books has been somewhat illuminating regarding the debate between poststructuralism and identity politics and relevant to the dissension among varying feminist perspectives. The anthologies of the early or mid-1980s were generally applauded when they appeared and were seen as correctives to women's invisibility in theater history. Keyssar's *Feminist Theatre* also garnered favorable reviews; her book analyzes plays by women through a more or less traditional critical approach.

Case's book, on the contrary, is a historical/critical/theoretical study with a polemical force that has made it subject to two aggressively unfavorable reviews. Gabrielle Cody, writing in *Performing Arts Journal*, chastises Case for a "lack of intellectual rigor" and an "inability to rise above [her] rhetoric."[9] This attack on her scholarship, in fact, seems to mask Cody's discomfort with Case's politics. Cody particularly lambastes Case's work on Greek and Elizabethan stage conventions, criticizing her for reducing "thoughts to ideology, literature to sociology."[10]

Cody misreads Case's thesis by attempting to locate her work within the sociological criticism from which Case points away. For example, Cody challenges Case to investigate Sophocles' and Euripides' women for their strength as characters. In her chapter on the Greeks, Case states explicitly that the feminist critic or historian, reading Greek theater history through its production practice rather than its texts alone, can no longer view these representations as in any way linked to the lives of real women.[11]

Similarly, Cody accuses Case of insulting women by "avoiding the images in Shakespeare (often the only representations of female power in Elizabethan England) by emphasizing his techniques of production."[12] But production is exactly Case's point. She insists these texts be read through living cultural history, rather than detaching them into a transcendent sphere. Case's poststructuralist approach does not focus on ahistorical content or images but, instead, analyzes the representational apparatus and the ideology that it enforces through theater history.

In her parting shot Cody writes that Case's book "posits that women have been robbed of their own representations throughout theatre history, but a more inclusive mimesis is possible through the creation of a feminist-identified culture."[13] This statement directly contradicts Case's final assertion that "the production of signs creates the sense of what a person is rather than reflecting it (in the traditional mimetic order)."[14] Case's approach is, in fact, antimimesis, and Cody does her a disservice by consigning her work to a radical feminist ghetto of feminist-identified culture in which theater is a validating mirror.

Joyce van Dyke's lead article in the *Women's Review of Books* contrasted Case's book with the Betsko/Koenig interview collection and Hart's *Making a Spectacle* anthology. Van Dyke applauds the collection of interviews as "energetic, lithe, funny, vivid," then goes on to deplore the "considerable gap between feminist critics and feminist playwrights." She calls Case's story a "lopsided one" and implies that she is more of a semiotician than she is a feminist. Van Dyke suggests that Case's work is selectively exclusionary and "does not admit the existence of what it leaves out,"[15] such as the women who did perform on the Continent during Shakespeare's era and the wealth of women's theater work that happened after Hrotsvit and Aphra Behn, on whom Case focuses in an early chapter.

Van Dyke feels Hart's anthology is more "balanced" in its view of contemporary women's theater and engages her critique with Yolanda Broyles Gonzalez's piece on the women of El Teatro Campesino, in particular. Her article takes its most ideological turn when she begins to summarize the ramifications of the three books she's reviewed. Van Dyke feels that feminist critics place themselves at a remove from work by living writers to focus on the arena of "critical combat." Suddenly, references to critical militarism ground her review:

> There are a number of governing metaphors that shape literary criticism today . . . [b]ut the prevailing metaphor is the militarist one, and feminists seem to have adopted it as enthusiastically as other critics. In this climate, the critical vocabulary of attacks, defenses, tactics and strategies seems natural and inevitable. Critics are praised as "brave" and "daring"; "discipline" (with its implications of hierarchy and punishment) and critical "rigor" (not just phallic but suggestive of military bearing, and other life-threatening or lifeless forms) are frequently equated with

intellectual respectability. . . . There are other metaphors available to criticism that would be more in keeping with feminism:
for instance, the theatrical metaphor. . . . It suggests a collectivist
enterprise, one that is at least potentially non-hierarchical. It
proposes a life-giving and pleasure-giving activity in an arena of
liberation from gender and other prescribed roles. It wel-
comes . . . a multiplicity of styles and personal voices.[16]

Van Dyke's equation of feminist criticism with life-threatening
militarism is extremely disturbing. Her comments reek of the most
virulent forms of radical feminist ideology. Her suggestion that criticism is male-like unless it's life-affirming implies that, unless the
feminist critic once again places herself fully in the service of the
playwright—the ultimate creator, the idealized mother of the dramatic text—she is participating in an imperialistic, nihilistic act that's
merely an exercise in power.

As feminist performance critics and theorists move farther into
the project of distinguishing the feminisms and their criticisms
from the amorphous mass of pluralism, a peculiar backlash has
begun to operate. Liberal feminists such as Gabrielle Cody get
uneasy when the canon is attacked; radical feminists such as van
Dyke refuse to take responsibility for their own positions as critics,
since they regard criticism and theory as male-like; and materialist
critics get trashed for their willingness to be "daring" and "brave,"
for attempting to chart new pathways in performance theory's
territory.

Although my sympathies are clearly with materialist feminist
theorists and therefore cloud my so-called objectivity, I truly don't
understand the response to Case's book, in particular. There appears
to be something very threatening about the first feminist book to look
critically at theater history, to suggest radical revisions of canonical
texts, and to sort out various strands of feminist ideology from a
theoretical perspective. The ideological (state) apparatus swings into
effect to protect its interests. But what surprises me is that relatively
alternative publications such as *Performing Arts Journal* and *Women's
Review of Books* are complicit in this repression. The critical attacks
(despite radical feminist claims to be anti-aggression) seem part of
feminism's general backlash against theory.

A Personal Defense of Theory in Discourse

Because poststructuralist theory questions the authenticity of experience as truth, many feminist theorists have been attacked as jargon-wielding elitists who have no political project and who trivialize years of political action organized around radical feminist epistemology. This is not the intent, as I know it, of theory. Poststructuralism simply questions liberal humanist notions that men or women are free individuals capable of mastering the universe and points out the way in which ideology is masked as commonsensical truth.[17] Poststructuralist performance criticism looks at the power structures underlying representation and the means by which subjectivity is shaped and withheld through discourse. These are intensely political projects.

But, rather than arguing the implications of such a poststructuralist perspective, some feminist academicians and activists attack the project of theory. Black feminist critic Barbara Christian, for instance, in her article "The Race for Theory," reasserts the accusation that theory silences.[18] She believes that theory became popular when marginalized minority writers were successfully clamoring to be heard in academia.

Christian criticizes theorists for ignoring black women writers to immerse themselves instead in the verbal gymnastics of famous white men. She implicitly charges that, because feminist poststructuralism acquiesces to the death of the author, it's complicit with a reactionary silencing of women authors. Christian is not the only woman to voice these concerns, and from a certain perspective the point she raises is valid. In theater much of the recent dissension over theory comes from a similar unwillingness to unsettle playwriting as one of women's primary activities. If we agree that the author is dead, how can we continue talking about women playwrights? Feminist poststructuralist theories, however, don't intend to kill off women authors a priori but, rather, to simply enlarge the consideration of texts to take into account the meanings that are constructed in performance as well as on the page.[19]

Christian angles her argument through a racial perspective, insisting that her race theorizes from the basis of its experience as minority. Other women attack theory by insisting that their experiences of oppression keep them from using its language. How can I, as a feminist theorist, respond to these concerns? How can I negotiate the differences between Christian and myself? Christian s[?] works in literary criticism to save her own life. I work in th[..], save mine. Theory allows me to articulate my differences from a feminism I first learned as monolithic. Theory enables me to see that there is no tenable position for me in the totalizing strategies of radical feminism and that I can align myself profitably elsewhere.

Through theory I can articulate the roots of my own identity in the conflicting discourses of lesbianism and Judaism and know that there is no comfortable place for me within any single discourse. Theory enables me to describe the differences within me and around me without forcing me to rank my allegiances or my oppressions. As feminist critic Gayle Austin would say, theory enables the divided subject to fall into the cracks of difference and to theorize productively from there,[20] knowing that truth is changeable, permeable, and, finally, irrelevant.

The irony of articulating my own experience as a defense of feminist poststructuralist performance criticism is not lost on me. The pervasive glorification of experience, and the testimonial strategies used to enforce it as truth, require that I, too, throw myself back on positions that theory otherwise allows me to detach from.

Positionality and Location

Feminist postmodernism happens in theory. Our experiments are conducted at conferences and in universities, and most often on paper, rather than on big stages sodden with spectacle. Feminist postmodernism does not play indulgently with meaninglessness or plurality, charges that might be leveled against some postmodern performance auteurs. Feminist postmodernism is committed to meaning, to sifting through the referents of material reality and drawing blueprints of their construction that can be historically revised and changed.[21]

Positions of identity are equally historical. Elin Diamond, on a panel about feminist criticism at the 1988 Women and Theatre Program preconference, remarked that positioning is utterly provisional, that once you have a position you inherit issues of identity that you want to put into crisis.[22] My challenge as a materialist feminist performance theorist, then, is to reposition myself constantly, to keep changing my seat in the theater, and to continually ask, How does it look from over here? To ask myself, How would Barbara Christian see this, and how might she and I prod each other to look differently? Working in theory allows such fluidity, since the only productive position for the theorist is balancing precariously on the edge of the differences between, among, and within women, who are the site of conflicting discourses in which there is no immutable truth.

NOTES

This article expands on papers presented at the New Languages for the Stage Conference in Lawrence, Kansas, October 1988, and at the Modern Language Association convention in New Orleans, December 1988.

1. Roland Barthes, "Death of the Author," *Image-Music-Text*, trans. Stephen Heath (New York: Noonday Press, 1977), 142–48.

2. Elin Diamond, "Refusing the Romanticism of Identity: Narrative Interventions in Churchill, Benmussa, Duras," *Theatre Journal* 38, no. 3 (October 1985): 273–86.

3. Teresa de Lauretis, "Issues, Terms, and Contexts," in de Lauretis, ed., *Feminist Studies/Critical Studies* (Bloomington: Indiana University Press, 1986), 9.

4. See Jill Dolan, "Is the Postmodern Aesthetic Feminist?" *Art & Cinema* 1, no. 3 (Fall 1987): 5–6; and Sue-Ellen Case and Jeanie Forte, "From Formalism to Feminism," *Theatre* 16, no. 2 (Spring 1985): 62–65.

5. Helen Krich Chinoy and Linda Walsh Jenkins, eds., *Women in American Theatre*, rev. ed. (1981; reprint, New York: Theatre Communications Group, 1987); Karen Malpede, ed., *Women in Theatre: Compassion and Hope* (New York: Drama Book Specialists, 1983); Helene Keyssar, *Feminist Theatre* (1985; reprint, New York: St. Martin's Press, 1991); Kathleen Betsko and Rachel Koenig, eds., *Interviews with Contemporary Women Playwrights* (New York: Beechtree Books, 1987).

6. Jill Dolan, *The Feminist Spectator as Critic* (1988; reprint, Ann Arbor: University of Michigan Press, 1991); Sue-Ellen Case, *Feminism and Theatre* (New York and London: Methuen, 1988); Lynda Hart, ed., *Making a Spectacle: Feminist Essays on Contemporary Women's Theater* (Ann Arbor: University of Michigan Press, 1988).

7. Case, *Feminism and Theatre*, 19.

8. Hart, *Making a Spectacle*, 4.

9. Gabrielle Cody, book review, *Performing Arts Journal* 11, no. 2 (1988): 117.

10. Ibid., book review, 117.

11. Case, *Feminism and Theatre*, 25.

12. Cody, book review, 117.

13. Ibid., 118.

14. Case, *Feminism and Theatre*, 132.

15. Joyce van Dyke, "Performance Anxiety," *Women's Review of Books* 6, no. 4 (January 1989): 1, 3.

16. Ibid.

17. See Chris Weedon, *Feminist Practice and Post-structuralist Theory* (New York: Basil Blackwell, 1987).

18. Barbara Christian, "The Race for Theory," *Feminist Studies* 14, no. 1 (Spring 1988): 67–80.

19. When I gave a version of this article as a talk at Brown University in May 1989, playwright Paula Vogel, who teaches at Brown, pointed out that many women playwrights are still struggling to live, literally, in the mainstream theater context, which makes the metaphorical death of the author something of a moot issue for them. Poststructuralist theory, she implied, which describes a moment in which authorship is dispersed across various reception strategies, seems premature for women playwrights who have not yet gained access to the author's position.

20. Gayle Austin, comments made on "Elucidating Terms and Issues" panel, Women and Theatre Program Preconference, Horton Grand Hotel, San Diego, August 1, 1988.

21. Because of its concentration in theory, feminist postmodernism has been vulnerable to assimilation by academic critics. The implosion of what might be called "apolitical postmodernism" and the feminist variety poses a very real problem for feminist critics determined to employ theory for political ends. The question resides, once again, in discourse—even publishing an article such as this one [originally] in *TDR* makes the movement's issues available to a readership outside its purview. Yet for feminist theory to become familiar and useful to those inside the movement, who have political investments in its utility, it seems important to speak through the public forum journals such as *TDR* offer. For recent feminist discussions of the potential of postmodernism toward social change, see also Linda Hutcheon, *The Politics of Postmodernism* (New York and London: Routledge, 1989); and Linda Nicholson, ed., *Feminism/Postmodernism* (New York and London: Routledge, 1990).

22. Elin Diamond, comments made on "Feminist Criticism" panel, Women and Theatre Program Preconference, Horton Grand Hotel, San Diego, August 2, 1988.

Chapter 4

Gender, Sexuality, and "My Life" in the (University) Theatre

When I turned twenty-one, coming out into my own sexuality meant beginning many years of relative exile from theater production, even though acting and directing first breathed life into my sense of the possibilities of this both public and private forum. I grew from a teenager who, at a local theater school, had enthusiastically played roles across gender and across generation (Mrs. Malaprop in Sheridan's *The Rivals*, for instance, was one of my famous performances) to a frightened college freshman in a professional theater training program who was being indoctrinated, through the theater practice that had once liberated her, into gender and sexuality roles she was ill equipped to play. Ingenues, and what I read as their utter submission, their vacuousness, their weakness, were anathema to me for reasons I could barely articulate in 1976. I only knew that my inability to do well in movement classes was somehow related to my alienation from my own body, which was somehow related to my thorough incompetence at the heterosexual role-play the professors in Boston University's theater program were casting me to do.

After one particularly painful experience playing the ditzy female in a scene from *Lovers and Other Strangers*—cast across from a young man I'm now sure was gay, although I didn't have those words at that time—I dropped out of the theater program and declared English as my new major. My self-imposed exile from theater practice created a critic, and later a feminist and a theorist, whose perspective was fueled by her desire to recapture or at least to describe what had so seduced her about the theater and what had then so wretchedly been snatched away.[1]

When I returned to theater practice as an assistant professor of theater and drama and women's studies at the University of Wisconsin (UW)–Madison, I wanted to create a climate for student actors that would insure against the kind of betrayal I experienced in actor training.[2] I also wanted to test out in practice the theories of gender and sexuality performance I had thought about in my critical writing and in my courses. And I wanted to create a production that would engage with the life of Madison's multiple communities, one that would attempt to form a dissenting community that might disagree with itself, talk across itself, differently, expectantly, together.

Returning to theater production offered me an opportunity to explore, with bodies in space, some of the current thinking in feminist theories about gender and sexuality. The performance of gender is a crucial concept in contemporary feminist thinking, as it has been conceptualized by thinkers such as Judith Butler and Teresa de Lauretis as well as other scholars in the burgeoning field of gay and lesbian studies.[3] The performance of gender in everyday life is now being carefully denaturalized in these writings, but performance in theater remains a place where feminist theory can be tested and enacted. I was able to use the University Theatre at UW–Madison to fashion such a deconstructive theatrical laboratory for conceptualizing disruptive, radically new and different performances of gender.[4]

My laboratory constituted itself rather arbitrarily at first. Our University Theatre selects its season by a more or less democratic process, through which faculty, staff, and students submit titles to a selection committee that then reads a number of plays and chooses among them for those that best suit the needs of student actors and designers and that might most tantalize the tastes of local audiences. This process is often more conservative than radical. Because our mainstage season supports itself, there's a real necessity to choose titles that will maintain a reasonable cash flow for the University Theatre. While it might seem that institutions of higher learning should be free from the vagaries of an intensely capitalist American theater market, our department can make no gestures to such purity without doing itself a real disservice.

When I proposed Marlane Meyer's play *Etta Jenks* to the play selection committee in 1990–91, I thought the text might speak across our various constituencies and be unusual enough to interest people who don't frequently come to see our productions. Despite our mandate to provide our own income, I've maintained that it's possible to create new audiences from the many eclectic communities that form the nucleus of cultural consumption here in Madison. For example, I thought that *Etta Jenks*, given the right spin and the right marketing, might appeal to the local feminist women's community and could provide for the university and intellectual communities the occasion for a complicated discussion about pornography, representation, censorship, free speech, sexuality, and performance.

Choosing *Etta Jenks* to work on in this way was almost gratuitous. I didn't like the text very much, since I read it as located staunchly within the antipornography feminist movement to which I am not sympathetic. But it seemed to provide the occasion I sought for creating communities of dissension in our audiences and one of physical and intellectual empowerment among the actors in the cast. These twofold objectives of my return to theater practice through feminist theory seemed possible to explore, if not to achieve.

Meyer's play is collected in Julia Miles's edited collection, *Women's Work: Five New Plays from the Women's Project* (1989). Like other recent collections of plays about "others" on the American theater's landscape, Miles's anthology marks itself by its difference from the canon to which it would add.[5] The title's reference evokes production: the production of cultural meanings marked by their location within gendered identities. Meyer's play, too, figures in complicated ways the products of women's work, by constructing the female body as an image and by representing sexuality as a kind of economic production. These various productions imply a set of choices, made by the characters who represent their producers and their consumers, which seem structured to allow for the kind of deconstructive treatment we gave Meyer's text.

The play tells the in many ways stereotypical story of the "naive" young woman from somewhere in the middle of the country who comes to L.A. to be a film star. Within moments after getting off the train she is accosted by a man who wants to be her pimp. Fending off his advances, she takes up with a deaf man who offers her a sleeping room in his blind brother's house.

The play positions these disabled men as Etta's protectors, but even their moral propriety and their insistent railings against pornography can't keep Etta from sliding into what the play describes as the depravity of the porn industry, when her money and her illusions run out. Etta does one porn film, then several, becomes a star and then a producer. As time passes, she loses a friend, who was also a sex worker, and—again, according to the script as written—her soul and her sexuality. She is left at the play's end with the sexually diseased hired killer who is her lover, drifting.

Meyer's text positions itself within the feminist antipornography critique in several ways. An author's note, which precedes the text in Miles's anthology, describes all the characters except Etta, Burt (the deaf man), and Sherman (his blind brother) as "possessed of a certain animal quality, subtly suggested through makeup or gesture, the effect to be not cartoonish but queer" (116). The "tragedy" of male mutation into animals, also evoked by the Robert Bly poem that serves as the epigraph to Meyer's play, structures the plot's progress, as Etta's hardly picaresque journey moves her from would-be saviors like Burt to actual murderers like Ben. Ben, the slimy porn king, describes the snuff films he eventually produces as just a "particular type of commodity." "It's a market," he says to Etta, with implicit indifference. "You can't begrudge the market" (163). The evolutionary chain, for Meyer's male characters, heads straight down, toward the depravity of committing murder for money.

But, alongside such a dismal reading of men as the ultimate purveyors and consumers of the objectified female body, it's possible to position the women in the play as potentially resistant to the hegemony of the male gaze. The sex workers whose lives Meyer describes can be more nuanced, their possibilities more complex than the one-dimensional quest for economic and representational power to which she assigns the men. Etta, for example, likes sex at the beginning of the play and is described (albeit by Burt) as aggressive and free with her body and her desire. When she does choose to make her first porn film, Etta knows she "looks fine" (132) and later understands that she's "good at it," that what she insists on calling her "business" (136) makes her "feel like I'm really here" (137).

While Meyer offers agency to these women only in a porn context that the play resolutely damns, there is a thematic gap between the porn star as subject and porn star as object that remains available for productive exploitation by female actors, who can be encouraged to see their characters resistantly in performance. In other words, enough space remains between a kind of active agency depicted by women characters in the text and the passive objectification to which they seem tied to allow for productive commentary. The play works as a "narrative of progress" of Etta's growth into self-assurance as a woman, somehow in spite of Meyer's moralizing about her journey.[6]

By contrast, Sheri, Etta's sex worker friend, insists that her relationship to her subjectivity can be detached from the boundaries of her body, separated from both its appearance and its exchange value in a representational economy organized by men. When, in an early scene, Sheri and Etta audition for a small, nonpaying Equity waiver theater administered by an officious director, Sheri insists, "I am not my body," after the director dismisses her as the wrong type for the role (124). Sheri later provides a kind of mystical discourse that works to free her from the gendered constraints of her own corporeality. As she and Etta and Kitty, another sex worker, prepare to film a scene, Sheri describes a yogi in India who "had mastered dematerialization to such a degree that he could vanish at will." Meyer implies that Sheri in fact saves herself from destruction in one of Ben's snuff films by "disappearing the body" (133) and leaving behind only a strong, "overpowering" scent of gardenias in the air (165). Although what actually happens to Sheri remains ambiguous in the play's plotline, her apparent vanishing act can be read as a positive manipulation of the body's materiality, an act of self-preservation conducted at an almost molecular level.

Etta, meanwhile, reconfigures the objectified body not by disappearing it but, rather, by remaining rooted to the exigencies of female flesh by staying in the porn industry and revising the rules of the marketplace in which it trades. Etta understands, implicitly, that part of her desire to be a "movie star" connects with a search for her own identity that can only be validated through monetary exchange on a representational economy. "People are giving me money . . . 'cause of who I am," she says, when she describes her dream to Sherman. Etta's pragmatism colors her romantic daydreams, as her choices inevitably connect to her worsening economic circumstances. Sherman tries to dissuade her from getting involved with Ben by describing him as "primordial ooze," but Etta doesn't flinch from her curious resolve. "I could use three hundred dollars a day" (128), she responds to Sherman. "And you know, it could be these films are artistic" (129). Once she's become successful in the industry Etta also refuses Burt's wistful desire for a domestic partnership in strictly practical, economic terms:

Burt: I don't want you to go.
Etta: If I keep working like this, I'll make more money than my
  lawyer.
Burt: Well, is that the point? Money?
Etta: Yes.

(135)

Sherman, the blind man whom Meyer employs as the play's prophet in a highly conventionalized manner, insists that Etta's lack of identity in fact keeps her from finding her place in the theatrical market. Sherman points to "archetypes" such as Marilyn Monroe, who crashed and burned after her exploitation as a kind of cultural projection screen. He predicts that Etta's dream will eventually degrade her, since what he sees as pornography's ultimately carnal mind is "necessarily death oriented since the body is always in a progressive state of decay. The earth begins to crawl up inside you..." (128). If the female body, tied to its own corporeality, cannot disappear, Meyer suggests it's doomed to enact the throes of its own death, the inevitable by-product of sexuality's seduction.

Meyer intersects these themes with overlapping metaphors, so that Etta's dream eventually bleeds into the "race memory" of a culture that needs movies as illusions that "function to keep you from seeing how shitty life is" (147). A kind of Darwinian economic ethos comes to drive Etta's choices, as she rises through the ranks of the porn industry from star to producer. Meyer intimates that the cost Etta pays for economic power in an industry dominated by men includes the erasure of her own sexuality. At the end of the play Etta forms a relationship with Max, the killer she's hired to eliminate Ben. Max and Etta seem attracted by their mutual antipathy for sex:

Etta: I hate sex.
Max: Me too, it's dirty.
Etta: I don't want to have sex with you is what I'm saying.
Max: I don't blame you—I have a disease.
Etta: Okay, Max. You want to fall in love with me, do it—you
  probably deserve it.
Max: Who said anything about love?

(162)

Although this scene could be read as the logical outcome of two morally depraved lives, in which sexuality becomes perverted in a deathlike, repulsively diseased body, it could also be read more resistantly as the end of the pipe dreams about gender relations that once fueled Etta's quest for stardom. Although the lines Meyer writes could make them either perverse or pathetic, there's also a pragmatism about Etta and Max that might offer a new, different model for sexual relationships at the play's end.

In the last moment of the play a young woman named Shelly arrives at Etta's office looking for film work, apparently to begin the cycle of "illusion" and "despair" over again. But Shelly's desire is different; she wants to be a legitimate actress, but she also already works in the sex industry as a dominatrix (intimately connected to power and sexuality) and doesn't hold Etta's romantic illusions about being a movie star. Shelly reclaims the intersections of power and representation, romance and sexuality, illusion and reality, that the text has troubled and judged throughout its action. Unlike the young Etta, Shelly knows exactly what kind of movies the industry produces:

> Look, I think it's kind of a turn on to be naked in front of men, I mean . . . they like me and I can make them think I like them. I do it all the time. Not that it's really possible to like them, 'cause they're, you know, maggots. But they don't know what I'm thinking, how I laugh at their sick needs. I'm already a great actress, you know what I mean? (172)

The discourse of love and romance is already distorted for Shelly, since she performs, self-reflexively, knowingly, what men want to see, without sensing herself implicated or objectified in the process. Her exchanges with men even seem to empower her, as she treads the line between "action"—the fantasies for which her clients pay—and "reality":

> I just came from my other job, I'm a dominant. Listen, do you ever do whip movies? 'Cause I can really use a whip. I just about killed this guy the other night. I start wailin' and forget it's just action. Sometimes I think, how it would be to just . . . well, you know? . . . It could be a public service. I bet the city would pay me. (173)

In Shelly's constellation the public service she might provide enables a highly ironic reading of her occupation as morally correct.

In scenes like these *Etta Jenks* clearly moralizes against pornography by positioning the women who work in the industry as victims of their own troubled childhoods and moral failings. The text elides long exposition, picking up its action in an insistently present tense. But many of the characters relate brief stories of actual abuse and incest that appear to explain and justify their involvement in pornography: Ben's father was a drunk (138); Etta's father and her mother's father "were the same person" (138); Shelly's stepfather "took" her when she was twelve (172).

These psychological flaws, implanted by dysfunctional families, create a kind of empathy for the characters that also allows spectators who consider themselves "healthy" or "normal" to distance themselves from the characters' misfortunes and describe their problems as individual, rather than social. These flaws also encourage spectators to read the play through a twelve-step discourse, which positions Etta as recognizing and then recovering from her "problem" with pornography.

But Meyer's text is open enough to allow a production concept to push against some of its easier assignments of moral blame, its vaguely self-righteous liberal humanism, and its antipornography feminism. Given the resurgence in arts censorship promoted by the New Right's incursion into the representation of sexuality, I wanted to use the occasion of the production to launch a discussion about what I see as the pernicious similarities between the antipornography stance in feminism and other proposed limitations on free speech.[7] By unsettling some of the play's gendered moral assumptions about how representations of sexuality always victimize women, I hoped to engage audiences in a more complicated debate.

Casting across Gender

I was initially attracted to *Etta Jenks* by the openness of its structure. The action unravels in nineteen brief scenes with a virtual lack of standard exposition; the dialogue is staccato and schematic; and the characters are stereotypical and familiar enough to deconstruct easily. My main strategy for pushing at the play's limits was to cross-gender cast several of the key roles. Not only did this choice begin to dislodge some of the play's most readily apparent meanings; it also empowered the female actors in the cast to work against their usual positions as sexualized, passive objects in the canonized texts of mainstream American theater. Ben was played by Krista Bourquein, a woman whose blond hair and fair skin usually gets her cast in ingenue roles. We cast another, more androgynous-looking woman, Susan McCully, as James, the coked-out lackey who brings women into the porn business but isn't competent enough to keep track of them. McCully identifies as a "bisexual lesbian"; in casting her, we had some hesitations that spectators would read her as a lesbian in the role and that the blame we were trying to complicate would be displaced from men to lesbians.[8] But, ironically, in production McCully was convincing enough that the great debate over her performance was whether or not she was really a man. The homophobic response we had feared was elided by spectators' inability to read the layers of McCully's performance of gender.

Because men playing women historically accrue a great deal of attention, I wanted to limit their cultural fascination and so cast many more women as men in *Etta*.[9] In addition to Bourquein and McCully's cross-gender work, one of Etta's customers, Dwight, and the hired killer's helper, Alec, were also played by a woman. Zoe Beckerman is a small, slight woman, who stylized her performance as Dwight enough to read as clearly playing at what turned out to be a rather pitiful male role. As Alec, Beckerman and the man playing Max (Scott Isaacson) turned into a kind of parodic Mutt and Jeff (or Laurel and Hardy or even Thelma and Louise).

Only one man was cast as a woman. Todd Ison, the actor who plays Clyde, the pimp Etta first meets at the train station, returns soon after as Kitty, a kind of blonde bimbo stereotype in the text who makes porn films with Etta. In his first scene as Kitty, Ison wore a bodysuit of lacy, light blue lingerie (by costume designer Irma Mayorga), through which his hairy chest was clearly seen. He wore women's makeup, raised the register of his voice, and "feminized" his gestures, but he didn't play the role as camp. As Sheri describes the possibilities of dematerialization, Kitty can't quite comprehend how escaping from her body might be an act of survival. For spectators observing this exchange through the fascination of a male body dressed in seductive, transparent female undergarments, Kitty's body was undeniably there and difficult to imagine vanishing.[10]

In a later scene Kitty has gotten pregnant and visits the now powerful Etta for advice. Kitty's attachment to the idea of bearing a child positions her within dominant American religious discourse, which applauds impoverished, unprepared women for carrying babies to term, who then become pathetic possessions that can in no way compensate for the deprivations of their mothers' lives. Since a man played Kitty, some of the situation's stereotypical qualities were transformed. Dora Lanier, as Etta, played her as patient and kind, and Ison, as Kitty, empathized with her plight and wound up ennobling the character. A woman playing the role might have been read, to some spectators, as simply reifying the young, working-class woman's lack of choices.

For McCully, who played James, it was much harder to embody her second role as Shelly, the young woman whose entrance marks the end of *Etta Jenks*. McCully's experience illustrated feminist theory about femininity as masquerade, which McCully exploited by playing Shelly as a consciously constructed lesbian femme.[11] The danger in directing and performing the play's final scene is to belittle Shelly, to construct her as an unwitting victim of her own false sense of power. But in our production there was a rapport between Shelly and Etta, perched together in the light on the edge of Etta's desk, that indicated a kind of sisterhood of power and possibility, a yoking of sexuality to business in a profitable, rather than exploitative way.

When Shelly strips to show Etta her "goods," as it were, the moment is frank and fun, rather than threatening and voyeuristic, as was Etta's earlier moment taking her clothes off for Ben.[12] Etta informs the younger woman about exactly what she can expect from the porn industry, and they sit together, implicitly contemplating the possibilities of a life in the business and outside of it. The lights (designed by Shoshanna Segal) seemed to encircle the two women warmly, and, rather than fade into the traditional blackout that ends most productions, the lights brightened to full intensity, as Mama Cass's song "Dream a Little Dream of Me" faded up on the scene and the curtain call began.

Production and Reception at the Intersection of Gender Construction

Early in the rehearsal process we held a gender workshop for the people cross-cast. The actors, dramaturgs, directors, and staff, which happened to be all women that night, sat together talking in a modified consciousness-raising fashion about how gender assignments had been made for us through our lives and the conscious and unconscious ways we had acquiesced or resisted them.[13] We described and developed a gender continuum that later informed the acting choices, on which zero became hypermasculinity (represented by someone like Sylvester Stallone or John Wayne), twenty became hyperfemininity (a spot snared by Marilyn Monroe and "Jessica Rabbit"), and ten became some sort of neutral that we continually troubled.[14] We asked, Can you ever really achieve androgyny, and should you want to? Can your body ever read as though it's without gender, or only in combinations and levels of gender that move more fluidly from masculine to feminine and back? If biology remains, can gender be fully erased, even if we accept it as a construct? These are the questions we posed as we enacted and embodied points on the gender continuum.

In workshop it also quickly became clear that gender can't be performed without considering ethnicity, class, and sexuality. The easiest impulse with Ben, for instance, was for Bourquein to play him as a kind of lower class, heavy-footed, slack-mouthed cur. It was much harder, but much more compelling, to work at playing him as an elegant man, closer to seven or eight on the gender continuum than zero. Thinking about sexuality in relation to gender also helped us conceptualize some of the other characters in Meyer's constellation. For example, Spencer, Ben's partner who would make art, rather than "smut," was played higher on the gender scale and was also conceived as bisexual or gay.

We realized that even the roles that weren't cross-gender cast would require the actors to investigate their gender markings. Gender reads as a relation—of parts of the body to the whole, of bodies to one another, of the body to its context—so, for example, even though Etta wasn't a cross-gendered role, it soon became clear that her character performed gender in various and different ways as her position in the porn industry changed and depended on other gendered and classed character positions. These choices—often developed by the actors—worked to make it harder to "blame" any one character on the basis of stereotypical correlations between gender and power, or gender and morality.

The performances of gender the actors embodied, whether or

not they were cross-gender cast, intrigued spectators and encouraged them to think about the relationships in the play as part of social arrangements that structure not only pornography but also businesses of any sort, theater of any sort, and gender of any sort.[15] But, as Judith Butler reiterates in *Gender Trouble*, there are material risks to transgressing the proper performance of gender.[16] For instance, for lesbians in leather who are often mistaken for men by hostile people who somehow know they are women, the consequences of gender transgression are felt experiences in their performances in everyday life. The University Theatre setting of our production contained the risks, in some ways, for the performers in *Etta Jenks*. For Krista Bourquein, playing Ben with a sock in her bathing suit to represent his penis in the beach scene (an image that always got a laugh); for Todd Ison, pretending to feel a womb he doesn't have to "quote" Kitty's growing attachment to the redemptive idea of bearing a child; for Zoe Beckerman, playing Dwight in a skewed wig and glasses as the quintessential mama's boy nerd and playing Alec as a wired, wild gay man—these impersonations take place as a relatively safe experiment in a controlled intellectual setting. I think these actors learned something about their own education into gender roles. From their comments in discussions after the production, I think their attachment to those once naturalized roles has been profoundly, productively shaken. I think what they learned will permit them to take risks outside the university's security.

For Susan McCully, playing James in pointed-toed boots and a tasteless red jacket and playing Shelly in spiked heels, a skin-tight short shirt, and the leather outfit and garters of a dominatrix, the experience marked her relationship to gender differently. Performing Shelly's frank and open femininity was much harder for McCully to achieve as an actor. Although many spectators assumed that James was the stretch for her, since the role crossed gender, Shelly's masquerade was more profound. McCully jokes that she was typecast as James but that, from playing Shelly, she learned to appreciate the power of femininity. I was gratified that such experiences were possible within our cast. And, given my own history as an acting student, the process for these actors was as important to me as the product for the audience.

The risks of our transgressions into dominant and local discourses about gender and sexuality, pornography and the conventions of theater, became evident in postshow discussions.[17] Spectators' anxieties over the subversions the actors embodied were voiced either with hostility or with the condescension of those who think they're morally (and politically) pure enough to chastise those who have fallen.

The production concept, although it pushed against the author's intentions about pornography, was purposely ambiguous in its meaning. It's not clear whether Etta really leaves the business at the end or if she and Shelly will start a new, revised, partnership of porn. Spectators were profoundly unsettled by this ambiguity and continually demanded statements from me and the actors about what we intended the production to mean. Much of this disturbance about ultimate, fixed meaning settled on the cross-gender cast roles and spectators' confusion and fascination by what they were seeing. If they could know gender, they could have knowledge, in the fullest sense.

This anxiety over what and how people know is amplified by the text, which insists on relating knowledge to the possession of bodies that continually elude capture. For example, when Sheri disappears and James is implicated, Etta screams at him: "Goddamn you! I knew her." James responds: "So you knew her? Big deal. Know somebody, it makes a difference" (156), automatically questioning, through his own experience, the efficacy of knowledge as protection. After Ben's murder Spencer echoes the complaint, fuming at Etta: "I KNEW Ben. We went to school . . . okay? I mean, his mother knew my mother. We used to piss in the same toilet, for Chrissake!" (169). Rather than imply some tenable connection, such bodily knowledge only confirms the boundaries in the play that separate the characters.

Partly because certainty over gender roles was clearly denied in our production, a host of uncertainties about everything in the play seemed to be bred for spectators, who wanted to *know* what we meant. They complained that the certainty of possessing knowledge was denied them. For instance, they asked what happened to Sheri, whom the plotline describes as dematerializing, escaping from her body in a moment of extreme danger, and then reappearing, possibly, probably, ambiguously, somewhere else, unseen but safe, later. People wanted to *know* what really happened to her and doubted that she actually was able to "disappear" her body. For people determined to read the play through its original antipornography values, the possibility that a female body could control itself could only be relegated to fiction, which very much challenged these spectators' determination to see the play as *real*.

I think some of this tension about what "really" happened, which insists that the events of the play are real, rather than fiction, came from how profoundly unsettling it was for some spectators to see a kind of falsity laid over something as "natural" as gender. People who objected to what they read as the anti-antiporn pitch of the production implied that we were belittling women who work in the porn industry by parodying them through gender play. A certain truth had been brooked, a moral certainty displaced. I think uncertainty is productive and useful, especially around an issue like pornography, which everyone seems to know the "truth" of, though mostly secondhand. The absolute desire to see women as victims of the porn industry was thwarted in our production by some of the cross-gender choices, and the converse, that is, seeing female sex workers as people with agency, with economic and sexual choice, appeared very frightening to some people.[18] The lack of psychological choice in the performances and the insistently distanced Brechtian acting style also frustrated spectators' expectations about empathy and sympathy. As a result, the cross-gendered characters received much of the attention in postshow discussions.

No one wanted to talk about Etta's choices, perhaps because she remained a "biological" woman who chose to become successful in the sex industry, who used her sexuality to her own profit and was therefore even more threatening. Performer Dora Lanier, who played Etta, is a very strong actor; the clarity of her choices and her singularly unsentimental interpretation of her role startled spectators more than I think anyone was willing to articulate. Lanier's unconventionally attractive appearance and her vivid use of charismatic presence made it very difficult to see her as a victim of her choices within the pornography industry. In some ways, for some spectators, it was easier to describe the anxiety provoked by gender impersonation than to really examine their responses to a strong woman who chooses to make money with her own body.

Interestingly, although the gender work in *Etta* was played seriously, the production made no attempt to convince spectators to "believe" in the characters in a strictly Stanislavskian sense. But spectators are trained so well to believe that they fill in the gaps so that they can read the characters as real, refusing to buy their status as fiction. There's also a refusal, in that kind of response, to see gender as detachable from the bodies that wear it. The choices we made were meant to display gender as gesture, as clothing, as a fiction, not as a biological truth.

The acting style was Brechtian throughout, including many moments of direct address to the audience, and a conscious quoting of the roles by the performers meant exactly to disrupt any kind of traditional believability. We offered the characters as outlines marked off by the performers' use of Brechtian *gestus* and our considerations of the Brechtian "not/but." We wanted spectators to be able to see the many layers of gender through which we were asking them to read the characters and printed the actors' full names in the program.

But some spectators floundered on the shoals of biology and went hunting for truth. McCully, who played James and Shelly, even wrote a long program note about the challenges of her roles. But still spectators were fascinated with discovering the "truth" of her gender. The conventions of realist spectatorship perpetuate themselves so readily that even a production clearly marked as revisionist was read as real. For example, until the moment she mentions the pregnancy many spectators thought Kitty was a transvestite. Very few realized that the man playing Kitty had also played Clyde at the beginning, even though the double-casting was intentional. American spectators in proscenium houses seem so schooled to look for truth that, even though our production was highly stylized and disruptive, some spectators, seeing a man dressed as a woman, could only see that as real, and therefore transvestism, not as a layered interpretation of gender as a performed role.

Because of some spectators' perplexed responses, and because of others' astute, multiple readings of the choices we made, our gender experiments were successful in opening up a wider, more complex discussion about gender, sexuality, pornography, and representation than is usually available in the relatively politically correct communities of Madison. Although there is resistance here to a hegemonic feminist line, the local women's bookstore still refuses to sell lesbian pornography; UW students recently held a referendum about whether *Playboy* and *Penthouse* should be sold at the student union; and the university administration wrote a "hate speech" rule that only later was declared unconstitutional. The play was produced in the context of Madison's debates about pornography, which we foregrounded with an extensive lobby display compiled by dramaturgs Bernd and Czekay that juxtaposed images of pornography with images from advertising in a lively, confrontational manner.

Lured by the enticement of our preshow entertainments, which we billed as a "pornography do's and don'ts midway" and a "museum of the gaze," and curious, perhaps, about the controversial context we'd built around the production, the lobby before the show was filled each night with juxtapositions: our "typical" University Theatre subscriber, over sixty, wearing comfortable shoes, and unwilling to participate in the dildo ringtoss that was one of our lobby carnival attractions; students from the department's "Introduction to Theater" course, who reluctantly allowed themselves to be interviewed by our "mock" media hounds, who roamed the lobby with a videocamera and fake microphone soliciting people's views about pornography each night; faculty from other departments, who read the lobby literature and visuals posted on the walls with fascination and perplexity; feminists from Madison's women's community, who also wore comfortable shoes and approached our parodic, polemic juxtapositions of pornography, mainstream advertising, and gay and lesbian images warily, watching for pictures or practices that might be objectionable to women; and lesbians from Madison's working-class bar culture (or from my own feminist theory class), who have, either by virtue of class or race or by virtue of resistance, embraced alternative sexual practices and the gender signs that go with them as a way of performing their opposition to the gender reifications of politically correct feminism.

The mix of style and politics that mingled in the lobby each night, adhering to people who filed into the theater to see the play, many of whom had never before attended our University Theatre, did create the dissenting, eclectic community I had hoped for our production. The postshow discussions were lively, even dangerous, as spectators asked difficult questions and the actors and staff fielded them openly. The production came to be about much more than women's status in pornography, and for that I'm grateful. I'm interested in why the pornography industry is reserved as America's place of horror, as the pit of all evil, by feminists and liberals and conservatives alike. Read metaphorically, the so-called pornographic imagination infects, or influences, all businesses and all representations by analogy.[19]

Antipornography feminist activist Andrea Dworkin, w... discusses the excess of pornography, pounds her podium and says: "This is real. This is true." Dworkin was invited to speak on the University of Wisconsin–Madison campus during the fall 1991 semester, under the auspices of "Porn Week," a series of pornography awareness events sponsored by student groups. As Dworkin's speech illustrated, the events were mostly framed from an antipornography feminist perspective. In the process of her lecture she reified the female gender as a site of victimization and erased female sexuality as a practice with agency. I can't presume to pound out on a different podium—in a lecture hall or in a theater—my own ethical sense of reality and truth. I'm concerned, in theater production and reception, with how you locate yourself on the edge of an issue. How do you not impose ethical answers but, instead, open a discussion of where the edge is and how it shifts?

Brecht, from whom we borrowed many of our production strategies, was a male Marxist who had a particular standpoint his work was invested in proving. How do you produce theater with multiple standpoints, none of which add up to an easy "for or against" answer? How do you create audiences with multiple identifications, without pandering to some reductive common denominator? How do you work against a text as a kind of found object, to create contradictions so full that spectators have to look at them in complicated ways? How can theorizing theater practitioners rephrase the questions and invite audiences to respond to the contradictions they see through their own various ethics? These are the questions that fascinate me about interrogating the performance of gender and sexuality through theater reception and production. Our production of *Etta Jenks* posed these questions and created a multivocal community whose responses to it offered partial, productive answers.

NOTES

My title is a somewhat ironic appropriation of Konstantin Stanislavsky's memoirs, *My Life in Art*, trans. J. J. Robbins (New York: Theatre Arts Books, 1948). Early drafts of this article were presented as a lecture at the "Performance and Gender Colloquium" at Southern Illinois University, March 6, 1992, and at the University of North Carolina at Chapel Hill, March 20, 1992. I'd like to thank all the participants at both events, whose feedback shaped these thoughts.

1. This rethinking of my own involvement in or exile from theater practice has become a recurrent theme in my recent work. As feminist theory written by white middle-class women like myself reembraces the importance of personal narrative, my own theorized experience in theater production seems useful to include in critical writing. See, for example, my "Peeling Away the Tropes of Visibility: Lesbian Sexuality and Materialist Performance Practice," *Theatre Topics* 2, no. 1 (March 1992): 41–50, for another recent positioning of theory in relation to my own experiences in theater practice. The style of my writing here is also partly inspired by Paula Bennett's description of the link between her own sexual awareness and the circulation of desire in her theater practice, described in her unpublished manuscript "Gender as Performance: Shakespearean Ambiguity and the Lesbian Reader."

2. This is not to say that students at the University of Wisconsin–Madison are experiencing the same painful gender enculturation I received as an undergraduate theater major. I think the work we did on *Etta Jenks* was possible, in part, because of the supportive work and progressive thinking of the University's theater and drama department acting faculty.

3. See, for example, Judith Butler, *Gender Trouble: Feminism and the Subversion of Identity* (New York and London: Routledge, 1990); and Teresa de Lauretis, *Technologies of Gender: Essays on Theory, Film, and Fiction* (Bloomington: Indiana University Press, 1987).

4. See my article "Gender Impersonation Onstage," in Laurence Senelick, ed., *Gender in Performance: The Presentation of Difference in the Performing Arts* (Hanover: University Press of New England, 1992), 3–13 (first published in *Women & Performance Journal* 2, no. 2 [1985]: 5–11), for an early argument about the stage as a laboratory for progressive gender experimentation. For other recent work in feminist performance theory and criticism, see Sue-Ellen Case, ed., *Performing Feminisms: Feminist Critical Theory and Theatre* (Baltimore: Johns Hopkins University Press, 1990); Gayle Austin, *Feminist Theories for Dramatic Criticism* (Ann Arbor: University of Michigan Press, 1990); Lynda Hart and Peggy Phelan, eds., *Acting Out: Feminist Performances* (Ann Arbor: University of Michigan Press, 1993).

5. Marlane G. Meyer, *Etta Jenks*, in Julia Miles, ed., *Women's Work: Five New Plays from the Women's Project* (New York: Applause Books, 1989), 115–74. All other references will appear in the text. Julia Miles began the Women's Project in New York City in 1978 as a primary forum for plays by American women that might not otherwise be noticed by mainstream producing organizations.

6. These ideas developed in dialogue with an unpublished paper by Stacy Wolf analyzing *Etta Jenks* and Sarah Daniels's antipornography play, *Masterpieces*, entitled, "Is Sex (Still) as Immutable as the Weather?"

7. As part of this effort, Peggy Phelan was invited to speak to the produc-

tion through the ideas about the NEA funding controversy ventured in her two articles, "Serrano, Mapplethorpe, the NEA and You: 'Money Talks,'" *Drama Review* (Spring 1990): 4–15; and "Money Talks, Again," *Drama Review* (Fall 1991): 131–41.

8. In the extended program for the production McCully asks, "What does it mean to have a misogynist played by a lesbian? Do those meanings change when I tell you that I'd actually define my identity as a bisexual lesbian?" (*Etta Jenks* program, University Theatre, University of Wisconsin–Madison, 1991–92 season, 16).

9. See my "Peeling Away the Tropes of Visibility," for a discussion of how the differently cross-gendered performances of Oberon and Titania worked in the Asian/Experimental Theatre Program production *A Midsummer Night's Dream*, which I codirected at the University of Wisconsin–Madison with Phillip Zarrilli in the 1990–91 season. Many historians and commentators on the history of gender impersonation in American popular entertainments, for example, chronicle audiences' fascination with male-to-female drag. But, perhaps because of more unisex dress codes for women in contemporary fashion, women performing onstage in men's clothing doesn't seem to bear the same threat as men dressed as women. The psychoanalytic and ideological implications of the different valences in these acts are worthy of a whole separate study; see, for example, Marjorie Garber, *Vested Interests* (New York and London: Routledge, 1992).

10. Some spectators during talk backs admitted their confusion with the cross-gendered role, partly because, until the character discusses her pregnancy with Etta, these spectators thought the character was written as a transvestite. This interesting misreading of the production choice might indicate the lengths to which some spectators will go to see coincident gender performances laminated onto "biologically" sexed bodies.

11. In McCully's program note she says, "In my portrayal of Shelly there are still more levels of sexual and gender ambiguity if I choose to interpret her as a traditionally attractive and feminine lesbian. . . . How identifiable is a lesbian if she doesn't look butch? Are feminine women automatically defined as heterosexual?" (16).

12. Actually, neither performer really took off her clothes in our production. Our effort was to confront spectators with their own desire to see the performers'/characters' bodies. When Etta begins to strip for Ben in an early scene, the lights blacked out exactly at the moment when her arm pulled her shirt up over her head. Later, when Shelly "auditions" for Etta, she peels off a conservative skirt and blouse to reveal her leather dominatrix outfit underneath but never is naked. The choice to fully clothe the actors resists suggestions in the play as written that they be partially naked. A production of the play by Straw Dog Theatre in Chicago, which ran at the same time as ours, reportedly opted for full nudity, which fulfilled the kind of prurient desire that in some readings could frame the play.

13. The participants in this discussion included Bourquein, McCully, and Beckerman; stage managers Eileen Tatarsky, Mary O'Neill, and Lora Cerone;

dramaturgs Lisa Bernd and Angelika Czekay; and assistant director Stacy Wolf and myself as director. Doing such modified CR in the context of a highly theorized production proved to be more compelling than I think any of us might have anticipated. For myself, in that awkward position of authority as professor and director, risking a certain vulnerability by sharing my own stories of gender enculturation provided an important connection to my own history through this revised situation of theater production.

14. This continuum was also very useful in cross-gender work Phillip Zarrilli and I had done on *Midsummer Night's Dream*.

15. In addition, the music between scenes was used as pointed commentary and also foregrounded the gendered assumptions of all traditional representational narratives. Assistant director Stacy Wolf and I chose the music from secondary sources, culling cuts from *Raiders of the Lost Ark, Working Girl, Funny Girl, Gypsy, Chorus Line, Dirty Dancing, Casablanca, South Pacific,* and others. Played in a context in which gender was purposefully detached into masquerade, the music, too, seemed obviously hegemonic in its ideological encodings. Broadway and Hollywood musicals' complicity in gender arrangements is insidious, but it's also very easy to turn familiar songs against their own meanings through parodic juxtaposition. By blurring the lines between porn films and classic Hollywood films and musicals, and between pornography and erotica, we hoped to point out the constrictive gender assumptions fueling "romantic" representations of men and women in all narrative representations. See Linda Williams, *Hardcore: Power, Pleasure, and the "Frenzy of the Visible"* (Berkeley: University of California Press, 1989), particularly her discussion of the structural similarities between pornography and film musicals (123–24 ff.). She writes, "To a great extent, in fact, the hard-core feature *is* a kind of musical, with sexual number taking the place of musical number" (124). Williams's book was an important reference in our conceptualization of *Etta Jenks*.

16. See Butler, *Gender Trouble*.

17. Postshow discussions are typically held at least once during the run of each University Theatre production. We scheduled two discussions for *Etta Jenks:* a panel discussion with New York University professor Peggy Phelan and University of Wisconsin professor Noel Carroll and myself was held Thursday, February 20, and the usual "talk-back" discussion, facilitated by University of Wisconsin professor Bob Skloot was Thursday, February 27, both in the Mitchell Theatre.

18. During the process of conceptualizing the production, the dramaturgs Lisa Bernd and Angelika Czekay and I did a lot of research into revisionist feminist thinking on the position of female sex workers in porn. Frederique Delacoste and Priscilla Alexander, eds., *Sex Work: Writings by Women in the Sex Industry* (Pittsburgh and San Francisco: Cleis Press, 1987), proved an invaluable resource.

19. Peggy Phelan, for example, discussed during her visit to Madison the "pornography of capitalism," which resonates through any discussion of the pornography of representation.

PART 2
Sexuality and Visibility

Chapter 5

Desire Cloaked in
a Trenchcoat

"Desire Cloaked in a Trenchcoat" is maybe a corny image to inform an investigation of pornography, performance, and spectators. But the man sitting alone in a darkened theater masturbating under his coat while staring at the screen is an image engraved on our collective imagination. Male arousal by pictures is an accepted part of dominant cultural discourse.

The provocative relationship between sexuality and representation is revealed perhaps most blatantly in pornography. Pornography is an important locus for feminist critical thought because it provides a site for the intersection of feminist sexual politics and the politics of representation.

Whether you are for or against pornography, or straddle the anticensorship fence with "First Amendment" painted on it, pornography has to be dealt with as representation. As Susanne Kappeler points out in *The Pornography of Representation*, "Representation is not so much the means of representing an object through imitation (that is, matching contents) as a means of self-representation through authorship: the expression of subjectivity."[1] Antiporn feminists condemning pornography as both image and educator of male violence against women look for a match of contents by equating pornography and reality.[2] But pornography is more than simple mimesis. As representation, it helps to construct subject positions that maintain the strict gender divisions on which the culture operates.

The subject/object relations delineated by pornography are also paradigmatic of those structured by representation in general. Feminist film and performance critics argue that representation is addressed to the gaze of the male spectator. He is invited to identify with the active male protagonist portrayed in the narrative through voyeuristic and fetishistic viewing conventions. The male spectator shares in the pleasure of the hero's quest to fulfill his desire for the story's passively situated female.[3]

If all representation is structured by male desire, then sexuality is as integral a part of constructing spectator subjectivity in a Shakespeare production at Stratford as it is in live sex shows in Times Square. Any representation can be seen as essentially pornographic, since the structure of gendered relationships through which it operates is based on granting men subjectivity while denying it to women.

Kantian aesthetics propose that the only way to contemplate a work of art is through a certain detachment from reality. Disengagement allows the artwork a separate, "objective" existence and hides the fact of its authorship within a particular historical moment governed by cultural and economic considerations. Kappeler argues after Kant that the principles of aesthetic distance and disinterestedness motivate pornography as well as art. She suggests that, in the peep shows where men masturbate while watching women perform behind glass windows, the goal is not actually to fuck women. Rather, the goal is what she calls the "feeling of life, the pleasure of the subject" derived from aesthetic distance.[4] Kappeler says that the pornographic representation is even preferable, because it allows the total assertion of a man's subjectivity. Since there is no intersubjective action, the image of the woman behind the glass becomes a screen for the projection of a fantasy over which the male viewer has total control.

In "Bar Wars," written for *Esquire* in November 1986, Bob Greene provides a succinct example of the intersection of sexuality, pornography, and spectatorship on the representational economy. A bar called B.T.'s in Dearborn, Michigan, which usually presents topless female dancing entertainment, also offers what it calls "Rambo Wet Panty Nights." Black plastic Uzi submachine water guns are handed out to the customers. Then a woman—sometimes a regular B.T.'s dancer, sometimes an "amateur" volunteer—mounts the stage dressed in a skimpy T-shirt and underwear and stands covering her eyes and face while the men shoot their water guns at her vagina. Six or seven women perform each evening, and cash prizes are given to the women who do the "best" job of being shot at, according to the bar owner's subjective judgments. Greene doesn't describe the critical standards applied.[5]

This performative exchange is a cultural feminist's nightmare of the conflation of sexuality and violence. But, aside from this neat match of contents, it's an overt example of representation proceeding according to a pornographic model. The bar is packed with men drawn by a chance to become Rambo in the flesh. The elements of a prior representation, then, are mapped onto the performance at the bar. Sylvester Stallone and his Rambo movies are missing, but they're implied in the narrative.

In the Rambo films, as in most Vietnam films, the enemy—or the other—is an Asian race. In the paramilitary ambiance of B.T.'s bar, the woman onstage becomes the alien enemy, the other defined by her difference.[6] The floor manager at B.T.'s encourages the men with guns to think of the woman onstage as Vietnam or Libya or even Nicaragua. It's a neat way of eroticizing imperialism and keeping sexuality imperialist.

The men with the Uzis are implicitly identifying with Rambo as they aim, and they experience visual pleasure by projecting their subjective fantasies onto the passive woman. One man tells Greene: "I got her. She's hot; I know she likes it. She likes it, and she knows that I know she likes it."[7] But, if the woman's eyes were covered, how could this man possibly think the performer was acknowledging and enjoying a spray from his gun, except by fantasizing because he wants it that way?

What do the performers at B.T.'s think about allowing their bodies to be used as substitutes for Third World nations and becoming screens for projections of male fantasy? One woman tells Greene, "It's a power game." Unlike most, she doesn't cover her eyes when she performs. "I try to look out into the audience and make eye contact with as many of the men with guns as I can. A lot of times, they'll turn away. If a woman looks them in the eye, they'll turn away."[8] At issue here is the struggle for subjectivity. These men can't face the intersubjectivity of the woman's gaze. They must maintain the disengagement of desire inspired by the safe aesthetic distance of the representation.

Greene's article, of course, is governed by the exigencies of his own male gaze, and he doesn't mention whether there are female spectators in the bar. But, theoretically, where could a woman place herself in relation to this display? How could she position herself in front of a peep show window? The image of a woman sitting in a darkened theater wearing a trenchcoat is incongruous at best.

Whether or not female spectators can be placed in positions of power that might allow for the objectification of male performers or that might allow for the liberation of both gender classes from the oppressions of the representational gaze is an issue hotly debated in feminist film theory. As Kappeler and others have pointed out, simply trading gender positions isn't as easy as it sounds. While women in representation usually signify their gender class, the culturally sanctioned power of male subjectivity makes a similar signification very difficult. Women cannot simply express their subjectivity by objectifying men. A nude male in an objectified position remains an individual man, not necessarily a representation of the male gender class.

For example, Richard Schechner, while pondering these issues, described the activity at several sex clubs in Montreal in which males danced for females as examples of women adopting the male gaze. Schechner says that the male dancers

> stripped until fully naked. They played with their cocks and displayed the rest of their bodies in a way very parallel to what women do in strip clubs. . . . As a new male entered the stage, the dancer who was onstage went from table to table, and danced directly in front of women. The male dancer brought with him a little step stool so that his genitals were face level to the female spectator(s). The women tipped him. There was a lot of flirtation, kissing, and some genital playing.[9]

While this situation seems to reverse the traditional paradigm, male sexuality is still active, privileged, and displayed. The female spectators want the male performer to desire them. Similar conditions are implied by female dancers in clubs for male spectators. The female dancers aren't performing their own sexuality: their display implies penile satisfaction; their open legs and wet vaginas imply the possibility of penetration. In both situations the desire of female spectators or performers is subordinate to male desire.

According to the psychoanalytic model, since male desire drives representation, a female spectator is given two options. She can identify with the active male and symbolically participate in the female performer's objectification, or she can identify with the narrative's objectified female and position herself as an object.

I do not mean to propose a universalism when I use the term *female spectator*. For the materialist feminist women are differentiated along class, race, and sexual orientation lines that make it impossible for them to respond to any image as a unit. Part of the problem with the psychoanalytical model of spectatorship is just this tendency to pose universal "male" and "female" spectators who respond only according to gender. Part of my project here is to suggest that sexuality is as large a part of spectator response as gender and that, by altering the assumed sexuality of spectators, the representational exchange can also be changed.

Mary Ann Doane, in *The Desire to Desire*, writes, "There is a certain naiveté assigned to women in relation to systems of signification, a tendency to deny the process of representation, to collapse the opposition between the sign (the image) and the real."[10] Women remain part of Lacan's Imaginary realm, completely marginal to the signifying process. Since she cannot separate herself from the image, the female spectator cannot experience the mirror phase through which she might see herself reflected as a separate subject. Because Doane's psychoanalytic reading considers desire as a form of disengagement "crucial to the assumption of the position of the speaking subject," a woman cannot hope to articulate her desire in the representational space.[11]

Since she can assume neither disengagement nor aesthetic distance from the image, she is denied the scopophilic pleasure of voyeurism. Fetishism, which also operates particularly in the cinematic apparatus to provide visual pleasure, is also unavailable to the female spectator, since her originary lack dictates that she already has nothing to lose.

Woman as a psychic subject, then, is unarticulated in representation. Doane goes on to propose that women as social subjects are constructed merely as passive consumers invited to buy the idealized, male-generated image of the female body as a commodity displayed in the representational frame.

If the female spectator chooses to accept this passively constructed consumer position, Doane writes, "The mirror/window takes on then the aspect of a trap whereby her subjectivity becomes synonymous with her objectification."[12] Buying the idealized image of herself, she turns herself into a commodity to then be sold, as the performer already has. The positions of the female performer and the female spectator are collapsed into one: they become prostitutes who buy and sell their own image in a male-generated visual economy. They are goods in the representational marketplace, commodities in an exchange by means of which they are both objectified.[13]

The women performing at B.T.'s, for example, are sheer spectacle in a representational exchange constructed for the male gaze. Some of the women admit that they do it for the money, prostituting their subjectivity to the demands of the representational space. The owner of B.T.'s, of course, doesn't see it in so mercenary a light. He romanticizes the women's involvement, speculating that they are willing to perform because they come from disturbed backgrounds and need attention—a variation of *A Chorus Line*'s "What I Did for Love."

The idea that specularized, objectified women do it for the love of the male gaze is a concept perpetuated by dominant cultural discourse. In "Confessions of a Feminist Porno Star," printed in a feminist anthology of personal narratives called *Sex Work*, Nina Hartley acquiesces to this view. She says she is an exhibitionist, a woman who is aroused by being looked at. But she also feels she has some control over the production of her image. "In choosing my roles and characterizations carefully," she writes, "I strive to show, always, women who thoroughly enjoy sex and are forceful, self-satisfying and guilt-free without also being neurotic, unhappy, or somehow unfulfilled."[14] Hartley proposes that she can subvert the representational apparatus by adjusting the content of its images and giving the positive, active roles to women.

This is a kind of liberal feminist, matching-contents argument that has been used to justify generating feminist erotica. Some feminists think that, if women controlled the means of producing pornography, its representations would be different. But the genderized component of heterosexuality, with its inevitable constant of male desire, problematizes positioning women as the producers or subjects of heterosexual pornography. Heterosexual feminist erotica, such as the magazine *Eidos*, and much feminist performance art indicate that disarming male desire in the representational space requires "feminizing" the represented males or avoiding sexuality as an integral issue. These attempts are for the most part either unsuccessful—since the erect male penis is still a power-filled image even if it's displayed in a feminine, "natural" context—or banal, as sexuality gives way to the obfuscating realm of spirituality.[15]

Debi Sundahl, in her *Sex Work* essay called "Stripper," acknowledges the subject/object problem inherent in heterosexual representation. Initially, she says:

> The hardest part of the job was dealing with my feminist principles concerning the objectification of women. Dancing nude is the epitome of woman as sex object. As the weeks passed, I found I liked being a sex object, because the context was appropriate. . . . I perform to turn you on, and if I fail, I feel I've done a poor job. Women who work in the sex industry are not responsible for, nor do they in any way perpetuate, the sexual oppression of women. In fact, to any enlightened observer, our very existence provides a distinction and a choice as to when a woman should be treated like a sex object and when she should not be. At the theatre, yes; on the street, no.[16]

I find this a provocative statement. Sundahl suggests that subject positions onstage can be separated from those assumed in life. But she also suggests that bowing to the demands of objectification in theater is the only role a woman can play in the heterosexual representational space. Implicit in her argument is the idea that representation is driven by a kind of sexuality in which objectification is constantly assumed. But is all sexuality motivated by objectification? And, if not, what might happen to representation if the sexual desire motivating it were different?

There's a twist to Sundahl's story. She is a lesbian; she publishes *On Our Backs*, a lesbian porn magazine; and she started a women-only strip show at Baybrick's, a now defunct lesbian bar in San Francisco. Sundahl herself makes a distinction between her performance spaces, pointing out that the different cultural mandates of the heterosexual and lesbian contexts make the terms of the performative exchange very different, even if the images used or roles played are the same. Describing the show at Baybrick's, for example, Sundahl writes: "The dancers loved performing for the all-female audiences because they had more freedom of expression. They were not limited to ultrafeminine acts only; they could be butch and dress in masculine attire."[17] In other words, if they wanted to, the performers could assume the subject position rather than objectifying themselves. The butch-femme role play allowed the performers to seduce one another and the lesbian spectators through the constant of lesbian sexuality.

This context allows lesbian desire to circulate as the motivating representational term. The subject/object relations that trap women performers and spectators as commodities in a heterosexual context dissolve. The lesbian subject, according to Monique Wittig and others,[18] has free range across a gender continuum, and, to paraphrase Sue-Ellen Case, her role-playing through a "strategy of appearances"[19] disrupts the dominant cultural discourse representation mandates. Wittig says lesbians are "not women" and not men according to the way these gender roles are culturally constructed.[20] Since they are already outside a strictly dichotomized gender context, they are free to pick and choose from both extremes. There are no prostitutes on the lesbian representational economy because the goods have gotten together.[21]

In *Upwardly Mobile Home*, a production by the lesbian performance troupe Split Britches, Peggy Shaw has a monologue describing her character's trip to see the fat lady at the circus. She says the lights and the posters promised her entertainment, but she got much, much more. When she entered the fat lady's tent, Shaw says: "She knew I had come to see her being fat. She looked at me and I looked at her. I loved that fat lady." Rather than the fight for subjectivity that takes place in B.T.'s heterosexual bar, Shaw's exchange with the fat woman seems paradigmatic of the lesbian viewing experience. The recognition of mutual subjectivity allows the gaze to be shared in a direct way. Shaw tells *Upwardly Mobile Home* spectators, "You have paid to see me"—but the visual economy is now under lesbian control.

Lesbians are appropriating the subject position of the male gaze by beginning to articulate the exchange of desire between women. Lesbian subjectivity creates a new economy of desire. To borrow from Irigaray once again, lesbians "go to the 'market' alone, to profit from their own value, to talk to each other, to desire each other, without the control of the selling-buying-consuming subjects."[22] Rather than gazing through the representational window at their commodification as women, lesbians are generating and buying their own desire on a different representational economy. Perhaps the lesbian subject can offer a model for female spectators that will appropriate the male gaze. The aim is not to look like men, but to look at all.

Epilogue

Since reading Teresa de Lauretis's article on lesbian representation,[23] I've been rethinking the issue of desire and, with it, the whole of what Case calls the "psychosemiotic" theoretical endeavor.[24] When I attempt to wrench myself from the psychosemiotic subject considerations that have governed my work on the spectator, and that hinge on the question of desire in representation, I come up with the notion of spectatorial communities. This is where de Lauretis, too, seems to arrive in her exploration of how to represent lesbian differences, how not to reify the lesbian spectator as some new, unbroken, unified idol.

The hint of utopianism that creeps into my thoughts when I write about changing the entrenched gender dynamics of representation comes from my conception of lesbian subjectivit(ies) as one of the most challenging, fruitful areas in this field of investigation. According to the psychosemiotic feminist critical model, of which my argument here makes use, male desire is the variable in the representational exchange that upsets the balance of power, reinforces the gender dichotomy in art and culture, and proscribes heterosexuality as compulsory.[25] Male desire is not at all a factor in representations created by lesbians. As a result, the area of lesbian subjectivity seems a place to begin to envision new possibilities for representation.

Shifting my emphasis from the psychological construction of the individual spectator, however, brings me perhaps to a less utopian notion of lesbian spectatorial communities, separated and differentiated by class, race, and ideology. As de Lauretis chastises, changing the shape of desire from heterosexual to lesbian won't get the entire crisis of representation off our backs. There is no universal lesbian spectator to whom each lesbian representation will provide the embodiment of the same lesbian desire. Sexuality and desire and lesbian subjects are more complicated than that.

Although I might concede the utopianism of my writing on lesbian desire and am currently working to think within the contradictions, I can't concede or condone what some see as the necessity to "universalize" this model to heterosexual women and men. For instance, Linda Walsh Jenkins mistakenly suggests that "most of the leading [feminist theorists] in the middle 80s are lesbian" and complains that "the heterosexual female position has not been given much attention or articulation."[26] Jenkins fails to acknowledge that heterosexual women are in a more visible, privileged position in the culture than lesbians and have in fact been given a great deal of attention. The history of theater and performance studies, as well as its criticism and theory, cloaks its heterosexuality in a universal guise that leaves lesbian subjects invisible in its discourse. I am, as Wittig suggests, shifting the axis of categorization.[27]

Placing the lesbian subject at the center of the debate, rescued from the invisible margins, illuminates aspects of the arguments about representation that were clouded or unexamined. But my argument also has a personal and political component that aims toward the liberation of a sexual minority. Heterosexual readers unsettled by their absence from this debate might have to confront their own homophobia, just as I, as a white reader grappling with work by racial and ethnic minorities, am forced to examine my own racism. As the postmodernists insist, the center is constantly shifting. The shock might be finding yourself on the margins.

Afterthoughts, April 1992

From this remove—looking back on an article conceived nearly five years ago—"Desire Cloaked in a Trenchcoat" seems like a piece of theoretical history, a kind of Americana in the discourse about female spectatorship. Although I see glimmers of my own more recent thinking through the cracks of my argument here, the piece in many ways represents an earlier moment in feminist and lesbian discourse about spectatorship and "the gaze."

The recent theoretical move into cultural studies, for example, to supplement the critical paradigms of psychoanalytic research on the operation of desire, offers innumerable ways to reconceptualize the fraught exchanges between performers, spectators, and audiences in particular, historicized, localized contexts. In fact, the move into audience studies (described, in part, by Susan Bennett's recent *Theatre Audiences: A Theory of Production and Reception*) reconfigures the concept of the spectator as a singular position interacting with a representational text into a community of viewers responding multi-vocally to multiply meaningful productions.[28]

Whereas the female spectator in "Desire Cloaked in a Trench-coat" seems bound to the limited options of identification with the narrative's active male or its objectified female, new research in me-dia and film studies, just now being applied in theater studies, argues that spectators use representation in more active, complicated ways, that even within the inequities of gendered viewing resistance can be found and agency claimed. Such counterhegemonic practices now seem available to heterosexual female, as well as lesbian, spectators and audiences, in ways that the more singular, psychosemiotic explo-rations of desire once obscured.

Likewise, the eruption in the early 1990s of counterhegemonic lesbian discourse on sexual practice offers even more sites at which to look for alternatives to the "cultural" feminist representations of female desire than in 1987, when *On Our Backs* and the testimonies in *Sex Work* seemed indeed a brave new world. The new "economy of desire" has proven a legitimate capitalist one for lesbians as well, as publications such as the quarterly *Out/Look* (unfortunately now defunct) and Susie Bright's now notorious *Susie Sexpert's Lesbian Sex World*[29] have redefined the boundaries of the debate over lesbian and gay representation and sexual practice. The "pornography of capital-ism" now proves lucrative in new and different ways, as lesbians across a range of political and identity affiliations have bought and sold a differently eroticized gaze.

If "Trenchcoat" ends with a mandate to "appropriate the male gaze . . . to look at all," the flourishing alternative visual culture in lesbian and gay publications, bars, and boutiques seems to indicate a liberation of the gaze not only in the theater but also in the perfor-mance of everyday life. But maybe I'm still waxing utopian, as I know that costs continue to be exacted for what appear to be these newly found freedoms to gaze.

My first epilogue in this text challenges heterosexual readers to confront their own imminent panic at finding themselves on the mar-gin of lesbian texts and suggests that efficacious political work in representation happens when the center continually shifts, across gender, race, sexuality, class, and other identity and community lines. If I were to rewrite this article today, I would attempt to trouble even further the binary of margin and center, inside and outside, that structures my ideas and my text. The concept of a discursive center, even when it's composed of identity communities once "silenced," "oppressed," and "marginalized" by dominant discourse, seems less productive in 1992 than a less fixed, less stabilized, less monolithic concept of positionality, in which lesbians, too, can find their respective rugs continually pulled out from under them. Positionality moves us all around some other space than a center or a margin, through the complications of considering (and living) more crossed, intersected identities. Giving up the notion of a center, of a privileged, fixed position to which spectators might aspire, will have useful implications for reconsidering the focus and power of a unidirectional gaze.

My last thought—inspired in part by a lecture Peggy Phelan gave at the University of Wisconsin–Madison in March 1992 and in part by the new resonances rereading this article sounds for me—troubles the issue of visibility as a progressive, even transgressive value in representation, to which my work has been so attached. In her talk Phelan proposed a new model of political activism founded in undecidability, which would challenge what she called the impoverishment of the "economy of certainty." She pointed out that being able to see and to know and therefore provoke to action is a paradigm used to equal effect by the New Right as well as feminists and the New, floundering Left. Phelan challenged her audience to confront the provocation of doubt, to resist a causal link between representation and the real that requires a deep, profound revision of an investment in visibility as politically radical.

While I remain hesitant to fully divest from "looking" or from "visibility" as desirable on a representational economy, I am provoked by Phelan's challenge to rethink the terms of political resistance. How, in the production/reception paradigm that structures performance, can we cast the "provocation of doubt" over how we look and what we see? How can we unmoor identity from visibility—in some ways the logical extension of deuniversalizing the lesbian spectator, as de Lauretis offered—without leaving desire cloaked in a trenchcoat? Or is the trenchcoat, with its enigmatic potential to flash the desire it hides, a most efficacious political metaphor?

NOTES

1. Susanne Kappeler, *The Pornography of Representation* (Minneapolis: University of Minnesota Press, 1986), 53.

2. Antiporn feminism is very much in line with the cultural feminist politic, which maintains that the biological differences between men and women are the basis of their psychological and social differences. This stance translates into often prescriptive dichotomies that describe men's behavior as violent, women's as pacifist. Andrea Dworkin is the most vocal and visible antiporn cultural feminist; her book *Pornography: Men Possessing Women* (New York: Pedigree Books, 1979) is the bible of the movement. See Jill Dolan, "The Dynamics of Desire: Sexuality and Gender in Pornography and Performance," *Theatre Journal* 39, no. 2 (May 1987): 156–74, for a further explication of antiporn feminism in terms of feminist performance and criticism.

3. See Teresa de Lauretis, "Desire in Narrative," *Alice Doesn't* (Bloomington: Indiana University Press, 1984), 103–57; E. Ann Kaplan, *Women and Film: Both Sides of the Camera* (New York: Methuen, 1983); and Laura Mulvey, "Visual Pleasure and Narrative Cinema," *Screen* 16, no. 3 (1975): 6–18.

4. Kappeler, *The Pornography of Representation*, 61–62.

5. Bob Greene, "Bar Wars," *Esquire*, November 1986, 61–62.

6. For example, this link between the eroticization of imperialism and sexual imperialism is drawn in Stanley Kubrick's Vietnam film *Full Metal Jacket* (1987). When the American soldiers get to Vietnam in Kubrick's film, they are immediately initiated into an economy based on the exchange of Vietnamese prostitutes for U.S. dollars. The soldiers' options in the war context are sex or fighting, and the two inevitably blur. The slow motion, orgasmic quality of blood capsules bursting all over soldiers/actors falling in battle is unmistakably sexual. After a series of more or less faceless skirmishes with the Asian enemy, the film climaxes with the face-to-face murder of a sniper who, not accidentally, is a woman. Aggression toward an entire country is signified by what ends up as sexual aggression toward one alien woman, the dark territory incarnate. Substituting a woman for the alien Asian enemy cannot be coincidental. In Kubrick's film Vietnam is signified by a woman.

7. Greene, "Bar Wars," 62.

8. In ibid., 62.

9. Richard Schechner, personal correspondence, September 7, 1987.

10. Mary Ann Doane, *The Desire to Desire: The Woman's Film of the* 1940s (Bloomington: Indiana University Press, 1987), 1.

11. Ibid., 11.

12. Ibid., 33.

13. Gayle Rubin, "The Traffic in Women: Notes on the 'Political Economy' of Sex," in Rayna Reiter, ed., *Toward an Anthropology of Women* (New York: Monthly Review Press, 1978), argues that women have been use-value in a male economy at least since the kinship systems studied by Lévi-Strauss.

Luce Irigaray, in "When the Goods Get Together," in Elaine Marks and Isabelle de Courtivron, eds., *New French Feminisms* (New York: Schocken Books, 1981), suggests that, if women refused to "go to market," they could fundamentally disrupt the dominant culture's structure.

14. Nina Hartley, "Confessions of a Feminist Porno Star," in Frederique Delacoste and Priscilla Alexander, eds., *Sex Work: Writings by Women in the Sex Industry* (San Francisco and Pittsburgh: Cleis Press, 1987), 142.

15. Dolan, "The Dynamics of Desire," 157–61.

16. Debi Sundahl, "Stripper," in Delacoste and Alexander, *Sex Work*, 175–80.

17. Ibid., 178.

18. See, for example, Monique Wittig, "The Straight Mind," *Feminist Issues* (Summer 1980): 103–11, and "One Is Not Born a Woman," *Feminist Issues* (Winter 1981): 47–54.

19. Sue-Ellen Case, "Toward a Butch-Femme Aesthetic," in Lynda Hart, ed., *Making a Spectacle* (Ann Arbor: University of Michigan Press, 1989), 282–99.

20. Wittig, "The Straight Mind," 110.

21. See Irigaray, "When the Goods Get Together," for a full explication of the economic model.

22. Ibid., 110.

23. Teresa de Lauretis, "Sexual Indifference and Lesbian Representation," *Theatre Journal* 40, no. 2 (May 1988): 155–77.

24. Sue-Ellen Case, *Feminism and Theatre* (New York and London: Methuen, 1988), especially the last chapter.

25. See Adrienne Rich, "Compulsory Heterosexuality and Lesbian Existence," in Ann Snitow, Christine Stansell, and Sharon Thompson, eds., *Powers of Desire* (New York: Monthly Review Press, 1983), 177–205.

26. Linda Walsh Jenkins, in Jenkins and Helen Krich Chinoy, eds., *Women in American Theatre* (1981; reprint, New York: Theatre Communications Group, 1987), 373.

27. Monique Wittig, "The Point of View: Universal or Particular?" *Feminist Issues* (Fall 1983): 63–69.

28. Susan Bennett, *Theatre Audiences: A Theory of Production and Reception* (New York and London: Routledge, 1990).

29. Susie Bright, *Susie Sexpert's Lesbian Sex World* (San Francisco and Pittsburgh: Cleis Press, 1990).

Chapter 6

Breaking the Code: Musings on Lesbian Sexuality and the Performer

In a recent interview in *The Village Voice* lesbian comic Lisa Kron said her friends once warned her that being an out lesbian in comedy could limit her salability in mainstream clubs. But, far from finding herself ostracized, Kron says, "Now they see that I'm getting all this media attention, and maybe even *because* I'm a lesbian."[1]

Lesbians do seem to be garnering a certain amount of notoriety. Lesbian performances and performers are now infamous, and several recent collections of lesbian and gay plays have made what were once underground texts widely accessible. The "Feminist Diversions" issue of *Theatre Journal* (May 1988) leads with Teresa de Lauretis's essay on lesbian representation, and a June 1988 issue of the *Village Voice* is devoted to the gay sensibility in the arts.[2] These two sources could not be more different, yet their intertextual resonances speak favorably of the impact of theory on practice and vice versa. With the walls between lesbian theorists and practitioners newly permeable, and the new media attention to lesbian playwriting and performing, a host of questions is raised about sexuality as a transaction of meaning in performance and, perhaps in a more insidious way, the dangers of lesbian assimilation.

In the *Voice* WOW Cafe compatriots Lois Weaver and Holly Hughes make statements about the centrality of sexuality not only to lesbian performance but also to performance in general. Weaver remarks, "Performance is sex," echoing the sentiment of feminist theorists who have written about the workings of representation.[3] Hughes insists that "sex must be very compelling if you're willing to suffer everything you have to suffer to be queer in this society. I think

135

that heightened sexuality can give you a special appreciation of sen-
suality."[4] The erotics of communication are hotly evident at the
WOW Cafe in New York, particularly in Weaver's seductively femme
presentation of her lesbian self and in Hughes's raucous parodies of
lesbian sexual mores. The lesbian community's desires, which lurk
as a forbidden subtext in the dominant cultural milieu, become blatantly textual in this subcultural theater venue.

The lesbian body in these performances is a text inscribed with
the experience of moving through a heterosexual world, marked by
the expression of a sexual desire that is thrilling for its danger. Feminist theorists have debated the issue of desire in performance ever
since film critics proposed that cinematic narratives move along a
trajectory of male desire, which sutures the spectator to the image
through psychoanalytic identification processes.[5] De Lauretis reiterates this issue in her *Theatre Journal* article, analyzing lesbian critiques
of representation that hinge on the psychosemiotic conception of
desire.

In an essay called "The Dynamics of Desire," for example, I
proposed that lesbian representation makes a gesture toward rectify-
ing the problem of desire in narrative, since the obstacle of male
sexuality is absent from its frame.[6] De Lauretis argues, on the contrary, that the question of lesbian desire cannot be posed as such an
ameliorator without sinking into oppositional generalizations that
valorize lesbian desire over male.[7]

She also cautions against creating a transcendent, unitary position for the lesbian spectator that elides her class, her race, and other
social stratifications that make lesbian people different from one another. In my optimism over the possibilities of lesbian spectatorship
I may have fallen unwittingly into such a trap. De Lauretis slightly
shifts her emphasis from theorizing the psychosemiotic subject position in representation toward a notion of lesbian spectatorial communities in which sexuality is a "local" link among a "global" chain of
differences.[8]

De Lauretis cautions against making the local link of sexual preference definitive. But marginalized sexuality does give lesbian spectators one vantage point of an outsider's view on dominant cultural
representations. Asked by the *Voice* to define her perspective, playwright Hughes answers: "I like the word *gay*, although I think of
myself more as queer. I believe the strength in my work comes from

that perspective—my being an outsider."[9] De Lauretis theorizes such an outsider's position by proposing that marginalized lesbian spectators and lesbian representations struggle to alter the "standard of vision, the frame of reference of visibility, of *what can be seen.*"[10]

Lesbians as outsiders, who see what the dominant culture would render invisible, is a trope common to lesbian plays written from within the American fourth-wall realism tradition. For instance, Carter, the protagonist of Sarah Dreher's domestic drama, *8 × 10 Glossy* (1985), is a photographer with a penchant for climbing trees to document her family's crises, from which she remains strangely, painfully aloof. Lacey, in Jane Chambers's one-act play, *Quintessential Image* (1983), is a famous photographer whose images have been misread throughout her professional career. Jess, in Judith Katz's *Tribes* (1979), is a videographer who hides behind the lens of her camera to protect herself from participating in her ex-lover's family interactions.[11] These are just a few examples.

While the metaphor of marginality seems apt, these characters appear to be hampered by their plays' forms. The only viable positions for lesbian characters within realism appear to be as heterosexuals-in-transition, as they are in the "coming out" stories, or as observers, women who can *see* within the limits of the form but who still cannot *act*. The personal, local conditions of their concerns somehow mire them in the domestic drama ruled by heterosexuality. The lesbian is posed as singular, alone on the margins of what is really a heterosexual drama. Her community, which might allow her to *act* on what she sees, is absent, repressed by the exigencies of the realist text.

Musings on the question of what can be seen and who is seeing in representation embrace the position of the performer and the spectator and are inextricably bound to considerations of production modes and venues—and, implicitly, to a question of community. A performance text created by lesbian performers for primarily lesbian spectators will carry different meanings than a lesbian text created by heterosexuals for primarily heterosexual audiences. The possibilities of different performer/spectator configurations based on sexuality are innumerable, and the ramifications of their meanings become more complex and variable when race, class, and gender become part of the discussion.

Race and gender are clearly legible in the sign system that governs how bodies are read in performance. In her feminist explication of the semiotics of drama, Sue-Ellen Case points out that all signs are culturally encoded and that "the notion of encoding shifts the political implications of a theatrical performance from the interpretative sphere of the critic to the signification process of the performance, thereby assigning political alliance to the aesthetic realm."[12] In other words, production choices, particularly those that center on the representation of human bodies, are inherently political, because a person's race and gender have cultural meanings that bear ideological weight.

The subtext in the heated debates about cross-racial casting in the professional theater press is that people are grappling with the ideological, political, and economic implications of nontraditional casting choices.[13] These choices are generally made within a realist tradition built on an assumption of coincidence between the spectator and a play's characters. In the community of traditional white American theater the actor's body, as Elin Diamond suggests, is laminated to the character, and the spectator expects to identify with this hybrid icon as a unified sign.[14]

How could the body of a person of color—or a female body, in an instance of cross-gender casting—be laminated to a traditionally white male character without disrupting the expectations of spectators who could no longer identify? The spectatorial community, in such an instance, would be forced to recognize difference. Under realism they are accustomed to correlating neatly their identities with representation.

Performers are taught to identify with their characters, and spectators expect to identify with the performers, in what Diamond describes as a triangular, closed, hegemonic system of meaning.[15] The identification with representation on which American realism depends is analogous to the psychological processes detailed by Freud that theoretically form a person's identity.

Feminist theorists dissecting Freud's model have persuasively argued that people are burdened with prescriptive gender roles and resolutely created heterosexual by a process that is governed by social arrangements determined by dominant ideology. If realism is a mimetic site for such arrangements, theorists suggest that realism cannot accommodate feminism, because the reality it reflects is con-

structed by the dictates of a culture that assigns women an objectified, passive role, in which they are denied subjectivity.[16]

One could also argue that realism cannot accommodate people
of color, because the model it promotes reflects the social organization of white, male-dominated, middle-class families. Cross-racial
and cross-gender casting break the realist frame with an insistent,
Brechtian discussion of the cultural meanings race and gender bear.

The heterosexual assumption of realism also marginalizes lesbians and gay men, since the form presupposes a traditional nuclear
family arrangement. Lesbian characters, if they appear in such plays,
are usually peripheral to the heterosexual plot, ape heterosexual
models, or are read as empty, liberal attempts to acknowledge the
diversity of sexual preferences. Craig Lucas's *Blue Window*, for instance, includes a lesbian couple in its panorama of New York City
relationships, but, to a lesbian spectator watching the couple portrayed by heterosexual women, the relationship is, at best, false.

Lesbian performers could audition for such roles and perhaps
struggle to bring them a certain truth, given their construction by a
male author. But, generally, because of the economics of production
and the mainstream's preference for heterosexual realism, many professional lesbian performers act straight. Unlike race and gender,
sexuality must be seen to be known, must be performed to be read.
Because the signs of sexuality are inherently performative, the assumption of heterosexuality prevails unless homosexual or lesbian
practice is made textual.

Casting across sexuality occurs continually in professional theater but is never part of the roundtable discussions reported on by
American Theatre magazine. The unspoken assumption is that a performer's sexual preference is irrelevant to casting decisions and that
lesbian and gay performers will protect their careers by acting
straight.

Lesbian performers acting straight in realist plays are, in effect,
"passing." Historical necessity has accustomed lesbians to passing,
a complex sociological trick that allows a subversive identity to survive, albeit in a compromised, silent state. Butch lesbians at certain
points in history opted or were compelled to pass as men from economic, social, or emotional necessity, and even today femme lesbians
can pass as heterosexual women. While a lengthy examination of the

politics of passing is inappropriate here, as de Lauretis notes, "Clearly, the very issue of passing . . . is related quite closely to the frame of vision and the conditions of representation."[17]

Passing exacts high costs because it requires the muffling of lesbian identity under layers of culturally constructed gender roles. Yet to survive lesbians often become adept at gender impersonation. Some femme lesbians imitate, from necessity, the gender role in which they are cast, with its requisite sexuality.

But for lesbian spectators of passing performances the subcultural subtext is always there to be read. A lesbian's ultimate refusal of the role dominant ideology would have her play is manifest in her style, in the subtleties of meaning that shade her gestures, her gait, and her pose. A lesbian required to pass as a heterosexual, on the street or on the stage, is placed in the Brechtian position of commenting on her role, editorializing on the trappings of her impersonation *for those who can see.*

To the heterosexual spectator blinded by presumption these lesbian performers appear to be heterosexuals. These performers enter the representational debate as imposters, with their roles dictated by the form and their identities erased. The inability of traditional representational strategies to allow heterosexual women to be more than decorative prizes for male heroes works on lesbians posing as heterosexuals doubly to rob them of subjectivity.

Lesbians who attempt to enter representation as lesbians under the auspices of realism fall prey to the same constraints as those who assume heterosexual characters. Most of the coming out plays, which characterize the preponderance of lesbian dramatic literature, are realist texts, since they have a conventional (i.e., heterosexual) narrative to tell. Because the heroine of a coming out play is just becoming a lesbian, these plays tend to focus on her choice to leave heterosexuality more than on her adaptation to her lesbian lifestyle. These plays might be liminal, teetering on the threshold of change, but their conflicts are usually centered in the new lesbian's struggle to validate her identity against the negative definitions of the dominant culture.

The dominant culture gets a great deal of space in realist coming out plays which, given the ideology of the form, seems no accident. Chambers's popular lesbian realist text, *Last Summer at Bluefish Cove* (1980), is really a coming out story about the girl next door, who unwittingly rents a summerhouse adjacent to a home full of New York lesbians. Dreher's *8 × 10 Glossy*, which has won innumerable awards and is published in Kate McDermott's "first" anthology of lesbian plays, purports to be about a disaffected lesbian but is really about the process of her sister's coming out. Even Terry Baum and Carolyn Myers's lesbian farce *Dos Lesbos* (1981) cannot seem to escape the constraints of realism. Each of the revue's short, episodic scenes falls into a realist guise to narrate the lesbian couple's oppressive interactions with a reproving heterosexual world.[18]

The assumption of mimesis that is so embedded in realist strategies is sometimes maintained even in lesbian texts that step self-consciously away from fourth-wall conventions. *Chiaroscuro*, written by Jackie Kay for the Theatre of Black Women in London, is also a coming out story. The play mixes poetic, choreographed, ritualized exchanges that trade in the epistemology of cultural feminism with a realist story and scenes of a woman's tentative exploration of a lesbian choice. The four black women characters read as archetypal positionalities in a struggle for sexual and racial liberation that are often at odds.[19]

A central prop in the piece is a mirror, into which one of the characters peers to acknowledge her emerging identity as a black lesbian. The audience is also used as a mirror that, even in a ritual format, extends the expectations of representation as mimesis in which a correlation between spectator/performer/character identities is presumed.

The need to validate identities that are legislated against by the dominant culture remains strong in minority communities, and lesbian theater continues to function as a corrective to the invisibility of marginalized groups. Giving up the notion of theater as a place to image those who are elsewhere erased is difficult, even as feminists debate the efficacy of theater as mimesis. Barbara Smith ends her influential essay on black feminist criticism by pleading for a piece of literature that will show her "something better to be." "How much easier both my waking and my sleeping hours would be if there were one book in existence that would tell me something specific about my life," Smith wrote in 1970. "Just one work to reflect the reality that I and the black women whom I love are trying to create."[20] But can lesbian theater hope to reflect any kind of reality without relying on mimetic strategies that now seem ideologically loaded? Do the recent discussions of differences among lesbians refract the rays of lesbian representation's function as a flattering mirror?

De Lauretis and others question how lesbians might enter representation at all, given its history as a cultural discourse that denies the barest possibility of lesbian existence. Can lesbians only enter representation as outsiders who lurk—or leap, as popular lesbian musical lore would have it—around the edges of the heterosexual play or as somehow too-good, too-positive, too-transcendent role models for healthy lesbian integration?[21] After the coming out story ends sexuality becomes part of a lesbian's material experience, along with her gender, race, and class. These experiences are signs available to be read on a lesbian body, signs to which realism cannot do justice.

A lesbian is always embedded in the Brechtian not/but, because her sexuality distances her gender. In her work on the semiotics of gesture, which is based on Monique Wittig's writing, performer Sande Zeig proposes that lesbians must refuse to adopt the gestures of women and must create and study other systems of gesture that borrow freely from both genders.[22] The lesbian performer becomes an activist in Zeig's work. She never disappears under the mask of her character; she is always there, presenting herself as an issue. Her body becomes a political palimpsest of experience and resistance.

De Lauretis cautions, however, that "redefining the conditions of vision, as well as the modes of representing, cannot be predicated on a single, undivided identity of performer and audience (whether as 'lesbians' or 'women' or 'people of color' or any other single category constructed in opposition to its dominant other)."[23] The lesbian performer demonstrating her selves before a community of lesbian people shares, in de Lauretis's words, the "division in the self, the difference and the displacement from which any identity that needs to be claimed derives"[24]—that is, a story of difference(s).

This audience/performer configuration admits to its differences. The psychological acting techniques that presume identification between performer and character and the realist conventions that assume a likeness between spectator and character can no longer be relevant. The lesbian performer breaks the identification pacts of realism, in effect, to lead people in a discussion about what they *see* in representation.

Several lesbian performance texts written in the 1980s impart an implicit understanding that the variety of lesbian lives and the experiences of lesbian bodies cannot be expressed within the constraints of realism. Cherríe Moraga's *Giving Up the Ghost* (1984), for example, is a long prose poem that describes moments in a Chicana lesbian's experiences.[25] The playing space is dark, without set pieces, carved into spheres of activity simply by suggestive lighting. No pact of identification or suspension of disbelief is understood here. The audience, in fact, is named as part of the cast list. Its members are disallowed the distance that would let them aestheticize the performance. They are not required to identify, to see *themselves* in it—just to *see*. Moraga calls the audience "The People," those viewing the performance.

Early cultural feminist texts individualized their spectators under a humanist guise and addressed them with rhetorical questions that assumed a certain universality of women's individual experiences. Moraga's text, on the contrary, is careful to acknowledge that the audience is present as a component part of its meanings but addresses it obliquely as a community of viewers, who see through their own experiences of difference.

Building full-fledged "characters" from the parts Moraga describes would be difficult, if not irrelevant. Instead, the performers' bodies become laden with meaning in the moment of performance. The performers' cultural positionalities within race, gender, class, and sexuality must be clearly legible on their bodies for the written text's meanings to be fully present. The body here is not idealized as a vessel of gender, in which femininity is recuperated and reified.[26] Rather, it becomes the locus of resistance, in which cultural constructions of race, class, and gender collide with sexual expression to explode the margins of the text.

Giving Up the Ghost demands the presence of a Chicana lesbian body to carry its meanings. Who, then, can perform this text and under what production circumstances? And who can constitute the social audience it requires to change the conditions of what can be seen? The question of who can perform and who can *see* a lesbian text takes on a particular urgency in light of the recent surge in lesbian and gay play publishing. McDermott's anthology has been quickly followed by Jill Davis's collection of lesbian plays from Britain and by Don Shewey's *Out Front*, which includes two plays by lesbians among eleven gay plays. Are these plays published simply to be read? If not, who will perform them, and in what context?

Shewey's gay play anthology includes Holly Hughes's lesbian parody, *The Well of Horniness* (1983). Hughes's text, which began at the WOW Cafe, has also been performed as a radio play. The overblown, fantastic murder-mystery plot is backed by sound effects and the ominous organ tones of melodrama. The play's puns and innuendos—even its title, which lampoon's Radclyffe Hall's classic lesbian novel, *The Well of Loneliness*—rely on the subcultural language of lesbian community audiences to be meaningful.[27]

At the 1988 Women and Theatre Program preconference in San Diego, Hughes's text was discussed along with Moraga's on a panel entitled "Generating Texts."[28] For the audience of white, mostly heterosexual women who attended the panel, Hughes's text was generally received as much more accessible than Moraga's, which is sprinkled with untranslated Spanish phrases. Moraga's text was assigned a suspicious status as "other," since this particular readership could not fully appreciate even its language, aside from the cultural and sexual references that it embodies.

Hughes's parody, by contrast, was read as completely understandable. Many of the heterosexual women who read *The Well* enjoyed the experience and were for the most part unwilling to consider themselves as less than efficient readers of a white lesbian text. Some of them did admit—with a degree of resentment, in fact—that they could not find their way into the Chicana lesbian text. The racist undertones to some of the women's objections to Moraga's text were compounded by the heterosexism implicit in their assumptions that they could fully interpret Hughes's. Both positions imply an erasure of difference, while placing white, heterosexual women at the apex of a hierarchy of competent readers.

Since the panel discussion was meant to focus on the ways in which race, class, and sexuality create different meanings within different spectator/performer configurations, many of the women participating in the discussion were peculiarly blind to the ways in which their own positionalities affected their readings. Acknowledging difference, as well as racism and homophobia, might have been a more productive way to tease out the multiple meanings in these texts.

In the author's note that precedes *The Well* Hughes insists that all the characters be played by women, although one character is written as a man. "I'm pretty tough about this part," she warns. "No men in *The Well*, okay? I don't care if you're doing a staged reading in Crib Death, Iowa—no men."[29] The male character in *The Well* will have to be played by a woman. But who in Crib Death, Iowa, will play the lesbians? And who will be cast as the audience?

This problem was further illustrated at the Women and Theatre Program preconference in Chicago in 1987, when Sue-Ellen Case took exception to my suggestion that two heterosexual women read scenes from *Dos Lesbos*. My casting choice was based on my own doubts about the play's efficacy. I was, and remain, uncomfortable with its cloying sentimentality and consider it a farcical coming out story. But Case's objections centered on the fact that a heterosexual woman playing a lesbian usurps a minority voice. She becomes an imposter, organizing an alien experience under the rubric of her heterosexual privilege.

Case has pointed out elsewhere that the dominant culture has always imposed stereotypical masks on minorities through just such theater practices.[30] Blackface vaudeville routines and female impersonations were common and acceptable on American popular stages, and the Greek and Elizabethan traditions institutionalized the precedent of impersonating minority or underprivileged subjects. The ideological, political objection to such practices still holds. A heterosexual woman playing a lesbian for a primarily heterosexual audience absents the very subject the representation is purportedly about. Although *Dos Lesbos* is written by lesbians for lesbians, there would have been no lesbians represented in my proposed reading of the play.

In addition to its political and ideological dimensions, the incident posed certain practical considerations. For lesbian spectators a heterosexual woman would not be believable as a lesbian. As much as she might empathize or do visualization exercises to project herself into a lesbian role, a heterosexual woman will never know, in her body, what it feels like to be queer in a homophobic culture. She has not developed the survival instincts that would teach her the signals lesbians use to break the code, to signify and to read what dominant representations suppress. Realist acting techniques are as inadequate toward a heterosexual woman's impersonation of lesbian experiences as they would be for a white woman attempting to impersonate a woman of color.

But what does this imply? Isn't the requirement that only lesbians play lesbians reminiscent of realism's demand for a coincidence of identity? If only lesbians can play lesbian roles, and if only African-American lesbians and Chicana lesbians can represent themselves, and if only lesbian audiences will truly understand these performers' meanings, don't these texts remain ghettoized as projects for community theaters that simply validate the identities of their members?

My ambivalent, tentative response is to think not. The notion of audience as community revises the hegemonic position of the singular spectator formed by psychological processes. The isolated individual masked by the dark auditorium is replaced with visible groups of people formed and differentiated by their positions within the culture.[31] Now that feminist theory has developed a solid critique of the male gaze and the psychosemiotic subject position, perhaps a theoretical performance practice based in spectatorial communities divided within themselves will provide a way to make something else happen within performance. But to reduce this work to community theater, and to say that only lesbians should see lesbian performance work, denies the divided identities people live among, which de Lauretis and others describe so eloquently. People need to see, to change the conditions of their own vision, to stretch the parameters of what they *can* see. Lesbian performers just might prompt people into such a revised circumstance of sight.

NOTES

1. Quoted in Laurie Stone, "Funny Girls," *Village Voice*, June 28, 1988, 39.

2. Teresa de Lauretis, "Sexual Indifference and Lesbian Representation," *Theatre Journal* 40, no. 2 (May 1988): 155–77; and Richard Goldstein and Robert Massa, eds., "Sensibility and Survival: The New Gay Arts," *Village Voice*, June 28, 1988.

3. Quoted in Stone, "Funny Girls," 39.

4. Quoted in Robert Massa, "We Invented Irony," *Village Voice*, June 28, 1988, 38. For historical information on lesbian performances, particularly at the WOW Cafe in New York City's East Village, see Alisa Solomon, "The WOW Cafe," *Drama Review* 29, no. 1 (Spring 1985): 92–101.

5. The psychoanalytic work in feminist film theory is now well known,

but see in particular Laura Mulvey, "Visual Pleasure in Narrative Cinema," *Screen* 16, no. 3 (Autumn 1975): 6–18; and Teresa de Lauretis, *Alice Doesn't: Feminism, Semiotics, Cinema* (Bloomington: Indiana University Press, 1984), especially her chapter "Desire in Narrative" (103–57). See also Sue-Ellen Case, *Feminism and Theatre* (New York: Methuen, 1988), particularly her chapter "Towards a New Poetics" (112–32); and Jill Dolan, *The Feminist Spectator as Critic* (1988; reprint, Ann Arbor: University of Michigan Press, 1991), for further theoretical work on feminist spectatorship, psychoanalysis, and semiotics.

6. See Jill Dolan, "The Dynamics of Desire: Sexuality and Gender in Pornography and Performance," *Theatre Journal* 39, no. 2 (May 1987): 156–74.

7. de Lauretis, "Sexual Indifference," 164–70.

8. Ibid., 159.

9. Quoted in Massa, "We Invented Irony," 22.

10. de Lauretis, "Sexual Indifference," 171.

11. Sarah Dreher, *8 × 10 Glossy*, in Kate McDermott, ed., *Places, Please: The First Anthology of Lesbian Plays* (Iowa City: Aunt Lute Books, 1985); Jane Chambers, *Quintessential Image*, (MS., 1983); Judith Katz, *Tribes—a Play of Dreams* (MS., 1979). For commentary on *Quintessential Image*, see also Case, *Feminism and Theatre*, 78–79, as well as Dolan (Masters thesis, "Toward a Critical Methodology of Lesbian Feminist Theatre," Performance Studies Department, New York University, 1983).

12. Case, *Feminism and Theatre*, 117.

13. See, for example, Zelda Fichandler, "Casting for a Different Truth," *American Theatre* 5, no. 2 (May 1988): 18–23; and Hal Gelb, "Should Equal Opportunity Apply on the Stage?" *New York Times*, August 28, 1988, H3.

14. Elin Diamond, "Brechtian Theory/Feminist Theory: Toward a Gestic Feminist Criticism," *Drama Review* 32, no. 1 (Spring 1988): 89.

15. Ibid. See Diamond's full analysis for further work on the political implications of psychological realism.

16. See Gayle Rubin's influential deconstruction of Freudian theory, "The Traffic in Women: Notes on the 'Political Economy' of Sex," in Rayna Reiter, ed., *Toward an Anthropology of Women* (New York: Monthly Review Press, 1978), 157–210. See Catherine Belsey, "Constructing the Subject, Deconstructing the Text," in Judith Newton and Deborah Rosenfelt, eds., *Feminist Criticism and Social Change* (New York: Methuen, 1985), 45–64, for an explication of the ideology at work in classical realism.

17. de Lauretis, "Sexual Indifference," 174. For writing on passing as a part of lesbian history, see, for example, Joan Nestle's stories and essays in *A Restricted Country* (Ithaca: Firebrand Books, 1987). See also Sue-Ellen Case, "Toward a Butch-Femme Aesthetic," in Lynda Hart, ed., *Making a Spectacle: Feminist Essays on Contemporary Women's Theatre* (Ann Arbor: University of Michigan Press, 1988), 282–99, for an analysis of the social, political, and performative aspects of lesbian gender impersonations.

18. Jane Chambers, *Last Summer at Bluefish Cove* (New York: JH Press, 1982); Terry Baum and Carolyn Myers, *Dos Lesbos*, in McDermott, *Places, Please*.

19. Jackie Kay, *Chiaroscuro*, in Jill Davis, ed., *Lesbian Plays* (London: Methuen, 1987). See also Jewelle Gomez, "Imagine a Lesbian . . . a Black Lesbian," *Trivia* 12 (Spring 1988): 45–60, for an analysis of oppositions between race, ethnicity, and sexual preference in the context of literary criticism.

20. Barbara Smith, "Toward a Black Feminist Criticism," reprinted in Newton and Rosenfelt, *Feminist Criticism and Social Change*, 3–18.

21. De Lauretis, following a metaphor posed by Marilyn Frye, describes lesbian spectators as those who can see what the conceptual system of heterosexuality attempts to hide and therefore shift their attention to those who work around the margins of dominant images ("Sexual Indifference," 172). Meg Christian's song, "Leaping Lesbians," is the infamous popular parody of the perceived lavender menace.

22. See Sande Zeig, "The Actor as Activator: Deconstructing Gender through Gesture," *Women & Performance Journal* 1, no. 2 (1985): 12–17.

23. de Lauretis, "Sexual Indifference," 171.

24. Ibid., 174.

25. Cherríe Moraga, *Giving Up the Ghost* (Los Angeles: West End Press, 1986). See also de Lauretis, "Sexual Indifference," 174–75, for a theoretical explication of the piece; and Yvonne Yarbro-Bejarano, "The Female Subject in Chicano Theatre: Sexuality, 'Race,' and Class," *Theatre Journal* 38, no. 4 (December 1986): 402–7, for a historical–critical reading that locates the play within the cultural indices of the Chicana community.

26. I am thinking in particular of much cultural feminist performance art practice, best described and defended by Jeanie Forte, "Women's Performance Art: Feminism and Postmodernism," *Theatre Journal* 40, no. 2 (May 1988): 217–35.

27. Holly Hughes, *The Well of Horniness*, in Don Shewey, ed., *Out Front: Contemporary Gay and Lesbian Plays* (New York: Grove Press, 1988). See also Kate Davy, "Constructing the Spectator: Reception, Context, and Address in Lesbian Performance," *Performing Arts Journal* 10, no. 2 (1986): 43–52, for a critical description of Hughes's play *The Lady Dick*, a lesbian *noir* that features Garnet McClit, the character introduced in *The Well*.

28. The 1988 Women and Theatre Program preconference, called "Staging Feminisms: Practices and Theories," took place at the Horton Grand Hotel in San Diego, California, July 31–August 3. The "Generating Texts" panel took place on August 1 and was moderated by Juli Thompson Burk. Ironically, the undercurrents at this particular panel remained relatively subtextual, while other panels or incidents during the polemical three-day-long event proved more overtly contentious.

29. Hughes, *The Well of Horniness*, 222.

30. See Case, *Feminism and Theatre*, particularly her chapter called "Traditional History: A Feminist Deconstruction" (5–28). Case and I had our public discussion about this casting issue at the Women and Theatre Program preconference coordinated by Vicki Patraka at Mundelein College in Chicago, August 1987, during a panel I moderated called "Feminism and Realism."

For more analysis of the sometimes heated debates at this conference, see my book *The Feminist Spectator as Critic*, particularly chapter 5, "Cultural Feminism and the Feminine Aesthetic" (83–97).

31. Yarbro-Bejarano writes, "While the psychoanalytic concept of the spectator as a gendered subject is essential in the discussion of representations of sexuality onstage with the female spectator in mind, the notion of audience as distinct from spectator brings into play social, gender, and economic factors that also determine the reception of the text" (406).

Chapter 7

Peeling Away the Tropes of Visibility: Lesbian Sexuality and Materialist Performance Practice

This is an essay about sexuality and visibility, about theater and location, about performance and community. The trajectory I want to chart starts in a production experience I had in the spring of 1991 and also originates in a recent realization that the desire I've written so much about in my scholarship had somehow become a figure of speech.

The first stirrings of my own desire were felt for actresses, whom I revered at my local theater classes as a girl. Watching these women perform, I felt a charged exchange of presence—or mutual present-ness—that necessitated I be there to witness their visibility, to hear their words, to protect, in some chivalrous, latently butch way, their vulnerable *live-ness*. This painful, pleasurable, and mostly unarticulated desire came to be replaced over the years in my writing about theater by a passionate theorizing that fed me instead.

The charge of those old seductions flickered now and then, but, sitting with my critic's pen in hand, the desire that once unsettled my body, mediated by cultural mores and family taboos, was now mediated by desire, the trope, and didn't feel quite the same. I was caught, differently, in the excisions of deconstruction.

Then, that spring, I simply started doing theater again and, to my surprise, have found myself caught by the possibilities of a recon-structive moment. My work as codirector, with my University of Wisconsin–Madison friend and colleague Phillip Zarrilli, on a postmodern, revisionist, gender-bent production of *A Midsummer*

Night's Dream rekindled a history of identifications (to borrow Elin Diamond's evocative term)[1] with myself, of falling in love with women across the stage space. Working with Phillip, and assistant directors Stacy Wolf and Michael Peterson, and a cast of twenty students, and four designers, to fashion those moments of presentness multiply exchanged between actors and actors, actors and spectators, and spectators and spectators, I remembered that desire has a body.

This essay is meant to evoke for you what became for me an experience in which theory and practice really did meld in production. I learned things from *Midsummer* about the stakes involved in performing lesbian theories. The production and its process taught me to revalue the power of theater to engage local communities; taught me to respect the imagination and courage of actors willing to embody their own social constructedness, to deconstruct it, and reconstruct something else; and moved me to remember that these moments of strangers and friends, actors and spectators, crew and ushers sharing a vision in the crucible of theater really do resonate outside the institution's walls.

In his book *No Respect* Andrew Ross suggests that live entertainment can't be considered through mass cultural frameworks, because its movement through cultural distribution networks is of necessity limited.[2] But I think theater can exploit its lack of a mass audience, its specific localities, its communities, to recuperate the too often derogatory term *community theater* and escape the constraints of a perhaps more elitist avant-garde. There's something in theater's presentation of the live, palpable, endangered body onstage, viewed by live, palpable, equally endangered audiences, that retains a certain power.

I had taught *Midsummer* for several years in a class called "Theatre and Society," which allowed me to engage Shakespeare's comedy with feminist theories of homosocial exchange. In addition to reading the text as ripe for the deconstruction of its gendered orderings, complicated as it is by its own history as a cross-cast production, I found the text already self-reflexive about its status as representation. The mechanicals' rehearsals for their performance before the court are very wry and pragmatic about how representation produces itself, about the creation of the real as false and the false as real.

The text's theatrical metaphors extend into its insistent heterosexual couplings to suggest that the principal characters' shifting desires and allegiances, their state-ordered or drug-induced dalliances, can also be read as performative. If these sexual relationships are performances as crude as the mechanicals' before the court, the genders and desires that found them might also be unmoored from the natural. Postmodern parody might liberate a more provocative circulation of desire from the text.

There are many things to say about our revisionist production approach: how race became a signifier of resistance when we cast a black actor as Puck and doubled him as Philostrate and the master of ceremonies in our preshow entertainment; how cross-gender casting many of the mechanicals allowed us to look at gender as it intersects with class and race; how the Asian theater techniques we employed provided ways to create physically embodied *gestus.* But I'll limit myself to describing the journey of the lovers, to focus on sexuality as performance and the circulation of desire.

Asking young actors to think about gender and sexuality proved a challenge that was met only after many weeks of workshops and rehearsals, and only after the actors trusted that their agency would be respected in their explorations. The actors moved through a kind of recalcitrant mutual suspicion and an insistence, particularly from the youngest men, on their heterosexuality and their maleness—which became conflated immediately in workshops—to a willingness to demonstrate their bodies as masquerades and to let their desire and their pleasure more fully cross genders.

We set the production in a cabaret space, to concretize the link between the performance of theater and the performance of gender and sexuality. The Gilbert Hemsley Theatre, University of Wisconsin–Madison's convertible black box space, was gutted and reconstructed as what might have become the hottest bar in Madison had its life been extended after the run. Spectators entered across a mock proscenium arch and descended several stairs to a cabaret floor, which was strewn with clusters of small tables and movable chairs, all arranged around a circular, raised dance floor that served as one of our central playing areas. Spectators entered where actors usually star and were often immediately discomfitted by a sense of their own visibility.

Once off the proscenium stairs the ambiance of the theater felt much like a bar, in which a certain sexualized looking is always promoted. A "real" bar that served beer, wine, and soft drinks before and at the intermission of every performance lined one end of the room; a balcony with additional seating and a dramatic stairway to the cabaret floor faced the bar along the opposite wall; and a baby grand piano sat on an elevated platform near the proscenium, parallel to the stage manager's box from which the show was visibly (and sometimes audibly) called.

Since we staged scenes all over the room, the environmental configuration disturbed profoundly the standard one-way direction of the gaze. Our production offered the invitation to gaze along a wide range of options. Rather than deconstructing it from within the traditional proscenium structure through pointed Brechtian intervention (although we used that as well), we detached the gaze into a multidirectional circulation that made it suddenly a potent, palpable force available across a spectrum of spectating positions. Spectators were never sure where to look, as the performance happened all around them. As a result, they looked constantly, at the performers and at one another. The piano bar atmosphere of our preshow entertainments and the disco dancing that happened every night at intermission capitalized on and encouraged a watchful socializing.

The cabaret metaphor provided our spatial framework, one that served as a fluid way to transform from the Athenian court to the mechanicals' rehearsals to the forest and back again. The play's opening in Athens used the space as an upscale Yuppie fern bar. We set Athens as the crossroads of economic, patriarchal, white, and state power and, with the resistant arrival of Hermia to Theseus's court, proceeded to stretch apart and break those four bands of authority.

The mechanicals' scenes transformed the cabaret into a working-class corner pub, where Alan Jackson crooned on a jukebox and actors clad in work suits played pool. The descent from there to the forest, our third space, transformed the cabaret into a gay disco. To introduce the space, a disco ball cast moving light all over the room and the sound system played Gloria Gaynor's 1970s disco hit, "I Will Survive."

Our decision to turn the forest into a subcultural gay disco space allowed us to play out the transformations of gender and sexuality we intended to liberate in Shakespeare's text. When our Athenian lovers escaped to the forest, our intent was to return them, after the night's confusion, not to their heterosexual status quo but, instead, to a world much changed by the possibilities of the gay disco night.

To represent these possibilities we cross-gender cast Oberon and

Titania. Titania, played by a man, was conceived as a kind of punk drag queen. He wore high black heels, fishnet stockings, a vinyl miniskirt, and a black leather jacket, which he unzipped provocatively to reveal only a black rhinestone bra nestled against a somewhat hairy flat chest. Played by John Jaraczewski, as coached by our drag consultant Martin Worman, Titania was a "cockettish" provocateur, who carried a whip under her arm and often slapped it for emphasis.

Oberon, played by Darcey Engen in a style that echoed the seductions of a fashionable, sexy, butch lesbian, wore a sharkskin suit, high-heeled boots, an upturned, unbuttoned collar, and a loosened black tie. A felt hat, perched jauntily over Darcey's wavy red hair, gave her the right dyke-debonair look.

Titania and Oberon's first entrance was staged as a B-movie confrontation between two rival gangs. Backed by the song "Some Enchanted Evening" and partially obscured by a fog machine effect, Titania descended the balcony stairs as Oberon crossed the proscenium to "ill meet" her on the dance floor. We assigned both the fairy King and Queen bands of merry gay followers: Titania was surrounded by four actors dressed in jeans, leather jackets, and various ACT-UP and Queer Nation T-shirts, along with whistles, chains, and safe-sex paraphernalia. Their movement motif was a kind of aggressive tap dance, best illustrated later in their musical theater–style dance to Madonna's "Material Girl," which they offered as Titania's lullaby.

Oberon's fairies were conceived as a somewhat adulterated version of the cultural feminist analogy in gay male culture, called the Radical Fairies. These three performers (who were also double cast as Theseus, Hippolyta, and Egeus) wore neo-Grecian tunics and tights adorned with chunky fake fruit. Oberon's fairies moved in a flowing, narcissistic camp style inspired in part by Isadora Duncan. The effort to mix movement vocabularies and metaphors was intentional, as we didn't want to fix this subcultural gay bar forest space into a singular, idealized identity.

We took the opportunity to extend the production's topicality around issues of sexuality and performance by transforming Bottom into an ass represented by Senator Jesse Helms. Played with broad verve and a kind of intelligent thickness by Dora Lanier, Bottom reappeared after his transformation wearing a T-shirt titled "Know

Your Assholes," which bore an image of Helms, and a two-dimensional head mask in Helms's likeness. When our drag queen Titania fell in love with Bottom in his new garb, the implied parody of Helms's homophobic, antisex, antitheatrical crusading was quite fun.

When the Athenian lovers hit the forest, their transformation from heterosexual and gendered convention began. On Helena's "treat me as you would your spaniel" speech to Demetrius, Puck snapped his fingers, and the ACT-UP fairies blew their whistles to halt the action. Gazing at Helena's supplicating, supine figure, Puck said, in lines actor David Richards wrote himself: "This lame and dominant sexist vision needs a quick and bold revision. Fairies, revise."

Helena was rescued from the ravages of her rigid gender role and its compulsory heterosexuality by the ACT-UP fairies, who handed her a leather jacket and graciously took her part, taking turns playing at the masquerade of femininity. They also assumed Demetrius's role, to keep the construction of gender unstable and spinning. Constructions of gender, sex, and race were passed on with the Balinese half-masks that now represented Helena and Demetrius.

When the lovers fall asleep and are returned by daylight to their "natural tastes," Helena is once again a biological woman, but Demetrius, her obscure object of desire, is now a biological woman as well, and their love is lesbian. Hermia and Lysander are approved to be wed, over Theseus's and Egeus's prior objections, which in our production had something to do with the fact of Lysander's race. We cast Philip Effiong, a Nigerian student, in the role, playing opposite Krista Bourquein, a white Hermia.

Our parodic, multivocal production ended with a reminder, as Judith Butler might encourage, of the costs of gender transgression.[3] Cloaking the graveyard speech at the play's end in references to AIDS and sexual repression, Puck sounds a cautionary note, implying that, while our theater has been a liberated laboratory, there are still high cultural costs for interrupting the stylized repetition of gender acts.

Working on *Midsummer*, after years of writing about desire in performance, allowed me to reexperience it in the theater. Each night I sat at the bar and watched the show. I gazed and watched other people gazing, watched male and female actors perform for the many gazes that circulated in that production, all sexualized and particularized in ways I can't presume to know. I saw some spectators who couldn't look, mostly young white men who were daunted and embarrassed when Titania uncovered his rhinestone bra, walked right up to them, and directly invited them to gaze. But our production opened up a condition of visibility in which many gazes could be born and worn. We offered an invitation to look and to be looked at, knowingly and pleasurably, to look at the performers, to look at one another, to look at the possibilities.

It's not as important to me now, at least in the educational, academic theater context in which our production took place, that the visible correspond with some underlying identity—for instance, that a lesbian play a lesbian or that a gay man play a drag queen—but that these positions *be visible* in representation. Not under the plodding character psychologies of realism, but as performed possibilities. Most of our cast was heterosexual, perhaps, but after the production I think most of them understand their sexuality as a choice, not as a natural birthright.

At a public discussion of the production a lesbian from the Madison community complained that she didn't see any real "dykes" in the production, only straight women playing at it. One of the more earnest young cast members misunderstood her point and responded: "But I was gay. When I came out for the disco number, I was gay." And that's exactly the point. This young performer, probably for the first time in her life, wanted to be seen as a lesbian. Given the history of my own theorizing, I should have been unsettled by this exchange. After all, a straight woman was assuming the place I once might have insisted be saved for a "real," "live" lesbian body with its specific, material, perhaps visual markings. But in the context of theatrical pedagogy my allegiance was with the performer, who learned and desired to make visible somewhere on her own body a sexuality that representation usually elides. I learned that making these subject positions visible was more important to me than who inhabited them.

We often worked in workshops and rehearsals on the *gestus* of gender impersonation by devising gendered scales of behavior and talking about how to use and discard cultural stereotypes. But we never directed people how to play sexuality. I wanted those who played across sexualities to find their own comfort in their own bodies, somewhere around the locus of their own desire. The effort was to embody what perhaps you can't know, rather than to testify to what you do know—and that's partly how we gave desire free reign.

For me one of the most compelling moments in the many representations of desire encompassed by the production was Titania and Oberon's reconciliation, which we staged as a dance. Professor John Staniunas choreographed a steamy, Bob Fosse–style number to Sylvester's bluesy, suggestive song, "In the Cool of the Evening." Titania peeled off her leather jacket, flashed his black bra, and put on Oberon's jaunty felt hat. Oberon took off his jacket, tossed away Titania's whip, and then unbuttoned her own shirt and tied up its tails, revealing her own lacy white bra. Watching them dance their seductive reconciliation, I didn't care if I was watching two heterosexuals, a lesbian and a gay man, two men, or two women. I was seduced by the pleasure of the visual, by a luscious, fog-surrounded, theatrically lit moment in which my own desire was simply invited to project what it wanted (literally) across many layers of the constructed artifices of gender and sexuality.

Perhaps the theater really is the place to reinhabit subject positions that seem evacuated by theory, because it creates a space of danger without quite the same consequences, a space of play and potential. Maybe this can be a place to start. For many years I've been starting with the theory. I think for awhile I'm going to start with the theater.

NOTES

1. I first heard Diamond use this term in her lecture "Hystericizing Brecht," at the University of Wisconsin–Madison, March 30, 1990.

2. See Andrew Ross, *No Respect: Intellectuals and Popular Culture* (New York and London: Routledge, 1989).

3. See Judith Butler, "Performative Acts and Gender Constitution: An Essay in Phenomenology and Feminist Theory," in Sue-Ellen Case, ed., *Performing Feminisms: Feminist Critical Theory and Theatre* (Baltimore: Johns Hopkins University Press, 1990), particularly 273 and 278. See also Butler's *Gender Trouble: Feminism and the Subversion of Identity* (New York and London: Routledge, 1990) for further elaboration of the punitive consequences of "failed" gender performances, and for many of the theoretical ideas that informed our production of *A Midsummer Night's Dream*.

Chapter 8

"Lesbian" Subjectivity in Realism: Dragging at the Margins of Structure and Ideology

When lesbian subjectivity became part of the feminist theoretical discourse, discussions about its construction were located staunchly in an alternative performance tradition. The postmodernist, camp, collectivist performances of Split Britches and the WOW Cafe became the space of debate on the radical implications of lesbian desire's disruption of conventional paradigms of spectatorship. The lesbian work at WOW is very specific about the audience it addresses—an ad hoc lesbian community culled mostly from its East Village New York neighborhood.[1] The lesbian subcultural context and mode of production often make these performances illegible to the heterosexual reader/spectator.[2]

But partly because of the increased theoretical writing on lesbian performance, the work has gained a notoriety that enhances its marketplace value. As lesbian work is brought out of its marginalized context and traded as critical currency in heterosexual academic and theater venues, the question of the performance's "readability" becomes complicated.[3] What does it mean for lesbian texts to circulate on the heterosexual marketplace? Is a lesbian performance transported to a heterosexual context readable, or is it illegible because it is inflected with subcultural meanings that require a lesbian viewer to negotiate? Is the intentional obtuseness of its postmodern structure frustrating for the uninitiated spectator? Which is more frustrating, its lesbian content or its postmodern form? If lesbian performance is now being created for mixed audiences, will the new context prompt a return to more conventional forms and their meanings?

These questions raise the issue of realism's efficacy as a political strategy in lesbian representation. My task here is to return to realism, which has been eclipsed by the postmodern performance work in discussions of lesbian representation. My theoretical project is to explore how lesbian positions are constructed under realism's formal constraints and to answer revisionist feminist critics who suggest that dabbling in traditional forms might be an effective method of insinuating social change. The realist plays examined below cross a historical spectrum, from plays written by heterosexuals for heterosexuals to those written by lesbians and performed in lesbian, alternative, and mainstream venues.

These texts also address the theoretical problem of constructing lesbian subject positions. Much of the work on lesbian subjectivity in representation has been deconstructive, pointing to the possibilities of the lesbian position as excessive to representation's conventional codes. But in the process of deconstructing representation the lesbian subject position within it was unwittingly posited as essential and whole, unproblematized in the transcendent, unified position it had assumed. Teresa de Lauretis, in a 1988 *Theatre Journal* article, took the next step in the theoretical debate by explicitly deconstructing the lesbian subject position into a heterogeneous site of differences.[4]

The most politically and theoretically appropriate lesbian subject position now seems to be a deconstructive one. But the term *lesbian* seems evacuated, its meaning eternally deferred. For theorists who would continue to write from within a lesbian position—if only provisionally, and if only one among many—the challenge becomes to reconstruct lesbian subject positions without reinstating essentialisms. While theorists teeter between the deconstructive possibilities and the essentialist problems of writing on lesbian subjectivity, representations of lesbians in realism continue to construct their conditions of objecthood.[5] The realist structure offers unhappy positionalities for lesbians, the ideological inflections of which are crucial to mark. My project, then, includes an investigation of how realism constructs the term *lesbian*.

Realism and the Case for Readability

Janelle Reinelt, in a historical overview of feminist theory and performance, describes the first phase of feminist criticism as one that believed optimistically that realism "seemed capable of reflecting the 'true' (her)story of women's lives in a direct, unmediated manner."[6] Those were halcyon days, when the project of feminist criticism seemed simply to agitate for more positive images of women within traditional theatrical forms. Since then the Marxist critique of representation, as well as poststructuralism and postmodernism, has been pressed into service for feminism to explode the notion of coherent texts whose transparent language is capable of projecting a stable meaning.

The "new poetics" have thrown into doubt the project of inserting a feminist agenda into the realist guise.[7] "Unmediated" realism has since been theorized as a site in which ideology intervenes in a very material way to inflect the meanings of the text. The mystification of the author, and his or her singular authority over the construction of meaning in the text; the position of the spectator as the competent interpreter of the realist text; and the mimetic function of realism as a mirror that truthfully records an objective social portrait, have all been analyzed as elements of the pernicious operation of a form with dire consequences for women.[8]

Materialist feminist performance critics have profited from Catherine Belsey's work on classical realism, in which she states, in a much quoted passage:

> Classical realist narrative . . . turns on the creation of enigma through the precipitation of disorder which throws into disarray the conventional cultural and signifying systems. . . . [T]he story moves inevitably towards closure which is also disclosure, the dissolution of enigma through the re-establishment of order, recognizable as a reinstatement or a development of the order which is understood to have preceded the events of the story itself.[9]

The events that precede the story are the authorized narratives of the dominant culture, and the enigma that disrupts the social order is usually one that threatens its ideological fabric. As Jeanie Forte remarks, "In light of this definition, it becomes evident that classic realism, always a reinscription of the dominant order, could not be useful for feminists interested in the subversion of a patriarchal social structure."[10]

Forte, however, questions whether subversive texts in turn "give rise to politicized action on the part of the newly constructed reader."[11] She suggests that, because of its structural recognizability, or "readability," realism might be able to politicize spectators alienated by the more experimental conventions of nonrealistic work. Forte cites Terry Baum's and Carolyn Meyers's lesbian revue, *Dos Lesbos*, as a case of "pseudo-realism." By tempering its realism with Brechtian distancing and foregrounding strategies, Forte feels the text is able to thwart the ideological impositions of the traditional form.

Forte chooses *Dos Lesbos* to illustrate how its pseudo-realism might move spectators away from homophobia, but her own heterosexist ideology slips out in the moments of textual overstatement that belie the seamless argument of her text.[12] Forte says the play's "ribald humor . . . endears the audience to the characters, who are then able to communicate some of the not-so-humorous problems for lesbians to a sympathetic audience."[13] Such a formulation positions the audience as charitable toward lesbian pathos.

Forte goes on to propose that the "realist elements serve to promote enough illusion of 'real experience in the real world' . . . that the audience can identify (in a manner which has been culturally conditioned) with [the lesbian characters] as people who are just trying to achieve a measure of happiness."[14] Forte's point actually illustrates that the realist elements in *Dos Lesbos* threaten to elide the lesbians' difference from the heterosexual norm.

The play's realist elements construct them as palatable only if they can be seen as humorous, pitiful, or as no different from heterosexuals. In fact, Forte says, "Many readers find *Dos Lesbos* somewhat palatable, even if the content disturbs them, precisely because of its relative readability, its quiescent realism."[15] The readability Forte champions for realism makes difference acceptable only by constructing it as sameness. Lesbians disappear under the liberal humanist insistence that they are just like everyone else. Difference is effectively elided by readability.

Rather than the deconstructive possibilities of the lesbian position provided through critical theory, bourgeois realism reinstates the unitary, transcendent lesbian caught in a binary opposition with heterosexuality. Realism is not recuperable for lesbian theorists, because its ideology is so determined to validate dominant culture that the lesbian position can only be moralized against or marginalized. The lesbian subject most readable in realism is either dead or aping heterosexual behavior.

Lesbian Positions in Heterosexual Realism

To explore the pernicious effects of bourgeois realism on the lesbian subject, a comparison of significant texts at contrasting historical moments will be useful. John Clum's work on gay male drama makes a distinction between plays written from an "outside/heterosexual" and an "inside/homosexual" perspective that can be transposed productively to a lesbian setting.[16] Lillian Hellman's *The Children's Hour* (1934) is written from outside of lesbian experience. The text is paradigmatic of the manner in which the structural codes of realism operate to mark and finally purge the lesbian enigma from its bourgeois, moral midst. On a superficial level the narrative describes the emotional and economic ruin of two young women teachers by a psychopathic student who accuses them of lesbianism. The realist structure, however, damns Martha Dobie as an unsettling influence even before the lie about her sexuality has begun to circulate.

Hellman's description of the Wright-Dobie School for Girls presents the inevitable drawing room that demarcates the bourgeois family boundaries in which realism lodges its moral dilemmas. In the first scene Martha's eccentric aunt, Mrs. Mortar, instructs the girls in sewing and elocution.[17] Mrs. Mortar's flamboyant behavior is a parody of proper femininity, but the scene exemplifies the domestic normalcy in which these girls are inculcated before the threat of perversion disrupts their lives. Mary's entrance marks the first disorder in this otherwise socially regimented scene. Her dishonesty about her whereabouts and her easy manipulation of Mrs. Mortar's affections establish her as morally impure and frighteningly powerful, instituting the binary opposition of goodness and evil that frames the realist plot.

The presentation of the structural enigma, however, occurs with Martha's entrance. Hellman quickly establishes Martha's displeasure with her partner's, Karen's, pending marriage to Dr. Joe Cardin. The playwright loads her stage directions with subtext that implicates Martha as "unnatural": "MARTHA: (*Looking at [Karen].*) You haven't talked about marriage for a long time" (15). The binary "natural and unnatural" is set up alongside that of good and evil, as Karen responds impatiently to Martha's fears, "For God's sake, do you expect me to give up my marriage?" (16). Heterosexuality is naturalized and unassailable.

The discourse of heterosexuality is further authorized by Cardin's entrance. He has stopped on the way to the school to look at a bull a neighbor recently bought and predicts, "There's going to be plenty of good breeding done in these hills" (16). His proximity to animal procreation casts him as a virile, if domesticated, man whose marriage to Karen will be equally (re)-productive. Late in act 2, Cardin is again inscribed within a natural, reproductive site, when he tells his aunt, Mrs. Tilford, "We're getting the results from the mating season right about now" (45). When he loses his resolve to marry Karen after the trial, Cardin's manhood seems deflated by the authorized verdict of "unnatural" sexuality that taints his procreative scene.

Since Martha rarely gets to speak for herself throughout the play, her motivations and emotions remain accessible to the spectator only through other characters' interpretations. Her silenced position invites spectators—with their longing for information and their desire to know encouraged by the play's realism—to side with the narrative constructed against Martha. Although Mrs. Mortar has been established as an unreliable source of information, the spectator is able to believe her insinuations about Martha's sexuality through witnessing Martha's earlier emotionally ambivalent scene with Karen.

When Mary fabricates her story for Mrs. Tilford, she is able to persuade her grandmother of its truth by harping on Mrs. Mortar's reading of Karen and Martha's "unnatural" relations. Mrs. Tilford insists Mary "stop using that silly word" (37), but clever Mary knows she is making progress when she senses her grandmother's fear. Whispering her description of the alleged sexual crime into the older woman's ear, Mary doesn't even understand herself, but the spectator, directed by Mrs. Tilford's response, is voyeuristically invited to imagine the horrors of a lesbian encounter. The scene, which is never named aloud, is unraveled for their disapproval, and for their prurient interest. In a climate of sexual repression imagination breeds pornography.

Truth and justice weave their way through *The Children's Hour* thematically but also serve as tropes for its realist structure. If there is an enigma in realism, its structural shape is bent toward unraveling and expunging it. Evil young Mary functions as a metaphor for the inexorable push of realism toward knowing and ordering its truths through the discourse of power. Mary's power at the Wright-Dobie School, for example, comes from her ability to collect and use information. People's secrets become fodder for her manipulations.

Mary is somewhat aligned with Martha in the text's two binary systems. She is evil incarnate, and, given the gendered ideology the play authorizes, Mary's aggressive, manipulative behavior seems vaguely masculine. Mary is bad because good girls don't act as she does. But her pathological evil is contained at the narrative's end, easily managed compared to Martha's unnatural affections. Good and evil are familiar oppositions, but the threat of sexual perversity threatens not just moral probity but also the heterosexual base of an economic system badly shaken by the 1930s stock market crash and ensuing depression.

Martha's position threatens Karen and Cardin's heterosexual emotional and economic union. In effect, after the trial Cardin will be forced to marry both women. Persuading Martha to stay with him and Karen, he says, "You stay with us now. . . . I'll buy you good coffee cakes and take you both to Ischl for a honeymoon" (65). To spectators in the 1930s the prospect of supporting two women must have been perceived as daunting and worked to convince them of Martha's status as an albatross.

In her final scene with Cardin, Karen tries to retain her place in heterosexual discourse, claiming she can have a baby like everyone else (68). But the taint of lesbianism makes her a social outcast until after Martha's death, when the possibility of a heterosexual reunion is reinstated. Mrs. Tilford insists, "You must go back to [Joe]." Karen protests but admits "Perhaps" when Mrs. Tilford amends, "Perhaps later, Karen?" (77).

Martha, on the other hand, is allowed no such resurrection. She internalizes the guilt thrust on her by the culture. "I've got to tell you how guilty I am," she pleads with Karen. " . . . I couldn't call it by a name." (71). The social sphere gives her a name by which she acquiesces to the ideological pressure of her unnaturalness and dies. The enigma is purged and the social order reinstated.

Martha's story could be read, through a 1980s perspective, as the tragic isolation of a lesbian forced to deal with her sexuality through the distortions of the dominant culture. But such a literal reading too easily remains on the level of plot and does not adequately indict the form that narrates Martha's position. Martha merely fulfills the requisites of the realist plot, which is to create truths that serve its ideology. The play is not Martha's play and is not accurately about lesbianism.[18] The realist structure inscribes Martha as the problem to be purged. Her death is inevitable and serves the order of morality that informs the play's structural movement. The lesbian position is a convenient, expedient pawn in a narrative that insists on its own moral justice.

The realist structure's manipulation of the lesbian position becomes more complex in Frank Marcus's *The Killing of Sister George* (1965). Although the play falls within Clum's "outside" designation, its subcultural references and focus mark it more explicitly as a "gay" play.[19] The death of the lesbian is metaphorical in this case, since the lesbian position is carved into two levels through which representation itself intervenes.

Sister George is a character in a BBC radio drama located in the fictitious community of Applehurst, which exemplifies the traditional values of English life.[20] Some of the text's tension derives from the implosion of representation and reality, shaded by the irony of loyal Sister George's "real life" as a monstrous butch lesbian named June Beckwith. June fears for the life of Sister George, who is in fact eventually killed off from the series because her ratings have dropped. The dominant culture, represented by the BBC's Mrs. Mercy Croft, intervenes in June's personal life to reclaim her infantilized lover Alice—called "Childie"—back into the bosom of the family life that the BBC radio program enshrines. June is eventually punished and ostracized by the disjuncture between her real and representational lives, left loverless and drunk.

Alice and June's relationship is described as butch-femme, not through the definitions of a lesbian community that throws gender enculturation into spin but, rather, through the censoring, moralizing eye of the heterosexual mores the relationship is constructed to imitate.[21] June/George expresses her masculinity through vicious sadomasochistic power plays. The binary operative alongside good and evil in Marcus's play is that of masculine and feminine behaviors as inscribed over female sexuality. George, the butch, is described as cruel, evil, and irredeemable because her masculinity is a perversion of heterosexual manhood and of femininity. Alice is allied with dominant cultural values—she gets up before dawn to queue up for ballet tickets—and is described as appropriately feminine. Her sexuality is ambivalent; George casts aspersions on Alice's ability to faithfully refrain from liaisons with men. The possibility of her return to heterosexuality threatens George's hegemony.

Mrs. Mercy's intrusion into this distorted domestic scene displaces George into the enigma position, and, with Mrs. Mercy as the narrative agent of dominant cultural values, the text moves inexorably toward George's exile from the social order. Mrs. Mercy creates the narrative of Sister George's death—"leave it to the BBC, we know best" (381)—and refuses June the pleasure of revealing herself as the character's creator, since "that would spoil the illusion" (382).

Since June is robbed of Sister George, whose persona is June's only entry into dominant discourse, she is pushed closer and closer to her metaphorical social death. Mrs. Mercy offers to resurrect June Beckwith in a children's series called "The World of Clarabelle Cow," in which June would play the title role (403), but the halfhearted effort to recuperate June into femininity fails.

Once again the lesbian is positioned as external to the discourse of dominant culture by the realist structure. Sister George mounts her motorbike—an ironic reference to lesbian subculture—and is hit by a truck. June listens to Sister George's radio death with a morbid fascination. The fictitious community and the BBC's listeners mourn Sister George, while the actor who played her sits alone mooing plaintively. Marcus describes her final utterance as "a heart-rending sound" (411), painful since June cannot enter the role dominant culture has marked for her, and is therefore purged from it. The social order is restored, and June/George joins Martha in the graves of the dispossessed.

The play's subcultural references and its levels of gendered characterization could be read as referring ironically to constructions of both gender and sexuality in a heterosexual culture. But the vicious portrait of the butch lesbian makes such a revisionist reading difficult. *The Killing of Sister George* premiered in the United States in 1966, before the Stonewall riots of 1969 had begun the public uprising of gay liberation. The lesbian plays discussed below are located in the post-Stonewall ideology of the gay liberation movement and are inflected by the growing influence of the second wave of U.S. feminism. Both movements reconfigure the position of the butch lesbian.

But, when described through realist plays written in the mid-1970s, her narrative position remains consistent with the marginalized, immoral place constructed for all lesbians in the "outside" texts.

Lesbian Subjectivity and the Exiled Butch

Historians John D'Emilio and Estelle Freedman describe the radical contours of the early movement for gay liberation, citing tracts that launched attacks against the restrictive gender and sexuality assignations of the nuclear family. "Coming out" became the gay liberation movement's rallying cry, an act of "public avowal" that would help gay men and lesbian women "shed much of the self-hatred they had internalized."[22] Coming out, inflected with feminism's intersection of public choices and personal politics, represented "not simply a single act, but the adoption of an identity in which the erotic played a central role."[23]

The assertion of the erotic for lesbians became taboo when liberal feminism's analysis was imposed on lesbian existence in the early 1970s. "Sensitive to the reaction that the [feminist] movement was eliciting in the minds of Americans," D'Emilio and Freedman write, "many feminists sought to keep the issue quiet, to push lesbians out of sight."[24] The homophobia of liberal feminism prompted lesbians to splinter into separate groups, which combined an analysis of gender and sexuality oppressions.

The modifying adjective *feminist*, however, tended to focus the new lesbian analysis on gender and away from alternative descriptions of sexuality. While the new radical lesbian feminists identified their sexual practice along a continuum of "woman-identification," the butch-femme behavior that marked lesbian subcultures in the 1950s and 1960s was erased and moralized against.[25] By the mid-1970s the sexual lesbian who engaged in butch behavior as a subcultural resistance to the dominant culture's gender and sexual ideology was silenced by feminism, her transgressive sexual desire "femininized" through the woman-identification that neatly elided active sexuality as a precondition for lesbianism.

At the same historical moment D'Emilio and Freedman document that the "gay movement adapted to the times, for the most part pulling back from its radical critique of the effects of sexual repression and instead recasting itself as a movement in the long tradition of

American reform."[26] The focus on transgression shifted to one on equal civil rights. Rather than asserting the radical difference of their lives and their critique, gays began to insist they were like everyone else and could imitate the heterosexual model in same-sex couples.

In such a setting the butch lesbian retains her difference and presents a dangerous threat to heterosexual, gay-assimilationist, and lesbian-feminist ideology. The butch in lesbian realist plays inflected by these ideologies remains ghosted as an anachronism from an un-enlightened time whom feminism has been unable to recuperate. Her isolation and the moral judgments launched against her by other characters place the butch in the position once defined for all lesbian subjects by heterosexuality. She becomes the enigma to be purged from the lesbian realist text.

Jane Chambers's A Late Snow (1974), for example, is a lesbian identity play inflected with the complementary demands of gay liberation as civil rights and early feminism's notion that the personal is political but not sexual for lesbians.[27] The play takes place in a secluded cabin at which, through a contrived series of events, a literature professor named Ellie is forced to scrutinize her alliances with four other women.

The realist narrative constructs Ellie's ex-lover, Pat, as a masculine, sexually rapacious, disruptive influence, a woman who is constitutionally incapable of maintaining a monogamous relationship. Pat's five-year relationship with Ellie dissolved when an affair Pat was having ended in tragedy and the other woman was killed. Chambers's choice to embed the butch in such a melodramatic narrative helps to elicit a moral stance against Pat. Not only is she an inveterate womanizer and a violent drunk; she is also guilty of manslaughter.

Quincey, Ellie's new lover, is a much younger woman to whom Chambers assigns the rhetoric of gay liberation. "Somebody has to make change happen," she intones. "Somebody who believes in the goodness of themselves and what they are" (306). Quincey insists that Ellie come out as the only proof of her self-love. Ellie argues, through pre-Stonewall knowledge, that she arrived at her sexual identity within a different historical era: "When I was your age, 'lesbian' was a dictionary word used only to frighten teenage girls and parents. Mothers fainted, fathers became violent, landlords evicted you, and nobody would hire you. A lesbian was like a vampire: she looked in the mirror and there was no reflection" (308).[28] Chambers sketches a continuum of lesbian identities inflected by history and slowly shifts each character toward the public avowal and self-acceptance gay liberation and liberal feminism demand be inscribed within monogamous relationships.

Only Pat is left at the far end of the continuum as irredeemable. The text's dim view of nonmonogamous sexuality allows Ellie to accuse Pat of hating women and hating herself (302). Compared to the romanticism of Ellie's relationship with Quincey and her budding attraction to Margo, Pat is staunchly pragmatic. All her anniversaries are celebrated on the same day, the date of which corresponds to the first three digits of her social security number (286). Her choice of gender roles is also pragmatic. "I never wanted to be a woman," sne says. "It's a crappy thing to be" (323). While her mobster father traveled the world, Pat watched her mother's circumscribed domestic life play out among babies, laundry, and groceries. Pat prefers the independence and mobility of a life that, for a pre-Stonewall, pre-feminism lesbian, could only be theorized as butch.

Chambers strains to win reasoned sympathy for Pat's choices but is ultimately swayed by the exigencies of the realist form and its production context. Pat remains the embattled transgressor in the context of a polite skirmish for equal lesbian rights, and the realist structure exiles her to the margins of its moral center. Happily riding off into the sunset of its liberal humanist ideology, *A Late Snow* leaves Pat adrift.

Last Summer at Bluefish Cove (1980) distances the nascent feminism that serves as the agent of the butch's demise in *A Late Snow*.[29] The text focuses on a lesbian community in which women are paired across age and class lines. Difference is implicit in their couplings. But Lil, the butch, remains the sacrificial victim of this realist text. Because she is dying of cancer, the narrative allows more sympathy for Lil's position, but it also insists on recuperating her into monogamy before she dies.

Bluefish opens on an inscription of Lil's butchness within her fishing expertise. Dangling her pole by the water, Lil seduces the fish:

> I see you circling down there. . . . [I]f you were a person, you know what we'd call you? A C.T. You nuzzle the bait but you don't put out. Now, I'm going to try a different approach, it's called courting. You're going to love it. . . . You're a terrific look-

ing fish, you know that, sweetheart? You're a real knockout. Now, don't get me wrong, it's not just your body I'm after. I love your mind, your sense of humor, your intellect, your politics. . . . I respect you, darling. I love you. Now bite, baby, bite. (8)

Lil is obviously adept at seduction, and even this one, witnessed by Eva, the unwitting heterosexual, is successful. Lil and Eva fall in love.

Months before her death Lil is ready to settle into what the dominant culture constructs as a legitimate relationship. She tells Eva: "I love you more than I have ever loved anyone. For the first time in my life, I understand why knights road miles to slay a dragon for their lady's hand" (77). Lil's butch aesthetic is still tinted with a chivalric code, but she is seduced into accepting the discourse of monogamous love. Eva's coming out story, however, prevails over the narrative, and Lil's death becomes the necessary precondition to Eva's independence.

If Chambers mourns the butch's passing in *Bluefish Cove*, she resurrects her in her last play, *Quintessential Image* (1983).[30] The play is the most self-referential of Chambers's work, referring directly to the realist conventions that dominate and control her early texts. The short piece is set in a television studio, in which cameras and monitors loom over the scene, providing layers of constructed representations.

Margaret Foy, a superficial, self-involved talk show host, has invited award-winning photographer Lacey Lanier to be interviewed. The presumption of a studio audience allows Foy to address the spectators in the theater directly, and the levels of spectatorship become implicit in the play's production of meanings. Enormous enlargements of Lacey's photographs, which appear to capture key moments in American history, hang on the set. The interview eventually deconstructs the images into the scene lurking like a palimpsest behind their creation; each image captures Lacey Lanier's failed attempt to photograph Belinda Adams, a woman she loved unrequitedly most of her life.

As Chambers focuses more directly on lesbian representation, the liberal and radical feminist analysis imposed on her earlier plays disappears. Lacey Lanier—with her wild hair, sensible shoes, "no-nonsense appearance," and tough vulnerability (3)—is Chambers's resurrection of the butch lesbian back into the center of her own narrative. Her moment in the studio is a failed attempt to reconstruct her lesbian truths. The eye of the culture pervades the set, and, through the closeted Margaret Foy, enforces its readings of her work, keeping her lesbian desire safely exiled from the frame.

Representation becomes a trope in the play, which allows Chambers to comment on the dominant culture's manipulation of images and the ideology they bear. Foy explains that the interview can be cut and edited, and she interpolates editorial remarks throughout her exchange with Lacey about which of the photographer's comments will be retained and which excised. Lacey eventually realizes that her appearance on television may be as misunderstood as her photographs and insists, "I don't want you clipping moments out" (17).

Trying to circulate her story from within dominant discourse, however, proves difficult, as Lacey learns that the image of herself on the tape can in fact do "something different" than she is doing (9). Lacey learns the tape is not strictly mimetic but constructs her position in a discourse over which she has no control. But, as she exits the set, Lacey goes off not to die, mute and marginalized, but to share the narrative of her life with Foy's lesbian lover, who wants to write a book about Lacey.

Only by commenting on the ideological codes of dominant representation can Chambers reconstruct a lesbian position outside of radical or liberal feminist ideology. *Quintessential Image* allows Chambers to break productively from the realist, Hellmanesque model of her earlier plays, in which bourgeois realism's inevitable moralizing finds its target in the transgressive butch lesbian.

These examples of lesbian realist plays follow the legacy of *The Children's Hour* and *The Killing of Sister George*, which epitomize the position of lesbians in realism as marginalized and moralized against by the narrative structure that surrounds them. The lesbians who survive in realism are the ones who look straight, who don't spin the sign system into the excess of butch-femme or other subcultural transgressions of sexual display. While lesbian performance in the postmodernist style works at constructing what has been called a "collective subject," realism isolates, marginalizes, and sometimes murders the lone lesbian, whose position is untenable.[31] The lesbian subject in realism is always singular, never adequately a site of the differences between or among lesbians, never described within the divided identity of the deconstructive mode.

A challenge for lesbian theory in the 1990s will be to reconstruct a tenable lesbian subject position outside of realist moralizing and somewhere between deconstruction and essentialism. Elin Diamond calls realism mimesis at its most naive, positivist moment and argues that it can be detached from the pernicious effects of its truth-value to "suggest ways in which feminist practitioners might avail themselves of realism's referential power without succumbing to its ideological conservatism."[32] Diamond argues that, rather than dismissing mimesis, feminism should "militate for the complex, different referents we want to see, even as we work to dismantle the mechanisms of patriarchal modeling."[33]

Reconstructing a variable lesbian subject position that will not rise like a phoenix in a blaze of essentialism from the ashes of deconstruction requires emptying lesbian referents of imposed truths, whether those of the dominant culture or those of lesbian radical feminist communities that hold their own versions of truth. The remaining, complex, different referent, without truth, remains dependent on the materiality of actual lesbians who move in and out of dominant discourse in very different ways because of their positions within race, class, and variant expressions of their sexuality—dragging at the margins of structure and ideology.

NOTES

This article was written during a July 1989 residency at the Wolf Pen Women Writer's Colony in Prospect, Kentucky, funded by the Kentucky Foundation for Women. The residency was shared with Sue-Ellen Case, Elin Diamond, Janelle Reinelt, and Vicki Patraka, with whom I engaged in continual discussion around the issues I am presenting here. Their insights ghost my own in this article, and their inquiries always provoked me. I am indebted to them for the support and encouragement they provided in the context of this writing. I am also indebted to Sallie Bingham for making our residency possible, and for the supportive, stimulating atmosphere she provided for feminist theoretical thinking.

1. For work on the history of the WOW Cafe, see Alisa Solomon's "The WOW Cafe," *Drama Review* 29, no. 1 (1985): 92–101. See Jill Dolan, *The Feminist Spectator as Critic* (1988; reprint, Ann Arbor: University of Michigan Press,

1991); Kate Davy, "Reading Past the Heterosexual Imperative: *Dress Suits to Hire*," *Drama Review* 33, no. 1 (1989): 153–70; and "Constructing the Spectator: Reception, Context, and Address in Lesbian Performance," *Performing Arts Journal* 10, no. 2 (1986): 74–87; and Sue-Ellen Case, "From Split Subject to Split Britches," in Enoch Brater, ed., *Feminine Focus* (Ann Arbor: University of Michigan Press, 1989), for writing on Split Britches and the WOW Cafe as well as the issue of lesbian desire and representation.

2. See Davy, "Reading Past the Heterosexual Imperative," for a discussion of *Dress Suits for Hire*, in which she argues that the semiotics of lesbian representation is intentionally organized to thwart heterosexual readings. Davy proposes a somewhat essentialist position for the lesbian performers in the piece, and Case, in a letter to the *Drama Review* ("A Case Concerning Hughes," *TDR* 33, no. 4 [Winter 1989]: 10–17), reads it as Shepardesque, transposing traditional tropes of the Old West to a lesbian context without radically changing their meanings. The question of this piece's legibility to heterosexual audiences is an important tangent to the discussion of lesbian realism that follows here. Additional debates about its production venues are set forth in the above cited issues of the *Drama Review*.

3. The performance narrative and production context of Holly Hughes's latest solo piece, *World without End* (1988), is somewhat revealing in this regard. In "Polymorphous Perversity and the Lesbian Scientist," (*Drama Review* 33, no. 1 [1989]: 171–83), an interview with Hughes, Rebecca Schneider remarked that Hughes's piece is "in some ways flavored by the recent appearances of lesbian theatre before more diverse audiences" (172). The mix of heterosexual and lesbian spectators might be the condition that allows Hughes to bring her bisexuality out of the closet in *World*. The piece is a long, autobiographical monologue about Hughes's relationships with her mother, other women, and men. Her usual maniacal, unpredictable stage presence is exchanged for the high-heeled, prettily dressed, lugubrious politeness of the family drama. Her adamant flaunting of her "polymorphous perversity" (173) constructs her as sexually autonomous but, in the process, unmoors her from the lesbian community that fostered her early work. Hughes has been domesticated by her own bisexual, bourgeois narrative.

4. Teresa de Lauretis, "Sexual Indifference and Lesbian Representation," *Theatre Journal* 40, no. 2 (1988): 155–77. See also de Lauretis, "Issues, Terms, Contexts," in de Lauretis, ed., *Feminist Studies/Critical Studies* (Bloomington: Indiana University Press, 1986), 1–19.

5. The notion of "objecthood" evolved in discussions with the women at Wolf Pen about the deconstructed lesbian position and the pitfalls of "strategic essentialism." I am indebted to them for their observations.

6. Janelle Reinelt, "Feminist Theory and the Problem of Performance," *Modern Drama* 32, no. 1 (1989): 48.

7. See Sue-Ellen Case, *Feminism and Theatre* (New York: Methuen, 1988), particularly chapter 7, "Towards a New Poetics," 112–32.

8. Sue-Ellen Case, for example, in "Toward a Butch-Femme Aesthetic" (in Lynda Hart, ed., *Making a Spectacle: Feminist Essays on Contemporary Women's*

Theatre [Ann Arbor: University of Michigan Press, 1989]), proposes that realism is deadly for women: "The violence released in the continual zooming in on the family unit, and the heterosexist ideology linked with its stage partner, realism, is directed against women and their hint of seduction. . . . the closure of [the] realist narrative chokes women to death and strangles the play of symbols, the possibility of seduction. . . . Cast realism aside—its consequences for women are deadly" (297).

9. Catherine Belsey, "Constructing the Subject, Deconstructing the Text," in Judith Newton and Deborah Rosenfelt, eds., *Feminist Criticism and Social Change: Sex, Class and Race in Literature and Culture* (New York and London: Methuen, 1985), 53, quoted in Jeanie Forte, "Realism, Narrative, and the Feminist Playwright—A Problem of Reception," *Modern Drama* 32, no. 1 (1989): 116.

10. Forte, "Realism, Narrative, and the Feminist Playwright," 116.

11. Ibid., 117. See also Laura Kipnis, "Feminism: The Political Conscience of Postmodernism?" in Andrew Ross, ed., *Universal Abandon? The Politics of Postmodernism* (Minneapolis: University of Minnesota Press, 1989), 149–66, in which, in the context of a complex discussion, she argues against modernist countercinematic practice as a political program in terms similar to Forte's argument for realism: "If the analysis of scopophilia in dominant cinema produces remedial cultural practices whose only audience is the traditional audience of high culture, it seems to suggest somehow luring the masses to *Riddles of the Sphinx* as a future political program" (156).

12. This description of the overstatement of realist narratives belying their ideological base is borrowed from Vivian M. Patraka, "Lillian Hellman's *Watch on the Rhine*: Realism, Gender and Historical Crisis," *Modern Drama* 32, no. 1 (1989): 128–45.

13. Forte, "Realism, Narrative, and the Feminist Playwright," 118.

14. Ibid., 118.

15. Ibid., 119. She goes on to argue that the readability of realism might produce a political response in some spectators by allowing them to recognize similar life experiences and raise their consciousness about difference. Recognition, however, might be problematized as an adequate precondition for political action and as effective feminist dramaturgy. Helene Keyssar, for example, in *Feminist Theatre* (New York: Grove Press, 1985), proposes that recognition is key to traditional dramatic theory and that perhaps transformation is the benchmark of the new feminist drama (xiii–xiv).

16. John Clum, "'A Culture That Isn't Just Sexual': Dramatizing Gay Male History," *Theatre Journal* 41, no. 2 (1989): 169–89. The inside versus outside distinction is helpful but also threatens a reinstatement of the essentialism that lurks when writing about marginalized communities. Because a lesbian writes from within the marginalized experience, are her truths "authorized" and therefore essentialized? This is a theoretical problem to worry about at another time, but one that hovers on the margins of my text nonetheless.

17. See Lillian Hellman, *The Children's Hour*, in *Six Plays by Lillian Hellman* (New York: Vintage Books, 1979). All other references will appear in the text.

18. Hellman insisted the play was about a lie, not about lesbians.

19. See William Hoffman's introduction to his edited anthology *Gay Plays* (New York: Avon, 1979), in which *The Killing of Sister George* is described as "probably the most famous play about lesbians ever written" (xxxviii).

20. Frank Marcus, *The Killing of Sister George*, in William Hoffman, ed., *Gay Plays*, 340–41. All other references will appear in the text.

21. See Case, "Toward a Butch-Femme Aesthetic," for a feminist theoretical discussion of butch-femme behavior in social and performative settings.

22. John D'Emilio and Estelle B. Freedman, *Intimate Matters: A History of Sexuality in America* (New York: Harper and Row, 1988), 322.

23. Ibid., 323. Coming out still plays a crucial thematic role in lesbian realist dramatic literature, although, eventually, the focus on such a transitional moment within the realist text traps the lesbian in a negative relation to heterosexual culture and disallows a full exploration of alternative lifestyles and sexuality. *Dos Lesbos* (see Terry Baum and Carolyn Meyers, *Dos Lesbos*, in Kate McDermott, ed., *Places, Please! The First Anthology of Lesbian Plays* [Iowa City: Aunt Lute, 1985]), for example, worries the issue of coming out at work and in the family so exclusively that the oppressions of the dominant culture outweigh the pleasures of lesbian life. Jane Chambers's *Last Summer at Bluefish Cove*, discussed below, although focused within a Long Island lesbian community, is distracted by Eva's coming-out story, her transition away from heterosexual choices. Sarah Dreher's *8 × 10 Glossy* (in McDermott, ed., *Places, Please!*) displaces its lesbian feminist heroine's traumas to solicit empathy for her married sister Julie and her divorced friend Dana, who are contemplating a lesbian affair. The coming out story, as represented in the realist tradition, is a fait accompli, the problem resolved, the deed completed by the narrative's end. Such a formulation elides the fact that, for most lesbians, coming out narratives lack closure, since the dominant culture operates under a heterosexual assumption that forces lesbians to continually reassert their resistant identities.

24. D'Emilio and Freedman, *Intimate Matters*, 316.

25. See Adrienne Rich, "Compulsory Heterosexuality and Lesbian Existence," reprinted in Ann Snitow, Christine Stansell, and Sharon Thompson, eds., *Powers of Desire: The Politics of Sexuality* (New York: Monthly Review Press, 1983), 177–205, for a radical feminist analysis of lesbianism as woman-identification. Case, in "Toward a Butch-Femme Aesthetic," writes that "the middle-class upward mobility of the lesbian feminist identification shifts the sense of community from one of working-class, often women-of-color lesbians in bars to that of white, upper-middle-class, heterosexual women who predominated in the early women's movement" (285). She also points out that the "ghosting of the lesbian subject" in feminism is a result of moralizing crusades such as the antiporn movement (284). See also Dolan, "The Dynamics of Desire: Sexuality and Gender in Pornography and Performance," *Theatre Journal* 39, no. 2 (1987): 157–74, for writing on the relationship between lesbian subjectivity and pornography.

26. D'Emilio and Freedman, *Intimate Matters*, 323.

27. Jane Chambers, *A Late Snow,* in William Hoffman, ed., *Gay Plays,* 281–335. All other references will appear in the text.

28. See Sue-Ellen Case, "Femimesis," an unpublished paper presented at the New Languages for the Stage conference in Lawrence, Kansas, October 1988, for a recuperation of vampire mythology in the context of lesbian representation.

29. Jane Chambers, *Last Summer at Bluefish Cove* (New York: JH Press, 1982). All other references will appear in the text. Kitty Cochrane, for example, the famous feminist in Bluefish Cove, is constructed as self-serving and self-righteous, her rhetoric belied by her life. Her best-selling book is a feminist tract in which she encourages women to "seize their sexuality" (18), but her fame requires that she keep her lesbianism closeted, since "the public is not ready" (27) to see it disclosed.

30. Jane Chambers, *Quintessential Image* (MS., 1983). See also Case, *Feminism and Theatre,* 78–79; and Dolan, *Toward a Critical Methodology of Lesbian Feminist Theatre* (Master's thesis, Performance Studies Department, New York University, 1983), for further analysis of the play.

31. See Case, "From Split Britches to Split Subject"; and Reinelt, "Feminist Theory and the Problem of Performance," for theories of the collective subject.

32. Elin Diamond, "Mimesis, Mimicry, and the 'True-Real,'" *Modern Drama* 32, no. 1 (1989): 61, 68.

33. Ibid., 62.

Chapter 9

The Body as Flesh: Or, the Danger of the Visual

Given the increasingly conservative political climate of this country, contestations over the meaning of images have never seemed so key to the maintenance and subversion of hegemony. Because the National Endowment for the Arts (NEA) distributes the funds that validate artistic images meant to represent some universal notion of the "American people," it has become an easy target for the right-wing ideologues who seek at all costs to control the country's representations. The protection of home, hearth, and above all the family demands that any image that challenges such values be erased from human vision, memory, and history.

The Jesse Helmses of the United States aren't the only ones legislating representation from ideologically, morally, and ethically righteous positions. Feminist communities, too, perpetuate their own censorship, dictating what can be seen, by whom, and why. For Helms it's Mapplethorpe's gay male sexuality that must be repressed from view; for cultural feminists lesbian sadomasochism (s/m) cannot be imaged or even imagined. Every movement needs a scapegoat to relieve its anxieties about difference.

Nothing is new about this debate over images and obscenity, but the furor over NEA funding has particular resonance right now for feminist theater studies. Our theory has encountered what Sue-Ellen Case calls the "essentialist vs. post-structuralist strife and stall," and what I have called the tension between deconstruction and reconstruction.[1] After several years of rigorous analysis of oppressive representations and the manner in which they marginalize gender, race, class, and sexuality differences, the logical next move is to theorize the construction of new representations that place the marginalized in the center of discourse. But, although poststructuralism and post-modernism have provided useful deconstructive tools, neither seems able to offer a reconstructive method, a road map to representations that will allow even provisional subjectivities to be expressed. Moving into a reconstructive moment requires taking what has been called the "risk of essentialism," to image identities that *must* be seen, both to be subversive and to survive.[2] But the problem is simple: What will those images and identities look like? Can we really construct "new" images, or can we only wrest new meanings from old ones?

In her engagement with the NEA debates, my colleague Peggy Phelan issues a provocative challenge. She writes:

> The art community must articulate the connection between vigorous artistic expression and the values of democracy. It must return again to some unfashionable but powerfully felt connections between artistic images and the moral imaginations of their viewers, and it must stress that every piece of art is part of an ongoing conversation with the history and future of the human imagination.[3]

Phelan's polemic stirs me but troubles me simultaneously. I am stirred by a call back to a system of belief, however fraught and destabilized, able to connect images with a productive moral imagination. This call returns to the meaningfulness of artistic expression and its effect, rather than a commitment to the deferral of its meaning and its context. But I'm troubled by the power inflections that surround the "morality" of the "democratic" imagination. For example, I have written favorably of lesbian sadomasochistic representations and explicit lesbian pornography as examples of sexual fantasy and practice that image gender and power in potentially disruptive ways. My hope is that lesbian porn and s/m can reinhabit old images with new subversions. But, if our task is to reclaim the moral power of images, whose morality can imagine anything like the excess evoked by violent exercises of power that elicit equally violent expressions of pain, all conducted for mutual pleasure? How can lesbian sadomasochism remain anything but amoral, beyond redemption, and therefore exiled from vision?

I think Phelan is imagining another moral system, one that could

accommodate these images and perhaps not define them
and therefore in need of redemption. But, if we're going to trade in
questions of morality, I propose that we need to look closest at images
that most disturb us, to address whose interest morality serves. The
NEA argument, as Phelan says, "is actually an argument about sexualities and their expressions," tinged with moral indignation over
sexuality differences from the fundamentalist Right.[4] The cultural
feminist arguments over lesbian s/m sound similar; s/m sexuality is
considered so immoral that some cultural feminist commentators suggest interfering with the civil rights of its practitioners. Reviewing the
1982 anthology of writings called *Against Sadomasochism*, Claudia Card,
for example, writes, "What *kinds* of rights should *anyone* have with
regard to s/m? . . . *Is* it justifiable to interfere with others' self-destructiveness on the ground that theirs is a product of or contributes to
self-destructiveness in others?"[5] Card and other writers in the anthology favor denying lesbian sadomasochists' civil rights to save them
from themselves. This language of redemption seems a logical extension of such moralizing.

Morality and sexuality are closely linked and regulated through
their representation, especially during moral panics like the one grip-
ping this country, which variously scapegoats obscenity, pornography, homosexuals, and people with AIDS, along with other so-called
sexual deviants. Gayle Rubin says, "Moral panics are the 'political
moment' of sex, in which diffuse attitudes are channeled into political
action and from there into social change."[6] She goes on to say that
"moral panics rarely alleviate any real problem, because they are
aimed at chimeras and signifiers. They draw on the pre-existing discursive structure which invents victims in order to justify treating
'vices' as crimes."[7] The struggle, once again, is discursive—who
wields the power to infuse which representations with what kinds
of moral judgments.

In the cultural feminist scene what seems most abhorrent about
lesbian s/m representation is the pleasure taken in sexual images of
power and pain. Cultural feminism insists on a kind of gender purity
(and I use that word quite intentionally, aware of its historical resonances with racial purity) that damns any intrusive connotation of
maleness. S/m practice is considered rigidly gendered. In her review
of *Against Sadomasochism* Card says the book argues that "s/m is misogynist whether practiced in same-sex or in opposite-sex relation-

ships, consensual or not, and regardless of who plays the 'woman.' "[8] The masochist is inevitably associated with powerlessness and victimization that is inevitably associated with women.

Psychoanalytic feminists have begun to theorize masochism as a kind of control. Linda Williams, in her work on s/m film pornography, suggests these films inscribe the masochist's power over the narrative.[9] But can the image of powerlessness, historically associated with women, be changed in a new historical and social context? Can the iconography of s/m be read differently when its meanings are traded by differently gendered and sexual agents? Lesbian s/m representations demand new readings of symbols whose history bear certain uncomfortable connotations. Symbols of pain, for example, like whips and restraints, reappropriated to a lesbian s/m context, become signs of pleasure and unbridled passion that, perhaps ironically, liberate the body on which they inflict such intense pressure. Symbols and practices that might be chilling or humiliating in "real life," because they are bound by fantasy and representation, take on new meanings.

But many of s/m's critics object to its use of symbols such as swastikas, with their incontrovertible historical connotations. Card points out that, in *Against Sadomasochism*, Susan Leigh Star asks "to what extent it is possible for individuals, or small groups, to determine the meanings of a symbol, such as a swastika," and she concludes Card goes on to say, "that 'change in symbolic meaning is possible only with a corresponding change in material conditions' and adds that she will feel willing to renegotiate the meanings of swastikas only when anti-Semitism no longer threatens Jewish existence."[10]

This raises a thorny issue, especially for me as a Jew. I, too, cannot look at a swastika without a rush of threatening associations with the history of my culture, which remind me that the safety I currently, apparently enjoy might be illusory. But what does such an argument imply, by extension? That certain symbols are claimed by history, caught there in a totalitarian and totalizing interpretation of their meaning? What does such a verdict portend for the disruption and reconstruction of meanings? And how can resistance be possible if power, as an effect of meaning, is always fixed? The swastika is a most emotional example, but all symbols are inherently powerful to someone.

Jon Erickson addresses this problem of symbolization and ownership in a recent *Theatre Journal* article, describing flag burning and other desecrations of our nation's preeminent sign of patriotism as "acts of transgression against the sacred status of a symbol 'owned' by the people who pay it respect and even die for it."[11] Erickson's argument unfortunately sinks into a kind of endless postmodern repetition of a stealing back and forth of meaning, which deemphasizes the very material power struggles that mark such raidings. But his observation that the appropriation of symbols into different contexts ridicules the ideological status of their original meaning and transfers their ownership is worth pondering. "To make something that belongs to others your own," Erickson writes, "you must transgress, that is trespass, across those boundaries separating what is yours from what is theirs. I make it mine, so the effectiveness that your meaning gives to it is devalued. This doubleness is at the core of both parody and travesty: the ridicule of authority."[12]

In some ways one could argue that lesbian s/m practitioners have stolen the signs of female gender that cultural feminism insists it stole from patriarchy and rearranged and complicated the question of gendered ownership, since it seems the sign of the feminine is partly what's at stake in the rift between these lesbian factions. If symbols are defined by contextual ownership, as Erickson argues, lesbian s/m should be a simple case of title transfer. But symbols and meanings are never transferred without a struggle in discourse that has crucial political, ideological, and historical investments, weighted differently across the balance of power. Cultural feminists, for example, are quite invested in reading signs of power and pain inscribed over female bodies as manifestations of male oppression, rather than female pleasure. These signs are caught up in a historically bounded system of language, but their exchange also has material effect, made most evident when they intrude on the body, as they do in lesbian s/m.

S/m advocate and author Pat Califia performs an appropriation of symbols and meanings that acknowledges their material attachment to human bodies, in marked contrast to Erickson's game of "capture the flag." Califia's definition of "macho slut," the textual figure honored by her latest collection of pornographic essays, extends the property metaphor back to the body, where perhaps, at least for women, it belongs, and makes very material the discursive struggle in which she engages. Califia writes,

Macho sluts are supposedly a contradiction in terms, like virgins and whores. The slut is, in [Andrea] Dworkin's parlance, male property . . . a woman who accepts male definitions of her sexuality. Instead, I believe she is someone men hate because she is potentially beyond their control. Whores are always accused of being lesbians because they get men to part with some of their property instead of becoming property themselves. . . .[13]

This property is unavailable for reappropriation.

And of macho, the other half of the contradictory lesbian s/m subject, Califia writes: "Someone who has machismo insists on his rights to dignity and defends himself and what belongs to him. . . . Women are not supposed to have machismo, to be macho, but then, we're not supposed to be sluts, either, and without machismo, a slut is just a commodity."[14] The juxtaposition of the two signs sets up a contradiction that empowers the lesbian s/m subject to move into new territories of meaning. The macho slut will protect the meaning she has wrested for herself and her symbolic property and refuse the incursions of those who, like Erickson and other clever postmodernists, would simply put her back into endless circulation.

The macho slut foregrounds the unleashed physicality of her body, its pain and pleasure, wrestling it away from domestic romantic propriety. Elaine Marks writes: "To undomesticate women would mean to change the relationship between nature and culture and seriously alter the configuration of culture as we know it. This can only be realized through the creation of images powerful enough to impress themselves on the reader's mind and to resist the pressures of misinterpretation."[15] The violence of the s/m macho slut is necessary to withstand her reabsorption into a commodity culture.

But who can inhabit such images, and who can look at them? And what does this macho slut look like? (Although I wonder why that's important to know. Would it be much more interesting if she couldn't be recognized?) On the cover of Califia's book she is a woman dressed in leather and chains, kneeling before the open fly of a person of indeterminate gender, also dressed in leather. Behind her stands another woman in a leather skirt, wearing fishnet stockings and knee-high boots, whose stiletto heel is balanced in the kneeling woman's waist. The sepia photography appears ripped, just at the place in the image where their faces would be. Is this the image that will stir its viewers to moral imaginings?

Like the cover image, Califia's stories are rough going. Their obsessive attention to detail reduces them to a chronology of bodily cavities and functions, but the images they evoke are seering. In her story, "The Calyx of Isis," for example, a woman is brought, in a leather body bag, to the dungeon of a women's bar and sex club, where eight sadists (or top) women are invited to torture her. The woman, Roxanne, is thus able to prove her devotion to her master, a woman named Alex. The eight tops inflict all sorts of extreme pressures on Roxanne's body; among other things they whip her and fist her and pierce her body with rings.

In Califia's crafting of this story the eight tops seem distinct, at first, but gradually their distinguishing characteristics fade, and all that remains is their actions. Roxanne, too, becomes reduced to a mere receptor. Her only access to agency is to express her response, which authenticates their actions. The characters Califia writes devolve into bodies in action or reaction, nearly undistinguished by sex or by gender. What's left appears to be the body as flesh.

This, for Califia, is where truth resides. "I do believe the flesh should not be despised," Califia writes passionately. "If the flesh is not sacred, holy, then we are trapped in the muck of the profane, because the body is all we have. All knowledge, reason, truth, beauty, it is all reducible to physical sensation and actions performed by the agency of the flesh."[16] The truth of the flesh, for Califia, is accessed through the mediation of pain. Is this descent to the corporeal limits of the body a descent into essentialism? Perhaps. But, if so, it's eerily detached from essentialisms of identity. Califia's is not an essentialism of gender, or even of sexuality, but an essentialism of viscera, of biology detached from its external markings, of lubricated limbs and orifices. Yet it's an essentialism marked by history, if, as Joan Nestle insists, for gay people "history is a place where the body carries its own story."[17] Is this the essentialism we need to brook to reconstruct new images?

It seems significant that my example here is fiction, rather than theater or performance or more visual representations. In fiction the body can be imagined, trespassed and transgressed, but, ultimately, its corporeality is kept at bay. In Califia's stories the body is revealed, probed, stressed to the limits of its endurance, but only in the fantasy of the text, only in the mind's eye, in which such imaginings are unbound by everything but ideology, a mind's eye in which transgressions come easier. How can such violent bodies—or such violence to the body—be represented onstage? In visual representation the flesh can never be represented without gender and sexuality. The historical connotations of those terms continually trouble their transgressive reconstruction in representation.

Rubin reminds us that "obscenity laws enforce a powerful taboo against the direct representation of erotic activities. . . . It is one thing to create sexual discourse in the form of psychoanalysis or in the course of a morality crusade. It is quite another to graphically depict sex acts or genitalia."[18] For this very reason the violent lesbian s/m body must be represented, to explode the old images of gender and sexuality and to test the limits of what can be seen. By staging this body, the theater can present the explicit danger of the visual and, in the extreme discomfort prompted by looking, force people to define the morality that keeps them from seeing.[19]

NOTES

1. See Sue-Ellen Case, "Introduction," in her edited volume, *Performing Feminisms* (Baltimore: Johns Hopkins University Press, 1990), 7; and my article "'Lesbian' Subjectivity in Realism: Dragging at the Margins of Structure and Ideology," also in *Performing Feminisms*, 40–42.

2. See, for example, "The Essential Difference: Another Look at Essentialism," Naomi Schor and Elizabeth Weed, eds., *differences* 1, no. 2 (1988).

3. Peggy Phelan, "Serrano, Mapplethorpe, the NEA, and You: 'Money Talks,'" *TDR* 34, no. 1 (Spring 1990): 8.

4. Ibid., 13.

5. Claudia Card, "Review Essay: Sadomasochism and Sexual Preference," *Journal of Social Philosophy* 15, no. 2 (Summer 1984): 45. See also Robin Ruth Linden, Darlene R. Pagano, Diana E. H. Russell, and Susan Leigh Star, eds., *Against Sadomasochism* (East Palo Alto, Calif.: Frog in the Well, 1982).

6. Gayle Rubin, "Thinking Sex: Notes for a Radical Theory of the Politics of Sexuality," in Carole Vance, ed., *Pleasure and Danger: Exploring Female Sexuality* (New York and London: Routledge, 1984), 297.

7. Ibid.

8. Card, "Review Essay," 43.

9. See Linda Williams, *Hard Core: Power, Pleasure, and the "Frenzy of the Visible"* (Berkeley: University of California Press, 1989), especially chapter 7,

"Power, Pleasure, and Perversion: Sadomasochistic Film Pornography," 184–228.

10. Star, quoted in Card, "Review Essay," 43.

11. Jon Erickson, "Appropriation and Transgression in Contemporary American Performance: The Wooster Group, Holly Hughes, and Karen Finley," *Theatre Journal* 42, no. 2 (May 1990): 225.

12. Ibid., 226.

13. Pat Califia, *Macho Sluts* (Boston: Alyson Publications, 1988), 20.

14. Ibid. When I taught Califia's introduction to *Macho Sluts* in my Lesbian Culture course, some of my students pointed out that Califia had decontextualized the notion of machismo and failed to adequately connect her metaphor to the ethnic communities in which, for men, machismo works most importantly.

15. Elaine Marks, "Lesbian Intertextuality," in Marks and George Stambolian, eds., *Homosexualities and French Literature* (Ithaca: Cornell University Press, 1979), 372. Marks refers here specifically to Monique Wittig's *The Lesbian Body*, trans. David LeVay (Boston: Beacon Press, 1986).

16. Califia, *Macho Sluts*, 19.

17. Joan Nestle, *A Restricted Country* (Ithaca: Firebrand Books, 1987), 9.

18. Rubin, "Thinking Sex," 289.

19. I am indebted to Vicki Patraka for the term *danger of the visual*, which she suggested to me in our many discussions during the writing of this essay.

Chapter 10

Practicing Cultural Disruptions: Gay and Lesbian Representation and Sexuality

Consider these scenarios:

1. At an art gallery and performance space in downtown Milwaukee, a long table at the entryway is set with colorful mints and peanuts and pink napkins decorated with black-lined hearts and flowers that announce "Happy Anniversary Peggy and Lois." The festive tone announces a real anniversary framed as a performance called *Anniversary Waltz*, which celebrates the ten-year relationship of Peggy Shaw and Lois Weaver, cofounders with Deborah Margolin of the lesbian feminist performance troupe Split Britches. *Anniversary Waltz* combines bits of "classic" Split Britches performances with a smattering of new material, held together with vaudevillian patter about relationships. The piece purports to offer a look at lesbian longevity; instead, although it shifts through the lesbian-specific iconography of butch-femme relationships, it constructs an innocuous glimpse into a more generic notion of coupleness.

2. Theatre X, also in Milwaukee, mounts a production of Robert Chesley's *Jerker, or the Helping Hand*, a play whose structuring device is pornographic phone sex between two gay men, one of whom eventually dies of AIDS. The text describes scenes of nonconventional sexual fantasy that inspire both men to masturbate. But the performers never enact the sexual fantasies or the masturbation indicated by the text. Their bodies remain

clothed and untouched, as their encounters move from completely anonymous, graphically sexual calls, to a relational intimacy based on knowledge of each others' voices and yearnings.

3. The fourth annual Lesbian Variety Show in Madison, Wisconsin, is disrupted by two acts that employ butch-femme and sadomasochistic iconography. In the context of a mostly lesbian cultural feminist celebration of femaleness, actions that represent taboo sexual practice intrude on the Variety Show's worship of gender difference.[1] The transgressive performances are decried in the local feminist press as representations of violence against women, and guidelines are drawn up to guard against the inclusion of such images in next year's show.

In the cultural and political climate of the 1990s what do gay and lesbian representations like these mean? Do their meanings read as assimilative or transgressive, now that dominant regimes of power and knowledge are once again branding homosexual representations as pornographic and obscene? The National Endowment for the Arts' (NEA) recently released guidelines to artists seeking to receive or keep their funding rely on the Supreme Court's 1973 definition of obscenity in the *Miller v. California* decision. Obscenity is defined as work that: (1) the "average person, applying contemporary community standards, would find appeals to the prurient interest"; (2) that "depicts or describes sexual conduct in a patently offensive way," particularly—according to the NEA—homoerotic and sadomasochistic activities; and (3) that "lacks serious literary, artistic, political, or scientific value."[2]

This definition relies on the commonsense knowledge of a generic viewer to determine obscenity. Historically, this viewer most resembles the white, heterosexual, male senator from North Carolina, Jesse Helms, whose outcry over the Robert Mapplethorpe and Andres Serrano exhibits prompted the new language of censorship to be attached to all of the NEA's funding awards.[3] The determination of behavior considered "patently offensive" is based on the standards of his dominant cultural community. If gay or lesbian community standards were applied to test obscenity, and if the assumed spectator of artistic work were a lesbian or gay man, commonsense connotations of prurience would certainly shift.[4]

But, as the feminist antiporn movement exemplifies, the radicality of such a shift cannot always be assumed. Some commentators even point to "the complicity of the anti-pornography movement in the larger moral panic," which, in part, has prompted the renewed vigilantism over obscenity. As Daphne Read notes presciently, "It seems reasonable to fear that new legislation [developed by Catharine MacKinnon and Andrea Dworkin] aimed at censoring or regulating pornography might be used more broadly to repress gays and lesbians, artists, and others . . . in spite of a feminist presence in the political process."[5]

Foucault suggests that, throughout history, what appears to be the repression of sexuality actually proliferates the different ways in which it enters discourse, some of which resist hegemonic power.[6] Perhaps the regressive outlawing of gay and lesbian images as prurient and obscene will prompt the reradicalization of their meaning effects in the 1990s. Perhaps representations of gay and lesbian sexuality will regain their potential to disrupt hegemonic meanings by invoking the excess of sexual practice, after a brief period of neutralizing assimilation into the dominant discourse on sexuality as alternative lifestyles and identities.

The furious discussion promoted by the congressional compromise measure to Helms's proposed amendment to the NEA appropriations bill is focused on representations of bodies, desire, and spectatorial pleasure that transgress the boundaries of white heterosexual propriety. For instance, Mapplethorpe's pleasurable (though some say objectifying) citing/sighting of black male bodies in classically sculpted poses, often with penises erect, implies sexual practices anathema to the virulently racist and homophobic likes of Senator Helms. By offering homosexual and cross-racial visual pleasure in flesh, they visually flaunt a rejection of compulsory heterosexual practice.[7] Exhibited in galleries and museums, the photographs take public representational space to image eroticized organs that simply by virtue of being seen contest dominant cultural regimes of knowledge and power about sexuality and race.

The possibility for transgression in such representations lies in the hint of sexual practice and seduction they envision, not in the gay lifestyle to which they refer, which superficially has come to resemble the quotidian routines of heterosexual relationships. Teresa de Lauretis, writing on lesbian representation, cautions that it is exceedingly difficult to alter the "standard of vision, the frame of reference of visibility, of *what can be seen*," since "the conventions of seeing, and the relations of desire and meaning in spectatorship, [remain] partially anchored or contained by a frame of visibility that is still heterosexual."[8] As a result, most representations of lesbian and gay sexuality remain mired in realist images of lifestyle and identity that fail to exceed the heterosexual frame.

The representation of sex politics as lifestyle, prompted partly by the Personal Is the Political slogan of the early white feminist movement, has limited efficacy in a culture in which lifestyles are so easily assimilated, commodified, and neutralized by dominant ideology. African-American feminist theorist bell hooks suggests that the emphasis on identity and lifestyle in white feminism, for example, has contributed to the movement's elitism and defused its ability to move social discourse. hooks says, "To emphasize ... engagement with feminist struggle as political commitment, we could avoid using the phrase 'I am a feminist' (a linguistic structure designed to refer to some personal aspect of identity and self-definition) and could state 'I advocate feminism.'"[9]

Saying "I am a lesbian" has been validated in cultural feminist discourse as speech that breaks the silence of lesbian existence under heterosexual hegemony. But in the 1970s and 1980s lesbianism's too rigid attachment to an identity politics of gender by terms such as "woman-identification" re-closeted active sexual practice.[10] Cultural feminism reified same-sex female relationships as a new and better version of the heterosexual family, a claim that has limited potential for changing the dominant discourse on how sexuality organizes culture and experience.[11] *Anniversary Waltz*, for example, is ultimately an assimilationist lesbian text because of its emphasis on romance and familial relations rather than sexual ones.[12]

A somewhat idealized lesbian family anchors the text's narrative of the vicissitudes of Weaver and Shaw's relationship: their partnership is inscribed as a marriage, from the pink table napkins on display in the lobby to textual references to the now twenty-year-old daughter the couple raised. Although Weaver and Shaw mock the conventions of heterosexual marriage by "lesbianizing" the familiar, deprecatory popular cultural patter about such relationships, their own partnership, though played as camp, remains the somewhat romanticized center of the text.

When they began performing together in the early 1980s,

Weaver's and Shaw's personal and performative butch-femme role-playing lent the couple a certain notoriety.[13] The antisex rhetoric of cultural feminism made their butch-femme display of sexual possibilities and practice—informed by what appeared to be an appropriation of heterosexual and male-female gender roles—a transgressive representation in feminist and mainstream contexts.[14] Early productions at the WOW Cafe, where Split Britches primarily performed, were often decried in feminist media as politically regressive because they employed butch-femme iconography and role-playing.

But in *Anniversary Waltz* Weaver and Shaw play with butch-femme iconography and roles only by trading the costumes of gender evenly between them. As the piece progresses through bits of the couple's performative and personal history, they peel off layers of costuming to reveal the signs of the opposite role underneath. Their manipulation of butch-femme solely as clothing moves it away from the transgressions of its historical signification. Rather than referring to sexual practice, like the Mapplethorpe photographs, the images that constitute *Anniversary Waltz* focus resolutely on lesbian lifestyles. Under the rubric of a long-term relationship the transgressive difference of alternative forms of lesbian sexuality once represented by the complexity of butch-femme drops out. Its costumes become empty sets of gendered clothing without referents to sexual practice or more than the most polite, nostalgic evidence of desire.

Extending hooks's analogy to "I practice lesbian sex" (in all its varieties), rather than "I am a lesbian," would initiate a discourse that might displace the emphasis on lifestyles and relationships and break open the sanctimonious strictures of politically correct lesbian identifications. A renewed focus on marginalized sex acts, instead of romantic, familial relationships, might reassert the transgressive quality of lesbians who enter the public sphere as representations. De Lauretis's cautionary analysis ends by apparently suggesting that only butch-femme lesbians can enter, together, the heterosexual frame of vision.[15] Making sexual practice blatantly visible on gendered bodies that wear this deconstruction of compulsory heterosexuality might still be a productively alienating act.[16]

Such a move might indicate a return to historical definitions of "deviant" sexuality as acts, rather than people. Eve Kosofsky Sedgwick, for instance, writes that in histories of sexual taxonomy "the proscription of particular *acts* called 'sodomy' (acts that might be performed by anybody), [were] displaced after the late nineteenth century by the definition of particular kinds of *persons*, specifically 'homosexuals.'"[17] Emphasizing the individual person over sexual acts or practice available for performance by *any body* inscribes homosexuality and lesbianism as biologically essentialized problems of lifestyle, rather than as social practices that constitute sex acts accomplished with agency differently through history.[18]

The choice of sex acts is what mark gay and lesbian bodies as different agents within history. Judith Butler proposes, "As an intentionally organized materiality, the body is always an embodying *of* possibilities both conditioned and circumscribed by historical convention. . . . [T]he body *is* a historical situation [. . .] a manner of doing, dramatizing, and *reproducing* a historical situation."[19] In the 1950s, for example, lesbian bodies coded with butch-femme iconography represented a transgressive accomplishment—the naming and practice of lesbian desire in a violently heterosexist climate. Lesbians who represented themselves as butch-femme in the 1970s bore traces of its courageous history, as they refused to retreat to the closet built by feminism. Even lesbian bodies of the 1980s and 1990s, when visible in representation, retain traces of the history of butch-femme resistance to dominant ideology that can still be accessed as transgressive. The disruption it symbolized can be realized by actively representing the desire and sexual practice to which butch-femme once referred. As Joan Nestle remarks, "For gay people, history is a place where the body carries its own story."[20]

The Mapplethorpe debacle indicates that speaking homo- or lesbian-sex, as opposed to identity, in public forums is still transgressive enough to activate the machinery of state power. Even if, as Foucault cautions, such transgressions don't exceed the discourse on sexuality but only set the poles of one extreme, the sex practice to which they refer contest the hegemonic principles of sexual difference that heterosexuality reifies. Representations of sexual practice that deviate from heterosexual acts threaten pornographic excess at sites accustomed to inscribing sex only as erotic, romantic love according to a heterosexual model.

In her book on hard-core film pornography Linda Williams offers a useful working definition of pornography as "the visual (and sometimes aural) representation of living, moving bodies engaged in explicit, usually unfaked, sexual acts with a primary intent of arousing viewers."[21] Making visible gay male or lesbian bodies in motion, engaged in sex acts, is perhaps one most radical way to disrupt dominant cultural discourse on sexuality and gender. The "primary intent of arousing viewers" might inaugurate a theory of reception based very materially—instead of psychoanalytically—on an invitation to participate in the seduction of alternative locations of desire.

It could be argued, then, that representing any sex act publicly is transgressive. Williams, in fact, argues that explicitness will demystify what Foucault calls the transcendent secret of sex. I agree and intend to suggest that imaging gay and lesbian sex in the public sphere, rather than imagining it in the private, moves toward Foucault's notion of a different economy of bodies and pleasure.[22]

Some performance forms and contexts, however, seem more capable than others of accomplishing the "making seen" of such sexual practice. Homosexuality's assertion of the same can hardly be accommodated in bourgeois realism, for example, which asserts moral and sexual bipolarity—right/wrong, good/bad, and male/female—and maintains heterosexual difference as its organizing principle.[23] In his article on dramatizing gay male history John Clum organizes his textual explications by designating certain plays as either "outside/heterosexual" or "inside/homosexual" perspectives on gay subject matter.[24] But the "inside" gay male texts in Clum's analysis that use realism to inscribe their heroic lovers into discourse exemplify the dominant culture's inability to see or to image the marginalized sexual practice that at least partly girds a definition of homosexual identity. Clum's discomfort with defining homosexual identity solely as sexual practice, signaled by his article's title ("A Culture That Isn't Just Sexual"), leads him to argue in favor of the representation of gay lifestyles rather than gay sex.

Nestle suggests the reverse, insisting that, for gay men and lesbians, "being a sexual people is our gift to the world."[25] But traditional theatrical forms tend to work structurally to keep the sexual gifts of gay and lesbian subjects invisible. Even in the texts Clum examines as favorably exploring gay male identity, realism approves the male lovers' sexuality as moral and right because it's romantic, not physical, and usually rewards their celibacy with death. There's a move in these "inside" texts toward the "outside" perspective, which legislates that sexuality be heterosexuality or not be imaged at all.

For example, in the incipient realism of Martin Sherman's *Bent*

(1979) and Robert Chesley's *Jerker, or the Helping Hand* (1986), both of which Clum discusses in his article, sex is exiled to a nonphysical plane.[26] *Bent* opens on the day-after, postcarnal denouement of Max's one-night stand with a leather-clad Gestapo flunky. Their evening of anonymous sex, replete with intimations of s/m play, is implicitly punished when SS troops storm Max's apartment. The wilder side of gay male sex is tinged with amorality by its quick equation with Nazi terror.

The physicality of sex at least referred to in the first scene is then elided situationally by the play's content. Once he is interred in a camp Max and Horst, the gay man he meets there, are constrained to verbal sex, the possibility of physical union eternally deferred by the watchful eyes of the guards. The men's surreptitious exchanges serve as a trope for the way realism operates on marginalized sexuality. Under the eyes of the dominant culture gay male sex must be expressed furtively, described but not performed, and must culminate in orgasms of affirming emotional love rather than physical transport—that is, erotics rather than pornography.

Williams suggests that the distinction between erotics and pornography—often posed by both dominant culture executors like the Meese Commission as well as by antiporn feminists, who too frequently travel similar ideological terrain—is loaded with moralizing that stifles a more productive inquiry into the representation of sex:

> The very notion of erotica as "good," clean, non-explicit representations of sexual pleasure in opposition to dirty, explicit pornographic ones is false. . . . The one emphasizes desire, the other satisfaction. Depending on who is looking, both can appear dirty, perverse, or too explicit. . . . We need to see pornography in all its naked explicitness if we are to speak frankly about sexual power and pleasure and if we are to demystify sex.[27]

Privileging erotica over pornography is particularly troubling in gay and lesbian representations, since the nonexplicitness of erotica continues to mask the difference of gay and lesbian sex. Likewise, realism helps formally to repress references to active sex, cloaking bodies and pleasure under a domestic guise of romantic propriety. Pornography exceeds realism by lifting the cloak to reveal the action; its explicitness offers material investigations into the discourses of power as well as pleasure.

Chesley's *Jerker*, since it's less realist than *Bent* at the outset and marks itself as explicitly pornographic, at first holds out potential to represent transgressive sexual practice in a radical way. *Jerker, or the Helping Hand* is subtitled, "A Pornographic Elegy with Redeeming Social Value and a Hymn to the Queer Men of San Francisco in Twenty Telephone Calls, Many of Them Dirty." First performed in 1986, the text is marked by the constrained sexuality of a community plagued with AIDS. The play confines its graphic descriptions of sexual practice to literally disembodied phone sex between two gay men, never performing their fantasies to set in motion the pornography of desiring, visible, moving homosexual bodies. Although they never meet, Bert and J. R. fall in love over the phone shortly before Bert dies of AIDS. The move toward an ill-fated romance disqualifies *Jerker* as pornography, because, as Williams says, paraphrasing Susan Sontag, porn is never primarily about the formation of a couple.[28]

Jerker's subversive potential lies in the ten or so phone calls before its descent into empathy for the loving and the dead. The phone calls begin as completely anonymous and aggressively sexual, almost clinical descriptions of sometimes sadomasochistic sex play. But the calls progress to an intimacy that makes the sex scenes they describe emotional, erotic, and relational, rather than pornographic. The fantasies culminate in J. R.'s fairy tale about three men who simply sleep together and don't have sex at all.

Theatre X's 1989 production of *Jerker* chose several Brechtian techniques to resist the text's pull toward theatrical and ideological convention. A male narrator was placed at a table behind the bifurcated set, from which he read aloud the stage directions. The directions throughout the published text indicate that the men literally "jerk off," although their erections, given realism's politesse, are carefully hidden under their bedclothes or their underwear. The two actors playing J. R. and Bert for Theatre X were fully clothed through the entire play, and, although they verbally announced their orgasms, they never touched their bodies. Often the performers' actions resisted the instructions read from the text.

Such a Brechtian intervention worked on the representation of gay male sexual practice in several ways. First, it quite literally refused to embody it by maintaining the distance of intellectual description. The fantasies related by J. R. and Bert were relegated even farther from physical inscription in representation because they remained narrative and even their orgasmic effects went unimaged. The inversion of the Brechtian *gestus* to nonshowing, nonaction, perhaps exemplified gay male social relations in the age of AIDS—sex relegated to telephone technology and history, imagination and nostalgia, and exiled, still, from representation.

Second, while gay male sex was verbalized in the Theatre X production, by choosing not to visualize it, the production suppressed the transgressions of pornography in favor of erotics and failed to actualize pornography's disruptive potential. Enacting the culminating masturbatory orgasms of *Jerker*'s sex fantasies might have been a more radical transgression of the ethical bourgeois performance space, less aesthetic than the critical distance imposed by even the Brechtian frame. The noninteraction of the performers would have adequately maintained the commentary on the isolation of sex bound by AIDS.

Because of its ideological and formal movement away from pornography into erotic realism, *Jerker* fails as a truly radical explication of gay male representations of sexual practice. But few lesbian texts come to mind that at least match *Jerker*'s frank descriptions of sex. The characters in Jane Chambers's and Sarah Dreher's realist plays, for instance, fall in and out of romantic love, but they rarely engage in anything more sexual than a hug or a kiss.[29]

Lesbian sexual practice remains repressed in these plays by the exigencies of propriety—both of the dominant culture and of the lesbian cultural feminist discourse on sexuality. The distinction in lesbian cultural feminism between erotics and pornography is marked by the iconographic representation of power on female bodies. Hegemonic antiporn feminism has so successfully infiltrated lesbian discourse in the 1980s that even erotica has been flattened out and carefully monitored for any evidence of politically incorrect sex practice. As Foucault might observe, however, such regimes of power seem inevitably to breed resistance. The 1980s also saw the "implantation of perversions" within lesbian communities.[30] The new visibility of sadomasochistic practices and representational styles seemed to replace butch-femme as the location of cultural feminist anxiety over imagining or imaging sexual practice between women.

But while "avant-garde" lesbians begin to textualize practices that cultural feminism still decries as pornographic, representing s/m as sexual style is still read as a violent invasion of lesbian cultural feminist erotic images. The fourth annual Lesbian Variety Show in Madison, Wisconsin, exemplified the friction between these opposing discourses. The Variety Show is a product of the city's lesbian cultural feminist community, whose demography is best generalized as young, middle-class, and white. In 1989 the show's preferred representations of the eroticized feminine body were disrupted by the intrusion of representations of gender, power, and sex that its context could only inscribe as pornographic.[31]

The first half of the Variety Show presented poets and musicians who crooned lesbian love verse in repetitive rhythms and equally repetitive chords. The cultural feminist-inspired ethos of "woman spirit" hung in the air like a musky mist, and spectators generally applauded the acts of empowering verbalization and sometimes interpretive movement that celebrated the erotics of femininity.[32]

Two back-to-back acts in the second half of the show broke the aura. In the first two women performed a lip-synch and dance routine to the rock song "Push It," by a group called "Salt 'n' Peppa." As the song began, one woman entered wearing a black leather vest, jeans, boots, and handcuffs at her waist, lip-synching and snapping her fingers to the beat. The lip-synching liberated this act from the naturalized cultural feminist representational economy in which the Variety Show had been trading, into a gay male performance tradition in which dressing up in gender roles and impersonating singers has a long subcultural history.[33] Suddenly, the Variety Show's folk-style, feminine aesthetic was disrupted by a large gay woman in butch clothing, furiously moving her lips to a rock song.

Rather than Weaver and Shaw's innocuous trading of gendered clothing, this act used its leather and lace to tease out the seduction of butch-femme as sexual roles. When the first woman's partner entered the stage, the butch-femme dynamic, and all of its class connotations, was secured. The second woman wore high-heeled black shoes, fishnet stockings, and only pasties on her breasts. She danced into the space to seduce the first woman, and the two acted out the song in a way that referred to sexual practice as it hadn't been before during the long evening. The sheer display of their bodies, layered with butch-femme and vaguely s/m iconography, inscribed the act within bar dyke culture, outside the hegemonic meanings of middle-class white feminism.

The next act outdid the transgressions of the first. In a much more stylized performance that quoted the conventions of body-building contests as well as gay lip-synch spectacles, two women powerlifters performed an interpretation of Barbra Streisand's song "Prisoner." The pun was intended, since the act's content included relatively explicit references to s/m.

As in the first act, bodies were present here in full force, clearly sexualized and also genderized, an admission of difference that the staunchly feminine show could not contain. At the opening of the act one woman stood facing the spectators with her arms crossed over her bare chest, wearing black jeans, black boots, a black watchcap, and mirrored sunglasses. As the Streisand song began, she flexed her quite well-defined muscles in a display that flattered her V-shaped body. Uncrossing her arms revealed her breasts as small flaps of skin; the practiced, constructed power of her body seemed to have tampered even with her biology. Femininity was startlingly absent.

Her partner, wearing a white tank T-shirt, cut-off jean shorts, and the ubiquitous black boots, knelt at her feet in apparent supplication. The two began a dance of sorts in which they posed and manipulated the power dynamic their bodies described. When the woman in shorts produced a studded collar and offered it to the woman in the mirrored sunglasses, indicating she would like to wear it, the audience booed loudly, and the performers broke their severe demeanor and laughed. Once the collar was fastened around the kneeling woman's neck, the one in mirrored sunglasses pulled her into sexualized positions of dominance and submission.

At the song's end, however, the power dynamic abruptly shifted as the kneeling woman rose to her feet and picked up in her arms the woman with mirrored sunglasses, who waved coyly to the audience and was carried off. The abrupt shift seemed to intend parody and also, for those willing to read it, offered a political meaning about the fluidity of power positions in sex and perhaps in gendered relationships and representation as well.

This act proved a radical disruption of a safely eroticized female space, by transgressors who performed sexual seduction through a complex assumption and deconstruction of gender roles inflected with power. For some lesbian spectators, myself included, the scene was clever and seductive, a reference to the "variety" of lesbian sexual practice. The performers' obvious self-consciousness seemed to intend the kind of playful discussion about lesbian sexual potential launched by proponents such as Susie Bright. But the scene has been described in the Madison radical feminist press as a pornographic act of violence against women. Newspapers for months after the event carried emotional outpourings that testified to the suffering this act caused. Relying on what Williams calls "naive realism," spectators claimed the images of so-called violence actually caused violence to be inflicted.[34]

As Williams suggests, after Walter Kendrick, pornography is really only defined by its censorship.[35] While Jesse Helms legislates against publicly funded displays of gay male sexuality in representation, the lesbian cultural feminist community perpetrates its own censorship by legislating the correct representations of lesbian sex. Imaging the explicit relationship between power, gender, and sex offends cultural feminist propriety.

Writing about sadomasochistic heterosexual pornography, Williams comments that, in art, "real sex, like real death, is unaesthetic and therefore out of place."[36] Because gay male or lesbian sex is completely out of place—unimaged, unimagined, invisible—in traditional aesthetic contexts, the most transgressive act at this historical moment would be representing it to excess, in dominant and marginalized reception communities. The explicitness of pornography seems the most constructive choice for practicing cultural disruptions.[37]

NOTES

1. Although some commentators feel the designation "cultural" is inappropriate, because it allows this brand of feminism apparently to corner the market on culture, Alice Echols's distinction between this more recent strain of feminism and the radical feminism that preceded it in the late 1960s and early 1970s is most persuasive. See Echols, *Daring to Be Bad: Radical Feminism in America, 1967–1975* (Minneapolis: University of Minnesota Press, 1989).

2. See William H. Honan, "Endowment Tightens Obscenity Rule," *New York Times*, July 11, 1990, B3.

3. For an excellent discussion of the political issues raised by the Mapplethorpe and Serrano exhibits and a chronology of the events surrounding the NEA censorship debates, see Peggy Phelan, "Serrano, Mapplethorpe, the NEA, and You: 'Money Talks,' October 1989," *TDR* T125 (Spring 1990): 4–15. *American Theatre* has also detailed the controversy in its government coverage over the past year.

4. For a cogent, poststructuralist feminist explication of the ideological implications of commonsense knowledge, see Chris Weedon, *Feminist Practice and Post-Structuralist Theory* (London and New York: Basil Blackwell, 1987), 75–80.

5. Daphne Read, "(De)Constructing Pornography: Feminisms in Conflict," in Kathy Peiss and Christina Simmons, eds., with Robert A. Padgug, *Passion and Power: Sexuality in History* (Philadelphia: Temple University Press, 1989), 282, 281.

6. See Michel Foucault, *The History of Sexuality*, vol. 1: An Introduction (New York: Vintage Books, 1980).

7. See, for example, Robert Mapplethorpe, *Black Book* (New York: St. Martin's, 1980). For an excellent reading of the intersecting racial and homosexual implications of Mapplethorpe's photographs of African-American men, see Kobena Mercer, "Skin Head Sex Thing: Racial Difference and the Homoerotic Imaginary," in Bad Object-Choices, eds., *How Do I Look? Queer Film and Video* (Seattle: Bay Press, 1991), 169–222.

8. Teresa de Lauretis, "Sexual Indifference and Lesbian Representation," in Sue-Ellen Case, ed., *Performing Feminisms: Feminist Critical Theory and Theatre* (Baltimore: Johns Hopkins University Press, 1990), 33, 35.

9. bell hooks, *From Margin to Center* (Boston: Beacon Press, 1984), 29.

10. This history of lesbian suppression under both radical and cultural feminism is now well documented. See, for example, Echols, *Daring to Be Bad*; and Sue-Ellen Case, "Toward a Butch-Femme Aesthetic," in Lynda Hart, ed., *Making a Spectacle: Feminist Essays on Contemporary Women's Theatre* (Ann Arbor: University of Michigan Press, 1989), 282–99. See Adrienne Rich, "Compulsory Heterosexuality and Lesbian Existence," in Ann Snitow, Christine Stansell, and Sharon Thompson, eds., *Powers of Desire* (New York: Monthly Review Press, 1983), 177–205, for the quintessential text on "woman-identified women."

11. See Jan Clausen, "My Interesting Condition," *Out/Look* 2, no. 3 (Winter 1990): 11–21, for a painfully honest discussion of the political and emotional strictures of life in a "new" lesbian family.

12. I attended the performance discussed below on June 29, 1990, at the Walker Point Art Center in Milwaukee, Wisconsin.

13. See Case, "Toward a Butch-Femme Aesthetic"; Sue-Ellen Case, "From Split Subject to Split Britches," in Enoch Brater, ed., *Feminine Focus: The New Women Playwrights* (New York: Oxford University Press, 1989), 126–46; and Jill Dolan, *The Feminist Spectator as Critic* (1988; reprint, Ann Arbor: University

of Michigan Press, 1991), especially chapter 4, "The Dynamics of Desire," 59–81, for explications of Weaver and Shaw's personal and performative roles.

14. For theoretical work on butch-femme role-playing as politically and culturally transgressive, see, for example, Case, "Toward a Butch-Femme Aesthetic"; Joan Nestle, *A Restricted Country* (Ithaca: Firebrand Books, 1987); Madeline Davis and Elizabeth Lapovsky Kennedy, "Oral History and the Study of Sexuality in the Lesbian Community: Buffalo, New York, 1940–1960," in Martin Baume Duberman, Martha Vicinus, and George Chauncey, eds., *Hidden from History: Reclaiming the Gay and Lesbian Past* (New York: New American Library, 1989), 426–40; Davis and Kennedy, "The Reproduction of Butch-Fem Roles: A Social Constructionist Approach," in Peiss and Simmons, *Passion and Power*, 241–56; and Joan Nestle, ed., *The Persistent Desire: A Femme-Butch Reader* (Boston: Alyson, 1992).

15. de Lauretis, "Sexual Indifference," 39.

16. See Elaine Marks, "Lesbian Intertextuality," in George Stambolian and Elaine Marks, eds., *Homosexualities and French Literature* (Ithaca: Cornell University Press, 1979), in which, referring to Monique Wittig's *Le corps lesbien*, she suggests that images "sufficiently blatant [. . .] withstand reabsorption into male literary culture" (375). The analogy might hold here.

17. Eve Kosofsky Sedgwick, "Across Gender, across Sexuality: Willa Cather and Others," in Ronald R. Butters, John M. Clum, and Michael Moon, eds., *Displacing Homophobia: Gay Male Perspectives in Literature and Culture* (Durham: Duke University Press, 1989), 59.

18. See Davis and Kennedy, "Reproduction of Butch-Fem Roles," for further discussion of essentializing versus more historical, social constructionist definitions of lesbian and homosexual identity.

19. Judith Butler, "Performative Acts and Gender Constitution: An Essay in Phenomenology and Feminist Theory," in Case, *Performing Feminisms*, 272.

20. Nestle, *A Restricted Country*, 9.

21. Linda Williams, *Hard Core: Power, Pleasure, and the "Frenzy of the Visible"* (Berkeley: University of California Press, 1989), 30.

22. See Foucault, *The History of Sexuality*, 1:156–59.

23. For an explication of lesbian subjectivities marginalized by realism's ethical and heterosexual codes, see Jill Dolan, " 'Lesbian' Subjectivity in Realism: Dragging at the Margins of Structure and Ideology," in Case, *Performing Feminisms*, 40–53.

24. John Clum, " 'A Culture That Isn't Just Sexual': Dramatizing Gay Male History," *Theatre Journal* 41, no. 2 (May 1989): 169–89.

25. Nestle, *A Restricted Country*, 10.

26. Martin Sherman, *Bent*, in Don Shewey, ed., *Out Front: Contemporary Gay and Lesbian Plays* (New York: Grove Press, 1988), 79–148; Robert Chesley, *Jerker, or the Helping Hand*, in *Out Front*, 449–92.

27. Williams, *Hard Core*, 227. Unfortunately, Williams's own text ends by describing newer porn films, created either by women or for heterosexual couples, which, although they explore options among a range of sexual prac-

tices, retain the monogamous ideal of the heterosexual couple as their textual and spectatorial standard. See, in particular, 229–79.

28. Ibid., 151.

29. See, for example, Jane Chambers, *Last Summer at Bluefish Cove* (New York: JH Press, 1982); and Sarah Dreher's *8 × 10 Glossy* and *Ruby Christmas*, in Kate McDermott, ed., *Places, Please! The First Anthology of Lesbian Plays* (Iowa City: Aunt Lute, 1985), 41–92 and 137–92, respectively. Holly Hughes's raucous play *The Well of Horniness* (in *Out Front*, 221–52) is reminiscent of *Jerker* in its use of language to break the taboo of homosexual discourse, but its transgressions remain verbal and cloaked in subcultural references. *The Well's* radio play genesis also works to repress the pornographic effects of bodies in motion to the margins of the text.

30. See Foucault, *The History of Sexuality*, 1:36–49. He writes, "The implantation of perversions is an instrument-effect: it is through the isolation, intensification, and consolidation of peripheral sexualities that relations of power to sex and pleasure branched out and multiplied, measured the body, and penetrated modes of conduct" (48). Cultural feminism's isolation of lesbian "deviant" sexualities saw porn magazines such as *On Our Backs* and *Bad Attitude* wrest their own piece of public discourse to transgress the law of politically correct sex developed by cultural feminist ideology. Pat Califia, s/m advocate and founder of the s/m support group Samois, published *Sapphistry*, a sex manual and disquisition on lesbian sexual variation that was in its third edition by 1988 (Naiad Press, 1988). Susie Bright, editor of *On Our Backs* and author of its Susie Sexpert columns, published a flamboyantly frank compilation of her essays in 1990, all of which describe and celebrate a loosening of lesbian sexual mores (*Susie Sexpert's Lesbian Sex World* [Pittsburgh and San Francisco: Cleis Press, 1990]).

31. I attended the performance discussed below on November 18, 1989, at the Barrymore Theatre in Madison, Wisconsin.

32. I don't mean to be facetious here, but I do mean to evoke the self-righteousness of these performances and the sanctimonious response they evoked.

33. The disjuncture between gay male and lesbian subcultures prompted by cultural feminism has recently been documented, in an effort to forge new alliances between the two groups as sexually stigmatized communities. Borrowing from gay male subculture, therefore, is a transgressive act in a cultural feminist setting. See Rich, " Compulsory Heterosexuality," for a historical example of feminism's betrayal of gay men. For work on the new alliances, see Nestle, *A Restricted Country*; and Gayle Rubin, "Thinking Sex: Notes for a Radical Theory of the Politics of Sexuality," in Carol Vance, ed., *Pleasure and Danger* (Boston: Routledge and Kegan Paul, 1984), 267–318.

34. See, for example, *Feminist Voices* (December 15–February 8, 1990, Madison, Wisconsin): 4, 6; *Feminist Voices* (February 9–March 8, 1990, Madison, Wisconsin): 11–13; *Wisconsin Light* (January 11–24, 1990, Milwaukee, Wisconsin): 5, 11. On "naive realism," see Williams, *Hard Core*, particularly 184–228.

35. Williams, *Hard Core*, 12.

36. Ibid., 38.

37. I would like to thank Stacy Wolf for her insightful comments in discussions around the issues in this article and for her thoughtful responses to preliminary drafts.

Index